Kasey to the Rescue

Kasey to the Rescue

The Remarkable Story of a
Monkey and a Miracle

ELLEN ROGERS

NEW YORK

In the interest of preserving confidentiality and protecting identity, some of the names and characteristics of individuals discussed within this book have been changed.

Library of Congress Cataloging-in-Publication Data

Rogers, Ellen.
  Kasey to the rescue : the remarkable story of a monkey and a miracle / Ellen Rogers.
     p.   cm.
  ISBN 978-1-4013-2341-7
  1.   Sullivan, Edward—Health. 2.   Quadriplegics—Massachusetts—Biography.
3.   Capuchin monkeys as pets—Massachusetts. 4.   Monkeys as aids for people with disabilities—Massachusetts.   I. Title.
  RC406.Q33R64   2010
  616.89'1658—dc22
                                                                              2010008265

Hyperion books are available for special promotions, premiums, or corporate training. For details contact the HarperCollins Special Markets Department in the New York office at 212-207-7528, fax 212-207-7222, or e-mail spsales@harpercollins.com.

Book design by Karen Minster

FIRST EDITION

10 9 8 7 6 5 4 3 2 1

We try to produce the most beautiful books possible, and we are also extremely concerned about the impact of our manufacturing process on the forests of the world and the environment as a whole. Accordingly, we've made sure that all of the paper we use has been certified as coming from forests that are managed to ensure the protection of the people and wildlife dependent upon them.

To Megan, Ron, Grace, Ned, Jake,
Maddie and Anna, Nonnie and Lynnie—
and to those watching down on you:
Ted, my father, Aunt Marion—
what heroes you created.

And of course to Kasey:
thanks for jumping in.

ACKNOWLEDGMENTS

KIDS, DOGS, MONKEY: *WE DID IT. I LOVE YOU.*

To the paramedics in Tucson: I don't know your names but I know you saved Ned's life. God bless you.

We have been very fortunate to have had love and support from so many people who have made a difference in Ned's recovery. I'm sure I've left out some inadvertently. To everyone, I thank you.

Brenda Copeland, my oh-so-wise and witty editor at Hyperion—sharing this roller coaster ride called *Kasey to the Rescue* has been an honor. Ellen Archer, Hyperion's president and publisher—your support has been so appreciated. Maybe it had something to do with Kasey knowing who's who instantly on the day we all first met on Ned's terrace. Kate Griffin and the Hyperion team—you are all great.

Susan Golomb, my agent, who recognized the power of Ned and Kasey's story when it was a simple query—not a chapter written. You've been the greatest champion a writer—and friend—could ever have. Terra Chalberg—your advice and ever-present help have been wonderful.

A giant and heartfelt thank-you to Joni Rodgers for your compassion, talent, and humor in helping me bring our family's story to life. Stay frosty, as I learned from you.

My mother, Lois Rogers, and my sister, Lynn, and her husband, Bob Vail—you are there for all of us every minute, every hour, every day. Patricia "Nana" Sullivan, for your lovely notes and calls to Ned. Big Ron and Terry Holsinger and, of course, Ron—the saying goes that you can't pick your in-laws, but if I could have, I would have picked each of you.

Our dearest family friends, who stepped up and stood with all of us through every moment of despair, hope, and joy: Judy and Wes, Heather, Quinn, Teddy, and Kyle Harrington. Judy and Don, Kate Helm Luethy, Annie and Susie Helm. Jane and Chris White (ILUFM) and their family. A monkey salute and love to all.

Helping Hands: Monkey Helpers for the Disabled. Your wisdom, dedication, and devotion to all the monkey helpers and their recipients have changed our lives. Megan Monkey: you're the best. Jill Siebeking, Andrea Rothfelder, and all the trainers—what a job you do. Bob Stern and Susan Keyes—thank you for your steady hands in guiding the direction of such a wonderful organization. Marie-Christine and Urs Jaeger-Firmenich, for your generosity and for becoming our friends. And Judi Zazula, for co-founding Helping Hands.

My many friends from growing up in Cleveland were among the first to call and support us. Bill Oberndorf—your love and support have meant so much to all of us. Rob Spring—a special thanks for the much-needed "assist" and for being there when I called. Margie Biggar, Christy Bittenbender, Poncho and Judy Bryan, Helen Gelbach, Betsy and Ted Hellmuth, Bill and Nancy Hellmuth, Jane Horvitz, Merry McCreary, Tyler Miller, Chip Oberndorf, Chip Spear, Jimmy Staples, Fred Stueber—all friends forever.

My Concord friends didn't ask "What needs to be done?," they just "did." Karen Sabatino, for your incredible generosity of time and love (as well as for our wheelchair-van misadventures). Mary Ann McCarthy, for always being there with a little laugh and a hug in the darkest days. Marti Berman, my fellow writer, dear friend, and chief instigator of Ellen Night. Joyce Brinner, Pattie Driscoll,

Jane Fay, Cathy Jenkins, Frankie Martinez, Elissa Sargent—all of whom looked after me, Ned, and my other children in countless ways. Dr. Don Driscoll—thank you for getting Ned into the best hands at Mass General and for mending each of my kids over the years. Lacey Gallagher and Joey Goodwin—you are both awesome godparents to little Grace. To all my kids' friends—thanks for being there for them.

My wonderful Brae Burn and book group friends, very special to me for many years: Pat Campbell, Kathy Callahan, Becky Epstein, Jan Johnson, Anne Margulies, Gene Miller, Julie Mirbach, Linda Thomas, Nancy Whitney, and so many others. You have been unfailing in keeping Ned's and my spirits up, not to mention your very generous support of Helping Hands.

Paula Harries, my friend and business colleague for way too many years, someone who drops what she's doing and drives 120 miles to be there for Ned. Kim Boucher, her kids, and her parents, Dot and Don Fay, who have become our family as well. Meredith Hanrahan, whose brilliance led me to agentquery.com and hence to Susan Golomb. Kimmy, Mer, and Paula: I love you.

Susan Davis, for totally adopting us in Atlanta. Brienne Johnson, Ned's friend, who's stuck by him through thick and thin and, I am proud to say, is now my friend as well. Rich and Andrew Montmeny—there in the very first horrific hours in Arizona, along with Marsha's love and prayers.

Nancy Martini, for taking care of my Megan when Megan was taking care of everyone else. Mary Luria, my legal eagle par excellence. Jane Cannon, who was among the first to hear my idea of *Kasey to the Rescue* and said: "I see it." Asturia Martin and Vilmar Pollack, for always being there for us. Brian Doherty for creating Ned's Room of Hope. Sari Botton for her clever and insightful thoughts. Nan Harbison and Rita and John Williams, for being the best neighbors a family could have. To all, thank you.

My heartfelt appreciation to the many medical professionals who have been instrumental in Ned's recovery. Dr. Stephen Hanks in Tucson, Dr. Lawrence Borges at MGH, and all the staff on White 12, along with Danielle, Kate, and Jen. Elana Shepherd and the entire staff—doctors, nurses, therapists, aides, volunteers—at the Shepherd Center: you are doing God's work. The Spaulding Rehabilitation Hospital team. Dr. Gary Stanton, Ned's neurologist at Emerson Hospital here in Concord, for his determination to free Ned from pain.

To Allison Thambash, Charity Collins, and the other PCAs and nurses—thank you for joining Team Ned and becoming a part of our family along the way.

And, finally, to whoever makes Monkey Chow—who knew?

CONTENTS

Kasey to the Rescue

You Can't Get There from Here

THEY SAY MOTHERHOOD AND SURVIVAL ARE THE ONLY PRI-mal instincts all animals share. It was a combination of the two that sent me careening down the Mass Turnpike that night. I was headed for the airport and didn't slow down as I groped to answer my cell.

"Megan?"

"Mom, I got you on a flight to Dallas."

"There's nothing nonstop to Arizona?"

"You can't get there from here," Megan said. "Dallas is your only option. You've got about forty minutes to get to the gate, forty-five minutes to make the connecting flight to Tucson. You'll be there before midnight."

"*Yes,*" I breathed, steering into the parking garage. Thank God for my go-to girl. "You're a magician, Megan. Thank you."

I hit the concourse running full out, my wheeled bag clatter-ing behind me, and charged down the jetway, pushing my fist against the searing stitch in my side. As I hoisted my bag into the overhead, I tried to remember what I'd thrown into it before dashing out the door. Didn't matter. All that mattered was mak-ing the flight.

Getting to Arizona.

Getting to Ned.

I slumped into my seat, instructing myself to breathe.

Oh, God. How can this be happening?

I powered down my cell and tried to organize the flowchart in my head. I was used to being the one with all the answers. I *liked* being the one with all the answers. I'd bounded through Boston's Logan International a thousand times before—places to go, people to see—so many business trips, each one "extremely important."

"It's *imperative* that I be there," I'd say. "I *absolutely have to* make this flight."

I guess life has a way of rewriting our personal dictionaries.

"Ladies and gentlemen, this is the captain. Looks like there's some traffic control issues down in Dallas. We'll pull back from the gate and wait for the go-ahead."

"Oh . . . no . . ."

"We thank you for your patience. Shouldn't be delayed more than an hour or so."

"*No.*"

I shut my eyes and worked to maintain the same mask of composure I'd tried to hold up for my daughter Maddie just ninety minutes earlier. She was with me when I got the call.

Are you Edward Sullivan's mother?

There was something about the way she said it.

Yes, I'm—I'm Ellen. I'm Ned's mother.

I could tell our world was about to fall apart.

Your son's been in an accident.

Critical condition. Extensive injuries. Significant blood loss. Emergency surgery. Come immediately. Hearing only my side of the conversation, Maddie had glanced up, her expression melting from curiosity to alarm. She covered her mouth with her hand, gasping strangled sobs, but I could only hold her in my arms for a moment, because then I was in motion, doing what had to be done.

"Miss? Miss?" I flagged the attention of a passing flight attendant.

"Yes, ma'am." Her pleasant smile faded to concern. "Are you all right?"

"No. No, I'm not. I can't be here for an hour. I have forty-five minutes to connect in Dallas. I have to be in Tucson. Now. Tonight. My son—he's a student at the university in Tucson. He's been in a terrible car accident. They said he . . ." The words were unspeakable, unthinkable, but I forced them out. "He might not make it through the night. Please. If I don't get there . . ."

The flight attendant nodded and squeezed my arm. "I'll be right back."

She left me strapped to my seat, fighting to swallow my panic.

I rested my head against the cool window, twisting the rings on my right hand: one for Megan, one for Ned, one their father gave me on our first anniversary. I sat up and scanned the aisle for the flight attendant, twisting the rings on my left hand: a signet ring my father gave me on my fifteenth birthday, a warm gold band from my grandparents' wedding in 1896. It's a nervous habit I have, twisting those rings, turning them around and around. It makes me feel connected to my life and the people I love. But now I looked down at those rings and realized my hands were shaking.

"Ma'am?" The flight attendant was back. "The captain asked me to give you this."

She handed me a sheet of paper torn from the flight log.

Air traffic control will give us special clearance into Dallas/Fort Worth and hold your connecting flight to Tucson.

I am a man of great faith and want you to know the entire crew is praying for your son. The Lord will make a way.

That note has never left me.

When we landed in Dallas, the pilot was waiting at the door to personally escort me to the connecting flight. I still get a lump in my throat every time I think of his kindness and the solid arm he offered as I matched his long stride through the airport.

Thank God for the good guys.

I made the second leg of the flight and hurried to my seat so I'd have a moment to check in with Megan.

"I just have a second," I told her. "Is everybody okay?"

"Maddie and I got Anna from her track meet," she said. "There were like a million people there, but we found her."

Thank God for big sisters.

"Did you tell her?" I asked. "Is she all right?"

"She's . . . We're all upset. But we've got things covered here. You have to hurry, Mom. You have to get there and make him be okay. Please, Mom, make him be okay."

Her voice was choked with fear and sorrow, but I'm the type who's not easily undone. I stuck to the stoic Presbyterian script: "We'll get through this, Megan. It'll be okay. I called Paula, and she's driving down from Phoenix so he's . . ."

So he's not alone, I'd started to say. But I knew better. Ned was utterly alone right now. This man who would forever be my little boy was adrift in the dark, separated from me by mountains, deserts, and two insanely tight flights. Thank God for Paula, the kind of friend who jumps in the car and drives 120 miles on a moment's notice. She's the type who's good in a crisis. So am I.

· · ·

I CONSIDER MYSELF something of a tragedy snob.

Having lived through some pretty terrible losses, I'm not easily undone. When I was twenty-four, I got married in a hospital sunroom down the hall from the surgical ward where my father fought for a few last months of life. My husband, Ted Sullivan, was diagnosed with cancer when our daughter Megan was just two and a half and I was eight-and-a-half months pregnant with Ned. Ted spent the next two years in radiation bays and infusion wards, our little family soldiering side-by-side through his experimental chemo, a grueling operation, and the long, sad hospice days before his death. When Megan was four and Ned eighteen months old, their father, my husband, was gone.

A second marriage brought two beautiful stepdaughters, Kerry and Mindy, plus my three youngest: Jake, Maddie, and Anna Kokos. But our blended family unraveled after Mindy died of melanoma at age twenty-three. That world-rocking loss was followed by a bitter divorce. My kids and I had only recently regained our footing.

Whenever I am away from home, my last waking thoughts are always a quiet inventory of my children. As the flight was cleared for takeoff, I closed my eyes and purposefully gathered them into my heart one by one:

Megan, whip-smart and beautiful at twenty-five, had recently married a true blue cop named Ron Holsinger.

Ned, twenty-two, had the boundless energy and blue-eyed charm of his father.

Jake, my gentle giant, was eighteen and about to graduate from high school.

Thirteen-year-old Maddie blossomed with creativity and un-furling fashion savvy.

And last, but not in any way least, was ferociously loyal Anna, twelve years old and completely able to hold her own in the high-velocity environment that was our home.

I'd managed to get myself and the kids (plus two puppies with myriad issues of their own) re-situated in a new house, juggling everyone's activities with the travels and daily operation of my own marketing consulting firm, a new endeavor I'd started after nearly thirty years in corporate high tech. A miracle of modern love and high-flying trapeze act of daily logistics, the Rogers-Sullivan-Kokos-Holsinger family was doing all right. We'd seen tough times before and gotten through them.

We'll get through this, I told myself. *We have to.*

WALKING INTO THE ICU at the University Medical Center in Tucson that night, I assumed I'd see Ned unconscious on a venti-lator. I fully expected the spiderweb of tubes, IV lines, and moni-tor wires. The apparatus of life support was nothing new to me, so I figured I was prepared—or at least as prepared as anyone could be—for what I was about to see.

I was wrong.

A massive steel frame encompassed Ned's head and shoul-ders. Solid bars abutted a heavy metal circle bolted to his skull by screws in his forehead and above his ears. Instead of the space-age technology you'd expect in a modern hospital, this looked like a medieval torture device. I gripped the bed rail with one hand and Paula with the other.

"What . . . what is that thing?"

"It's called a halo," said the nurse. "They put it on in surgery to secure his head to his neck."

I damn near fainted.

Inside the metal halo, Ned's face was astonishingly unharmed. He seemed a little puffy, and a small shard of glass had nicked him high on the forehead. The tubes into his nostrils, the respirator taped to his mouth and extending down his throat, and those screws—that huge, invasive bear-trap contraption on his head—it all seemed so surreal, so incongruous in combination with the beauty of his sleeping expression.

Hollow and frozen, I sorted through the questions crowding my brain and found the only one that mattered. "Is he going to make it?"

"No one survives this type of injury, Ellen. We're calling all over the country trying to find someone who knows how to treat a case like this." In time, I would learn to be grateful for this sort of candor. But that would come later. The doctor continued with a litany of specifics. Spinal cord injury. Major brain trauma. Organ damage. Blood transfusions. They'd removed Ned's spleen. (*What does a spleen do?* I wondered. *Is that important?* But he'd already moved on.)

"He's in a medically induced coma right now, so it's too early to say anything for certain." The doctor slid several X-rays and MRI scans onto a light board. "The major issue is the broken neck."

There was no misunderstanding the extent of the damage. The force of the crash had essentially decapitated him, snapping everything that connected his skull to his spine. The intense whiplash had stopped the flow of blood and oxygen to his brain long enough to produce the effects of a stroke.

"You can see the fracture of the C1 and C2 vertebrae here, and with this type of SCI—"

"SCI?" I interrupted.

"Spinal cord injury," the doctor said. "Unfortunately, Ellen, this means he'll be paralyzed from the neck down. Realistically, he won't be able to move, talk, or breathe on his own again."

I gripped Paula's arm, willing the oxygen to flow to my own brain.

"We can't tell if the spinal cord itself has been severed until the swelling subsides. More troubling is what we see here," he added, pointing to several places in the brain MRI. "When the brain is slammed back and forth inside the skull, we see 'shearing'—damage to individual nerve cells, which leads to breakdown of communication among neurons in the brain. As long as he's in the induced coma, there's no way to assess cognitive function. Even if he comes around, it could be a year or more before the damage is completely understood."

The doctor asked if I had any more questions, and of course, I had a thousand, but I shook my head.

I thanked him. He left.

I sat on a plastic chair. Paula sat with me.

A steady wasp's nest of activity surrounded us. Jarring alarms periodically cut through the racket of machinery, the sigh of the ventilator, the hiss of the deflating blood pressure cuff. I got up and paced the cramped space between the window and the banks of machinery keeping my son alive. Paula talked to me, the kind of quietly bolstering talk that isn't even about words, just the sound of a good friend's solid presence.

We were allowed to stay only an hour in the ICU. I glanced at my watch. Somewhere over the cracked expanse of the Sonoran

Desert, I'd made the conscious decision not to reset it—it was 3 A.M. at home. Keeping it on Boston time made me feel like I was still connected to my kids. I'd traveled backward in time. But not as far as I wished I could.

I checked into the hotel that would be my base of operation in the coming weeks. Paula brought wine and a little food to my room.

"How many times am I allowed to thank God for my friends?" I asked, trying to steady the glass between my hands.

"No quota." Paula smiled.

At the hospital the next day, I collected a couple of pillows for my chair and a blanket to wrap around my shoulders. I sat and stared out the window at the mountains. There was a gentle knock on the door, and a police officer came in with Ned's personal effects. One shoe, his backpack, keys, wallet, and cell phone. I took the familiar items, trying to see them in some kind of context.

"Can you tell me . . . what happened?"

"It was a single car accident," the officer said. "Witnesses observed him slow down, then lurch forward. He slammed into a brick wall at about forty miles per hour."

Investigators later speculated he'd either fallen asleep or had a momentary relapse of an old seizure disorder that had been brought under control with medication years earlier.

"Was he . . . Did he say anything?" I asked the officer.

"I'm sorry, I wasn't at the scene," he said. "I didn't see anything in the report."

The nurse checking Ned's IV glanced up. "I heard a paramedic saw his legs move."

"What does that mean?" I gasped. "Does that mean something?"

"Well—I mean, you never know—but sometimes . . . It could mean there might be movement in the future. But that's just . . ." She lowered her eyes to her paperwork again. "I'm sorry. I shouldn't have said anything. I don't even know if that's accurate."

I didn't care if it was accurate; it was hope, something to grab on to, and I would take it. Perched on this narrow outcrop of clinical answers and hedged bets, I needed some kind of hand-hold. A branch—a *twig*—the slenderest root of hope would do. I hugged Ned's backpack to my chest, desperate to hold on to whatever was left of this young man so full of life, this young life so full of promise.

I sat in the chair, my head tilted against the window, watching the medical flights on the helipad—landing, leaving, landing again in an endless rotation of deafening racket and bloody gurneys, trailed by woefully broken loved ones. There was no way any of us would ever return to anything resembling "normal."

You can't get there from here.

But you can get somewhere. And I was determined to find the way.

2

When You're Going
Through Hell . . . Keep Going

T HE CAPUCHIN'S EYES ARE UNCANNY AND WISE, AND KAS-
ey's are set in perfect proportion to her delicately expressive
face. She's covered with glossy, golden hair (*not fur,* Ned will in-
form friends who remark on its beauty and softness) and wears a
jaunty version of the tufted black cap that reminded fifteenth-
century Spanish explorers of the Capuchin monks back home.
Hence the name.

Kasey made the five-thousand-mile journey from a breeding
colony in Argentina to Boston in the spring of 1986. Only a few
months old, she'd already been selected by Helping Hands: Monkey Helpers for the Disabled, an incredible organization that places
specially trained capuchin monkeys with people who are paralyzed or suffer other severe mobility impairments. Someday Kasey
would literally provide a pair of helping hands (two pairs, if you
count her astonishingly dexterous feet) and offer gifts of independence and dignity along with lively companionship to a friend in
need. For the moment, however, she was busy exploring her new
world.

Kasey spent her "childhood" with a couple in Virginia who'd
probably call "lively companionship" the understatement of the century. Helping Hands has a nationwide network of foster homes
that gently acclimate young monkeys to the world of humans and
provide loving elder care for retired monkeys, and I'm told Kasey's

foster "mom and dad" have many fond memories of her. Quick as a lightning bug, insatiably curious, and far too clever to stay out of trouble, she loved to ride around with "Dad" on his bicycle. Tucked safely inside his shirt with just her head sticking out in the wind as they cruised the neighborhood, she created a stir wherever they went.

The care and feeding of a capuchin monkey is complicated, and Kasey is a high-maintenance diva. When I think of this couple's generosity (and I do think of it—often), I'm humbly amazed at the time, energy, and tenderness they invested in this tiny creature, all for the benefit of a total stranger. Her loving nature is a testament to their enduring patience and commitment. Knowing Kasey as I do now, it's not hard to imagine what a dervish she must have been as an untrained preadolescent.

She had a lot in common with my son, I imagine.

Spry and audacious from day one, they both had winning personalities: big sense of fun, small fear of challenge, the sputtering attention span of a gnat, and no patience at all for anything that smacked of giving up or giving in. I wouldn't say either of them was uncooperative, but they both had minds of their own.

About the time Kasey moved in with her foster family, Ned and Megan found themselves adjusting to the new "yours, mine, and ours" situation that came with my second marriage. My husband's daughters were a few years older than Ned and Megan. In an uncomfortable shift of the sibling hierarchy, Megan went from big sister to middle kid, and with the addition of Jake, Maddie, and Anna, Ned went from baby of the bunch to big brother. Our little family expanded to a three-ring circus of kids, pets, friends, and a steady parade of nannies and repairmen happy to cash in on the mayhem.

Ned was bright-eyed and rambunctious, solid and built close to the ground. He learned early how to get out of trouble with his ready grin and innocent "who, me?" expression. He was a study in perpetual motion, a little daredevil who lived to get air, forever working to perfect a new dirt bike trick or build the ultimate skateboard jump, never afraid to try anything. He never had it easy—with attention deficit disorder, learning disabilities, and a seizure disorder. But the challenges he faced inspired him to try harder. He learned to be cautious about his expectations, but unstoppable in pursuit of his goals. Trials of daily life trained him to become methodical and discriminating. He did well with strategy, process, known quantities—laying out his clothes for school, staying on schedule. Instead of pondering *why* or *if,* he cut straight to the chase with *how* and *when.* He was a keen observer of what worked for others, the same "monkey see, monkey do" methodology with which Kasey would later learn to perform specialized tasks.

As a teenager, Ned kept careful track of his grades, piling on extra homework if he saw himself slipping. He was game for anything and everything, determined not to let lack of experience or his learning issues affect his academic or athletic performance.

"I'm going out for the ice hockey team," he announced in his sophomore year.

"Really?" I said.

He could tell I was skeptical. It was completely unlikely. His entire ice skating experience consisted of one wobbly outing on a neighbor's pond. This didn't bother Ned a bit. Hockey was just another game to play, another case of "practice makes perfect." Mind made up, skates laced tight, he fell and got up and fell and got up again as many times as he had to until he made JV, then varsity. He worked his way onto the football team and won Most Improved Player, but baseball was his passion. Thrilled to play on a team at the top of their league's championship several years in a row, he excelled at the game and even got a few nibbles from colleges in Florida. With his high school diploma and big ideas in hand, he went off to the University of Arizona, filled with big brotherly dreams of leadership, motivation, and mentoring.

There wasn't a doubt in his mind or mine: Ned had a purpose.

"MS. ROGERS," a nurse chastised, "no cell phones in the ICU."

I nodded and smiled, thinking, *Yeah, try and stop me.*

My mother and my sister and the kids were far away, waiting on pins and needles for the smallest bits of information, and I was just beginning to wade through the logistics that come with calamity, trying to figure out who needed to know what and how to get hold of them. Ned's cell was filled with names and numbers I didn't recognize, a wealth of friends he'd made in his home away from my home. I started at the beginning.

"Ally, this is Ellen Rogers, Ned's mother. Are you a close friend of his?"

"Ned . . . ," she echoed. "Oh, you mean *Ed.*"

"Yes. I guess I do."

It was a little unsettling to think Ned was an entirely different person here, a man whose name I didn't know, whose friends were strangers to me. But isn't that what kids do when they leave home, become different people? His whole young life, Ned had wrestled with his nickname, correcting people when they called him *Ed* or *Ted.* But here in Arizona, where few people knew the New England nickname of *Ned* (and fewer knew that he was called

Ned to distinguish him from Ted, his father), he let it go. He became Ed.

"Ally, Ned's been in a terrible accident . . ."

I fumbled through the basic facts, implementing the harsh new vocabulary I'd acquired in the last twenty-four hours. (*SCI* and *halo* were only the beginning. Soon I'd know the meanings of *aphasia, apraxia, dysphagia, dysreflexia*—the glossary went on and on.)

"Oh, my God . . . poor Ed . . ." Ally struggled to assimilate this information that in no way coordinates with life as most college kids know it. "Is there anything I can do?"

"Just be here for him. Let his other friends know. And let Ned know you care."

Ally put the word out, and as the news moved swiftly through the phone tree, Ned's friends crowded his room with balloons, flowers, and love. I was grateful for the company and trusted that somewhere in the dark, Ned could hear their voices and would gain strength from it. One of his roommates brought me Ned's laptop, a desperately needed lifeline to an outpouring of support from family and friends that kept me going.

I've always maintained a healthy respect for my children's privacy, but photographs on Ned's hard drive rolled past in his screensaver: Ned and Maddie on the ski slopes, Ned and his friend Teddy hoisting a cold one at a sports bar, Ned with his friend Annie and Teddy's sister Heather in a limo on Teddy's twenty-first birthday. I drank in the images of my son, whole and upright, physically active and wide awake. The Ned I knew.

I heard a ringtone from his backpack. When I fished out his cell, the caller ID read "Little Bro."

"Jake?"

A little boy with a strong Hispanic accent said, "No, this is Mikey. Is Ed there?"

"This is Ned's— I'm Ed's mom." I waited for him to say something, and when he didn't I asked, "May I please talk to your mom, Mikey?"

"My grandma's here."

"May I speak with her?"

Mikey shuffled the phone to his grandmother, and I told her, "Ned's been in a terrible accident."

I reiterated the details I'd been spelling out over and over again to people who needed to know. The words had become wooden with practice, but Mikey's grandmother—obviously a mother with her own complicated story—was well enough acquainted with dry grief to recognize the sound of it.

"I'm so sorry . . . so sorry . . ." Her voice was choked and tearful. "He's a good man, your Ed. He's made such a difference for Mikey."

"How do you and Mikey know him?"

"He volunteers in the Big Brother program. Mikey's matched up with him. His little brother."

Of course. I had to smile at yet another vivid snapshot of my son, whose heart I knew well, even if I didn't recognize the places and faces around him.

"I'll pray for him every day," said Mikey's grandmother.

"Thank you. I appreciate that."

We needed all the help we could get.

On Saturday, Jake graduated from high school. I'd been planning a huge party at the house. Had I been there, all the bustle— hustling everyone out the door, cleaning and shopping for the party, prepping a lovely celebration—the doings of the day would have occupied all my thoughts. Instead, I sat looking out at the Arizona mountains while my dear friends Judy and Jane went to the graduation ceremony in my place. Maddie went with them and held up her cell phone so I could hear when Jake's name was called.

Megan took care of business at home and took charge of all things Maddie and Anna. Word spread quickly through our close-knit community of friends, and the girls were instantly surrounded with love, help, and home cooking. Paula returned to Phoenix, and Judy arrived in Tucson to prop me up. I was grateful for the company, but more importantly, I needed a second set of ears to help me take in the overwhelming information that was coming at me.

"Let's get a list going," she said, but I couldn't begin to get my head around it.

"I guess . . . Ned's apartment . . . he won't be going back there for—" I shook my head, not knowing what I meant to say. For a while? Forever?

"I've got it," said Judy. She went out for the day, and when she returned, she'd accomplished the task I couldn't face. His apartment had been cleaned and packed, his belongings shipped home, his trash put out on the curb, his toothbrush thrown away. Judy had given his bed and television to one of his friends. I could tell she was exhausted, but she sat with me in the hotel room and talked quietly until I could bear the thought of turning out the light.

Wednesday morning, six days after the accident, the doctors cut back the meds keeping Ned in the coma. We watched over the nurse's shoulder as she monitored his vitals. The pounding of my heart was louder than the beeping and grinding of the machines.

"Ned?" She leaned in at the first flicker of his eyelids. "Ned, you've been in a car accident. You're at the hospital in Tucson. There's a tube down your throat, so you won't be able to speak, but I want you to blink if you can hear me."

Judy and I were clutching each other—hoping, praying, shaking, waiting. What if . . .

He blinked. I exhaled for what felt like the first time in days.

"Ned, do you know your mom is here?"

Another blink. *Best. Blink. Ever.*

Both gratitude and fear overwhelmed me. Somewhere inside the steel halo, inside the broken body, Ned—or at least some part of him—was still here. The word "relief" doesn't begin to cover it, but with this reassurance came the enormity of the unknowns confronting us.

"What does this mean?" Megan asked when I called home. "Will he be . . . okay?"

I didn't lie to her or try to quantify the shifting meaning of the word "okay."

"He's fighting" was the best I could tell her. "Just pray for him to keep fighting."

Ned drifted between fitful sleep, mysterious fevers, and waking agony for twenty-two days, and I hovered, waiting for every precious eyelash of communication. One blink for yes. Two blinks for no. The pain medicines were reduced, and every once in a while, I could see a momentary lifting of the fog in Ned's eyes. It inspired a surge of hope in me, but there was also sorrow for my son. How would he—how *could* he—ever come to terms with the bleakness of his situation? This vital young man, always so healthy and gung ho. What would his life be now?

I kept asking the same questions and getting the same bleak answer: "It's highly unlikely that Ned will ever move on his own again. Or talk. Or even breathe without a ventilator. There can be no expectation of functional recovery with a devastating injury like this."

Devastating, they kept saying. The meaning of the word hit like a wrecking ball: to overwhelm . . . to render desolate . . . to lay waste. I understood what they were saying. I listened and nodded, but I couldn't accept it.

Not for Ned. Not for my son.

He would not fade away. He would not be forgotten.

Ned was strong and fit, a lifelong athlete, and one of the most motivated people I'd ever known. Even as a kid, he drove us crazy with his ongoing collection of *hoo-rah!* inspirational sayings. He could actually be a little annoying in his efforts to "inspire" others to do and be their best.

"Mom," Ned once admonished when he found me watching *Project Runway* with the girls instead of unpacking groceries. "Procrastination is the thief of time!"

Quoting Vince Lombardi was his favorite way to pester his siblings, especially Jake.

"There's only one way to succeed in anything, and that is to give it everything!"

And this was before Jake was even old enough to know what Ned was talking about. Four years younger and Ned's devoted shadow—for better and worse—Jake wanted to do everything his big brother did. Naturally, Ned wasn't always thrilled to have Jake in his entourage and loved to get a rise out of his sensitive little brother.

Home from college on spring break his sophomore year, Ned asked me, "Have you ever heard of the Dale Carnegie course?"

"Sure," I said, with a sinking feeling I was about to hear a lot more.

"A buddy of mine went to an open house—you know, the whole *How to Win Friends and Influence People* thing—and he was blown away. I think that course would really help me."

"How so?"

"Business capabilities, leadership, public speaking . . ." He ticked off the benefits on his fingers. "Seriously. It would be well worth the money."

"And by *the* money, I assume you mean *my* money?"

He disarmed me with a broad "well, duh!" grin and, of course, I forked over the cash. I wasn't sure the family needed any additional "motivation" from our chief inspirational slogan-ginner, but at least this would give him some new material to sling.

Now I scrolled through his catalogue of wise sayings, searching for one that approached the gravity of the occasion.

Yogi Berra: "It ain't over till it's over!"

Gandhi: "An eye for an eye leaves the whole world blind."

Dale Carnegie: "First, ask yourself: What's the worst that can happen? Then prepare to accept it. Then proceed to improve on the worst."

Reaching inside the halo, I stroked Ned's stubbled cheek.

"Winston Churchill," I whispered. "'When you're going through hell . . . keep going.'"

DURING NED'S fleeting periods of wakefulness, I told him about the heartening flood of unexpected emails, cards, letters, and gifts—hand-knit prayer shawls, CDs and DVDs, and all things Red Sox—coming to us from all over the world.

"Not just from friends," I said, "but from friends of friends— neighbors, ministers, prayer groups—total strangers from Australia, all over Europe and the U.S."

Ned's eyes opened wide.

"It's unbelievable. Every time I open my email, I find something from someone's mother's cousin or an old teacher's tennis partner. Uncle Bill, Karen, Mary Ann, Kimmy . . . so many people have called to say they're thinking of us. And everyone at home is pitching in, bringing food for the kids and helping out."

I was so touched by this outpouring of prayers, encouragement, and simple kindnesses. It was empowering to know that all these people, known and unknown, were pulling for Ned. And it was humbling, too.

"People all over the world are praying for you right now, Ned."

There was a vague crinkling at the corners of his eyes.

"Ned, are you . . . are you smiling?"

He blinked once. My heart jumped. Minutes later, he'd slipped away again.

As the days dragged on and his conscious moments expanded to fifteen or twenty minutes here and there, I tried to ease his mind and keep him thinking with movies and music. Damage to his optic nerves made his eyes rove, so focusing on the screen seemed more of a task than a pleasure. The blinked "conversations" were endlessly aggravating for him, more like interrogations, because Ned could only blink yes or no.

"Do you want the TV on, Ned?"

Blink blink. No.

"You want music?"

Blink. Yes.

"Rap?"

Blink blink. No.

"Hip-hop?"

Blink blink. No.

"Okay . . . um . . . what else is on the radio? Wait. Did you mean the radio?"

Blink blink. No.

"A CD?"

Blink blink. No.

"Do you . . . you want me to sing to you?"

Blink blink. No!

After a thousand painstaking questions and blinked answers, Judy said, "Wait—iPod?"

Long, slow blink. *Yes, for crying out loud. Thank you.*

"Of course, iPod. All his favorite stuff." I clapped Judy on the shoulder. "Way to go."

But her smile faded. "Where is it?"

"Ned, it wasn't in your backpack," I said. "Was it . . . in your desk?"

Blink blink. No.

A thousand more questions led us to the conclusion he'd had it with him.

"In your car? Are you sure?"

Blink. *Yes.* With a "sheesh" roll of his eyes.

"Okay. That's . . . that's doable. We'll find the car and get it. Right, Judy?"

Judy looked a little skeptical. But it was all his favorite music.

There was no way I'd be able to reassemble it for him if we had to blink our way through the entire Billboard Top 100.

I called the kindly police officer, and he told me where we could find Ned's car. Judy and I drove a long way out into the desert, to an expanse of rusty graveyards where thousands of totaled vehicles were stacked like pancakes, two and three stories high. We finally pulled through an electrified barbed wire fence to a tumbledown shack. A dusty "Drink Coke" thermometer on the wall read 110 degrees, and despite the heat, two Dobermans barked and slavered at us. The greasy proprietor seized the dogs by their choke chains and pointed us to a dilapidated golf cart. Judy and I exchanged a nervous glance, then clambered aboard. We were ferried back through the endless stacks of damaged cars. Suddenly, we spotted a heart-stoppingly familiar bumper sticker: "Red Sox Nation."

"There!" I commanded.

We lurched to a stop beside a brutalized remnant of black metal. Ned's car. His wheels. His freedom.

The hood of the Honda Civic had been folded and forced into the front seat. The dashboard and shattered windshield were spattered with blood. A medical midden—syringes, gloves, tape—littered the floorboard, and the steering wheel jutted impossibly close to the driver's seat. The sight sent a shock wave deep into my bones. The echo of the impact passed through every muscle in my body and left me trembling with grief and a belated terror I couldn't seem to find a place for.

After a long, stunned silence, Judy and I searched for the iPod. I managed to pry open the glove compartment. No iPod, but a flash of green snagged a glint of sunlight.

"*Oh!*" I made a small, involuntary sound.

Judy looked up from her search of the backseat. "What is it?"

"These two little jade dragons . . ." I held them on the palm of my hand. "I bought them for Ned when I was in Singapore on business last year." I took one last shuddering look at the mangled Civic. "They were supposed to protect him."

"Maybe they did," Judy offered.

I'm pretty buttoned-down—*All Talbots all the time,* my friends like to joke—and not one to put much faith in things unseen, but I kept those dragons close by, and I was humbly grateful for all the prayers that poured out for Ned in those long weeks. A priest came to administer the healing oils. Mikey's grandmother came to say the rosary. A woman who cleaned the room asked if it would be all right if she laid hands on Ned. The mother of the bellman at my hotel came and said prayers beside his bed. Someone sent a Cherokee shaman, who performed a ritual meant to restore Ned's energy. A stuffy hospital in Boston might have had a problem with this, but here in the free-spirited high desert of Arizona, it didn't raise an eyebrow.

"As long as there's no candles or smoke," shrugged the charge nurse as the shaman entered with eagle feathers.

"There's a black cloud over your family," the shaman told me. "It's suppressing all your energy."

A chill trickled down the back of my neck.

"Normally, people have a field of protective energy that extends about three feet all around them. Yours is like this . . ." He measured a meager inch between his thumb and index finger. "And your son's . . ." He shook his head.

"Do you think my son will ever walk again?" I didn't expect him to say the clouds would clear and everything would be fine, but I was desperate to hear anything other than the same dire prognosis.

"I don't see him walking. But I don't see him *not* walking." The shaman studied the mountains in the distance. "I see him neither alive nor dead. I don't mean to be vague. No one can say what's possible or impossible," the shaman said. "But you need to do everything you can to restore your own energy now and give whatever you have to your son."

"Anything," I said, and I meant it.

That night at the hotel, I lay staring at the ceiling. The shaman's words haunted me like lingering smoke. Neither living nor dead. Not walking, but not *not* walking. It made no sense. But I could feel the void in Ned's energy—and the daily sapping of my energy when I was with him. It was suddenly so clear. We needed to surround ourselves with life and love. We needed our family and friends.

We needed to go home.

3

Coming Up for Air

I N THEIR WILD HABITATS IN CENTRAL AND SOUTH AMERICA, capuchin monkeys have been known to make, use, and even share tools. This ability to manipulate their environment is evidence of their astonishing intelligence. In captivity, they display what scientists call an "affinity to humans." I'm inclined to call it compassion—maybe even empathy.

I've long believed that empathy is an animal emotion and that our most human behavior is essentially primate. There are so many occasions when words are the least effective form of communication. We've learned to speed things along with verbal shorthand, but the true language of love and connection is unspoken. Sometimes a touch, a look, or simple *presence* is more honest and eloquent than anything that can be said. In our struggle to control everything that goes on around us, we rationalize away gut response and censor open sentiment. Animals don't do that.

Neither do children. I saw this with Ned when he was just a baby. Born in the first year of his father's cancer treatment, Ned seemed strangely tuned in to what was happening. As soon as he was big enough to manipulate his own environment, he did everything he could to get his father's attention, pushing toys into Ted's hands, jumping on the bed, filling the room with noise and excitement. He and Megan wanted to be close to their daddy all the time. When Ted was too weak to do anything but watch TV,

Megan would sit in the crook of his arm while Ned rolled around like a playful bear cub between his feet. Even at the end, when Ted couldn't talk to or play with or even hold them, they were determined to be smack in the middle of his life and have him be smack in the middle of theirs, as if they instinctively knew their time with their father would be short.

I wondered then, after Ted was beyond the ability to communicate, if he could feel us there with him, if he knew what was in our hearts. And I wondered, watching my boy fight for life in this Arizona hospital, if he was aware of me standing beside his bed. He was so encumbered by equipment, there was no way to hold him, except in my heart. I tried to feel by instinct, by motherly intuition, what he was thinking, where he was headed. Whenever they raised his eyelids, shining a light into his pupils, I strained to see over their shoulders. All I could see was a bottomless, dry well as Ned fought off spiking fevers and raging infections.

Oh, Ted . . .

I hoped he was watching over our son. So much of this scene was sickeningly familiar: the trach, the IVs, and the drugs; the ambient sounds and restrained explanations. I'd hear some unwieldy fragment of medical jargon and think, *Oh, that's right, I remember that.* And the next moment, I was weak in my stomach, needing desperately for the outcome to be different this time. It was too late for "okay," but I was willing to settle for anything short of that unbreathable heartbreak.

Despite the treasured few moments of Ned's wakefulness, the doctors and staff remained pessimistic.

"The latest X-rays are showing that even with the halo, Ned's head isn't securely connected to his spine," the doctor explained. "The vertebrae could be fused, however, using a bone graft and hardware to rebuild his neck. It's risky and very delicate surgery and in Ned's highly compromised state, he may not survive."

"That sounds so complex, so scary," I said.

"Without it, Ned has virtually no chance for even minimal recovery. If it goes well, he could be stabilized. The halo could be removed. He'd be able to sit up," said the surgeon. "That would improve circulation and give him a fighting chance against pneumonia."

"What would you do if this was *your* son?" I asked him.

He paused for a long time, shuffling his papers, looking at his shoes. Then he looked me straight in the eye. "I'd fly him back to Boston for the surgery—to be near his family and friends. Then I'd get him to a spinal cord specialty hospital like Craig in Denver or the Shepherd Center in Atlanta as fast as I could."

I weighed all this as objectively as I could, factoring in hard statistics and Ned's quality of life. It all came down to one harsh reality: Ned had nothing to lose.

"We'll do it," I said. "We'll go back to Boston."

Thus began the process of relocation, a complicated square dance that would somehow coordinate a stable moment between Ned's hospital-borne infections with the availability of a Med-Flight plane staffed with a crew trained for advanced life support and the availability of a bed at Mass General in Boston. All this was dependent on a specific doctor agreeing to assume responsibility for Ned's care, and it would be woven through a tangle of red tape and insurance paperwork.

Every time Ned's fever went down, I was all over the phone. One day there was a plane but no bed. Another day, a bed but no plane. Day after day, there was always some piece of the puzzle missing, and while I waited, I agonized over the risk we were taking moving Ned at all. My birthday rolled around, and Megan sent me a framed photo of all three girls and our little dogs, Guy and Bailey. I held those jade dragons in my hand. *C'mon, you two, it's my birthday. Don't let me down.* The next day the stars aligned and we took Ned back to Boston.

Many times since Ned's accident, I've experienced moments of standing outside myself, observing a scene that seems utterly absurd. Surreal. This was one of them. A cloud of brightly colored umbrellas shielded Ned from the blazing sun as medics shifted him, the ventilator, and the bulky halo onto the impossibly tiny airplane: a fragile beating heart inside a massive metal cage.

"There's no restroom on the plane, so . . ." The pilot left the rest to my imagination.

I didn't eat or drink anything all day and spent the long flight folded onto a narrow metal ledge, nodding off, jerking awake, staring at the pages of a book.

When we landed in Boston, Megan and Maddie met me on the tarmac.

"Peanut butter," said Maddie, holding up a sandwich.

"Pinot Grigio," said Megan, offering a plastic sippy cup.

I hugged them for the first time in what seemed like ages, and we stood there, holding each other tight in the midst of this profound *happening* that had happened to our family. On our way to the hospital, I ate my sandwich and drank my cup of wine. Luxury beyond description.

Ned was installed in the ICU with an entourage of specialists, the full array of machines and monitors, and a new web of tubing and wires. I stayed by his side as long as I was allowed, then returned to the blessed, barking, coming-and-going chaos of home. For the first time in almost a month, I kissed my daughters good night, collapsed into my own bed, and closed my eyes to count my blessings and my brood, all in the same time zone, with a fortress of good friends around us.

In the morning, more rested than I'd been in weeks, I awoke with a solid sense of *get on with it*. But then, I'd had time to come to grips with what had happened. The same could not be said for the kids.

"I can't imagine how trapped and helpless he must feel," Anna told me with tears in her eyes. "Unable to move, unable to talk or cry or scream."

"I don't understand why this had to happen," Maddie said. "Why Ned? It's not fair."

"I don't know if there is any *why*," I told her. "If there is, we could just as easily ask why he didn't die in the crash, couldn't we? I believe things happen for a reason, but it's not like God punishes us. I think it's bigger than that. I've always believed God had a plan for him. And I still do. I'm trying to, anyway. I'm trying to at least stay open to it, and maybe . . ."

But that almost sounded like hope. And I had decided long ago that hope was a dangerous place to go. It fills your mind with the unreachable and crushes your heart with thoughts of what could be—if only, if only—but never is. I'd hoped when my father had cancer and hoped again through chemo with Ned's father. I'd hoped while my beautiful stepdaughter lay dying and kept hoping right up to the moment I signed divorce papers. And each time I was thoroughly devastated. Not anymore. I had to stay balanced. Guarded in my expectations. Realistic in my decision making.

The proficiently humming staff at Mass General stabilized Ned, preparing him—and us—for the highly complex and risky surgery that was but a few days away. He wasn't awake much, but we were able to visit him for a little while each day, and we talked to him about sports and what was going on in the world outside his room. The night before the surgery we were somber but steady, and the next morning at five thirty, I was back at Mass General, waiting with Ned until they came to take him into surgery. I tried to be as calm as I could for him. It wasn't easy. Fortunately, Ned was sleepy from preliminary medication they'd given to relax him. He drifted in and out, offering a blink here and a blink there as I blathered mindlessly, about nothing, to fill the space around us.

When transport arrived to take him away, I caught my breath and steeled myself to say . . . something. *Not good-bye,* I told myself.

"You can walk down with him," said the nurse. "At some point they'll stop you, but go ahead and walk with him if you want."

"Ned, do you want me to come with you?" I asked.

Big blink.

"Okay." I mustered a confident nod. "Let's go."

We rumbled down corridors, up a few floors in a large service elevator, down another long corridor to another giant elevator. With each jarring bump and swivel of the gurney, Ned grimaced in pain.

"Hang in there, Bud," I said. "I think we're almost there."

The elevator opened on the blazing lights and hubbub of the surgical floor, where dozens of nurses, aides, doctors, and cleaning people were purposefully and skillfully preparing for their morning operations. A nurse bustled over and checked Ned's wristband.

"Are you Edward Sullivan?"

Ned blinked yes.

"And you are . . ."

"His mom."

"Would you like to come with him into the pre-op room?"

I looked over at Ned. Another resounding blink. The nurse handed me a gown, cap, surgical mask, latex gloves, and paper boots, which I donned self-consciously. I didn't see any other family members outfitted this way—in fact, I didn't see any other family members—but I wasn't going to lose even a moment of being there with Ned if I could. I followed the nurse into a world of people who had only eyes; the rest of their bodies were completely swathed in scrubs. Once again that surreal feeling closed in on me. What was I doing, masked and gowned, in the OR of Boston's oldest and biggest hospital? Ned shouldn't be here.

I looked down at him and muffled, "I bet I look pretty silly in this getup."

He blinked yes and gave me another small crinkle of a smile with his eyes.

I thought of all the things I'd ever wanted to tell him. The things I *never* wanted to tell him. I wanted to grab that stretcher and take him . . . I don't know, to Mars, to Antarctica, to a time machine. Anywhere but here.

The surgeon approached.

"We're ready for you, Ned."

It was time.

"I love you, Ned," I said, looking steadily into his eyes. "You're going to do great. I know it."

He blinked up at me. I couldn't really kiss him, but I blew him a kiss and gave him a broad pat on his shoulder so he'd see my hand touch him, even though he couldn't feel it. As the OR nurses whisked him through the swinging doors into the operating room, I closed my eyes tightly and said some serious prayers—for Ned, for the surgeon and his team, for our family.

I cleared my throat, blew my nose, and tried to pull myself together, and as I did, I thought back to one of Ned's football games when the captain marched his defeated team off the field at half time, down 48–0. "Heads high, men," he said. "Heads high." With those words the players threw back their shoulders and put a little life in their step as they trotted off to the locker room. Pride. Courage. Hope. They were all there in those three little words.

Head high, Ned. Head high.

"IT WENT WELL," the surgeon told me in the exhausted post-op hours. "He's stable. Doing as well as we could have expected."

"Thank God," I said, and released a breath. "So now . . . what?"

"We'll keep a close eye on him to ensure that his body doesn't reject the hardware and bone graft or that there isn't any swelling in his brain. We'll need to keep the halo on for a few more weeks while things heal," the surgeon cautioned. "All we can do right now is watch and wait."

My least favorite mandate. I'm neither a watcher nor a waiter. My response to any situation is *do something*. Anything. Climb a building. Jog to Chicago. It was agony to sit on my hands while my son stood so precariously close to the edge. Ned came and went from consciousness, sweating through fevers, blinking brief, desperate responses through his pain and anguish, or just lying there wrapped in terrible stillness. The flow of gifts and letters continued, a source of comfort and strength. I never stopped being humbly amazed at the goodness in people.

Judy's son Teddy, Ned's longtime co-conspirator and road-tripping buddy, came in to say good-bye before leaving on a long-planned backpacking trip to Europe.

"I'm coming back, dude. And I want you to be here when I do." His voice rusty with tears, Teddy gripped Ned's hand and said it again, hoping Ned would hear him through the fever, over the inner roar of mind-numbing medication. "You be here, Ned. You hear me? You be here when I come back."

Ned finally blinked. *Yes.*

That moment still haunts me. It was just so wrong for these two boys, these twenty-two-year-old kids—to be having this conversation at all.

AS THE SWELLING RECEDED and the pain meds were reduced, Ned tried to mouth a few words when he had the strength, but the movement was so minimal, it was impossible to read his lips. This was another fresh hell. My boy—my talkative, charming, "I can do anything" boy—couldn't *say* anything. He was rendered silent. I thought that if maybe Ned could communicate a little better, we could help lift the burden of his mind, if not his body, so adding to the blinked yes-and-no conversations, we developed an alphabet card system where I'd run a finger across the letters until he blinked a "stop" signal, then start over again, running a finger to the next letter he'd stop me at, spelling out brief, stilted messages.

"A, B, C, D, E, F, G, H—"

Blink.

"H? Yes? Okay . . . A, B, C, D, E, F, G, H, I, J—wait. Was that for J?"

Blink blink.

"Not J . . . So was it I? H . . . I . . . What? Oh—*hi*. Hi. Okay. Hi, Ned. Hello."

It was tedious for us and insanely frustrating for Ned. Sometimes he'd just close his eyes and refuse to go on, but I persisted. I pushed. I needed to know what was going on inside him, and this hangman method was all we had.

What emerged, letter by letter, was a chicken-scratched portrait of a young man in enormous pain and despair.

"Ned? Can you hear me? Do you know where you are?"

M . . . O . . . M . . .

My heart broke.

"I'm here, Ned. I'm here."

H . . . U . . . R . . . T . . . B . . . A . . . D . . .

"I know it's bad. I know . . ."

I wished I could comfort him, offer words of encouragement, but I just couldn't fake it. All I could offer was myself.

"I love you Ned . . . We all love you."

H . . . E . . . L . . . P . . .

WHEN YOUR CHILD IS BORN, you see this tiny, robust creature crying for you, needing you, wanting you. You make a promise to yourself that you will do all that you can for him, that you will help him grow up strong and good, that you will show him the way, keep him from harm. You make that promise and you believe in it. You believe in yourself and the strength of your love. But it's not enough. It's never enough.

I'd pursued second and third opinions from top doctors and rehabilitation specialists in Boston, and they consistently gave me the same dismal prognosis delivered by the doctors in Arizona.

No movement.

Not a word.

Not a breath.

Ever.

What could I do for my son but be there for him? Help prop him up. Respect him with the truth.

For Ned, the dawning reality of his situation was as agonizing as the nerve pain that ripped through his extremities.

"Medically speaking, it's a good sign," his doctor told me. "The nerves are trying to find each other. Talking to the brain."

Talking?

"I don't understand," I said. "Paralyzed—doesn't that mean you can't feel anything? Are you saying there's a chance he could—"

"Ellen, there's always a chance, but you need to be realistic."

I was realistic, all right. But I hated that word. Hated what it was coming to represent, what it meant for my son and his future.

"They're trying to help, Ned," I told him time and time again. "The doctors . . . they're really trying. They're doing what they can, but . . . but . . . I'm not going to lie to you. It's bad, Ned. It's bad. You have to hang on."

So he hung on. Through the pain and the silence and devastation of his young life, for days he tried. And then, one morning, through a laborious round of alphabet torture, Ned spelled out:

I . . . G . . . I . . . V . . . E . . . U . . . P . . .

I stared at the letters, not wanting to see the words. My own handwriting on a yellow sticky note.

I give up.

Heartbreak flowed over me like ice water. My beautiful boy. Just weeks earlier he'd been hiking the high desert, barhopping with his crew, road-tripping to Sedona and Mexico, and dreaming of so many places farther flung than these. Now here he was. A prisoner in his own body. No foreseeable future outside this room. Only the continuing sigh of the respirator kept him from everlasting freedom, perfect flight. If it had been me, I'd have been begging them to end it from the start. It was nothing less than heroic that Ned had made it this far without giving in to the dark thoughts.

With an almost drowning sense of urgency, I searched out every option. New doctors, state-of-the-art research and technology— anything that might give him a reason to hang on.

"Ned? Wake up, Ned. Listen. A world-renowned acupuncturist from China is coming in to treat you . . . Ned?"

He expressed a moment of interest, then sank back into himself.

AT A TEACHING HOSPITAL, no doctor travels alone. There's always an entourage. After I spoke to Ned's attending physician about his crashing spirits, he showed up with a cadre of psychiatric residents. They crowded into the small space between Ned's bed and the machines that were keeping him alive.

"Here's a situation where we see little or no probability of improvement," the doctor told his disciples. "The patient is not a minor, but no medical directives exist."

They always held court over the nameless patient with an efficient, all-pro coolness. I knew not to take it personally, but I hated hearing Ned reduced to such a dry commodity. As for medical directives—living wills or dying wishes—why would such a thing have ever crossed Ned's mind? He was young. Invincible.

The psychiatric team peered down on him, debating the credits and debits of this sad state of affairs. The whole scene was like something out of Monty Python. The Flying Circus clustered at the foot of the bed. Every one of them was a caricature.

"Edward, you seem to be depressed," observed the tall and terribly chic woman in stiletto heels and lab coat. "Blink once if you feel depressed."

"Edward," said a bearded Freud wannabe with a thick Eastern European accent. "How do you feel about your injury?"

How would this guy feel if *his* head was bolted into the undercarriage of a '67 Buick?

"Edward," said a barely legal Doogie Howser type, "I'd like you to share three *feeling* words about your injury."

I could think of two right off the bat, but they leaned in with the alphabet cards.

"A . . . B . . . C . . . D . . . E . . ."

"I think I saw a blink."

"Was that a blink, Edward?"

"It wasn't a blink. It was a twitch."

As the frustration of the spelling game set in, they kept blathering at him louder and louder, as if the increased volume would make their questions less ridiculous or Ned's body less car-wrecked. Finally, I couldn't stand it anymore. I jumped from my chair to stand beside my son.

"For God's sake! He's paralyzed, not deaf."

Ned's eyes connected with mine, and I thought I glimpsed relief, maybe even a little amusement. But then he closed his eyes and didn't look up again.

"Antidepressants," recommended Doogie. "Lots of 'em."

Ned spiraled downward. The thought of losing him terrified me. This boy who'd made me laugh every day since he was born, who hummed with energy even in his sleep—how could he simply stop *being*? If I could have traded my life for his, I'd have done it in a heartbeat because trying to imagine my life without him was like staring down a dry well. I couldn't imagine how I would prepare my children for another tragedy. I sought the wise counsel of my mother, my sister, and a few close friends, and I didn't shy away from the conversation when Anna and Maddie broached the topic.

"We have to do everything we can to keep him going," I said. "But ultimately . . . it's Ned's life. It's Ned's decision, and we have to respect his wishes."

Maddie—always empathetic, filled with compassion—just couldn't go there. The next day, she was quiet on the way to the hospital, and as we entered Ned's room, she started sobbing. Trembling with emotion, Maddie stalked to his bed and pointed her finger in her brother's face.

"No, Ned! You do *not* give up. You always told me I could never, never, ever give up, so now *you* don't get to give up. *Ever.*"

Ned did his best to blink some feeble reassurance for her, and we sat in silence for a while, Maddie's face full of stubborn hope, Ned's eyes full of longing and agony. After a while, she took up the alphabet cards, and he offered her whatever small answers he could, even as another deep fever overtook him. Between his compromised state, the plethora of hospital germs, and the introduction of foreign bodies like the new hardware in his neck and the shunt draining fluid from his brain, some nasty thing was always trying to get the better of his immune system.

Days passed. He drifted in and out.

One morning, I came into his room to find the respiratory therapist intent over the monitor on the ventilator, pointing something out to a nurse who was a favorite of Ned's.

"Ellen, look at this." The therapist waved me in. "Right here. See? Every once in a while, he's breathing over the ventilator. Taking a breath before the machine can take it for him."

"*What?*"

"This is really significant. This means we might be able to wean him off the respirator." She paused, physically swallowing her excitement. "I don't want to get anyone's hopes up. But if he's willing to try . . ."

I'd done my best to be bulletproof when it came to hope, but this was a real possibility.

"Ned?" I turned his face toward me. "Ned, are you hearing this? Do you want to try?"

He blinked his wide eyes. Yes.

"Okay." I nodded, my heart in my throat. "Turn off the respirator."

"I'm right here, Ned," the nurse assured him. "I'm keeping my hand right on the knob, so if you can't—"

But Ned dragged in one labored breath. And then another.

The three of us stood over him in disbelief, afraid to breathe ourselves.

Ned took another breath. And another.

Something—not words, not laughing or crying, but something that had elements of all three—burst out of me.

"Good job, Ned!" The nurse whooped and cheered.

"You did it, Ned. You did it," I said over and over. "I'm so proud of you."

Ned was Mr. Cool. He'd always been cautious about getting ahead of himself, but he'd also been one who loved to kick butt and prove naysayers wrong. I saw a fresh spark in his eyes, and I was smug enough for both of us. Just a few days earlier I'd brought in a big-time specialist from another hospital who'd confirmed the bleak prognosis we'd been hearing from day one. I saw that guy on the street a week later, and I wanted to poke him in the eye. I wanted to grab him by the necktie and drag him back inside the hospital room so Ned could enjoy a hard-earned moment of *How d'ya like me now?*

It was a gradual process, building one breath at a time, but a few weeks later, Ned was off the ventilator. His original tracheotomy tube, which had let him breathe in and out via the trach bypassing the nose and mouth, was replaced with a "talking trach"—one that would allow air out of his natural airway and through his vocal cords to create a sound. A battery of horrific tests determined his larynx wasn't paralyzed, but everything was out of sync and his diaphragm had been compromised by his injury.

Speech was still impossible.

Ned was wretchedly disappointed, but there was good news, too. The uncomfortable nose tube, which had been the means of providing liquid nourishment, was taken out, and a "G tube," or feeding tube, was surgically inserted into his stomach. The halo could be removed, replaced by a nasty body armor–type neck brace, but at least it wasn't screwed into his head. He could be moved— with the help of four nurses and aides—to a special chair, so he could actually look out the window or down the hall rather than just staring at the ceiling. A few of the nurses even took him outside one day—the first fresh air he'd had in weeks.

There were also mysterious but intriguing results from the Beijing acupuncture doctor. When inserting and twisting needles in Ned's left elbow, the doctor could trigger a "twitch" in his right leg. Ned couldn't feel a thing, but we were told that the response meant that the pathways from his brain to his feet were still open.

With these small but not insignificant signs of progress (not to mention the antidepressants), Ned's spirits seemed to pick up. He'd started to give a little smile to the nurses and mouth "thank you" when they came in to help him. He toughed out test after test and didn't complain. One day, he made a kiss with his lips when I was leaving.

Could it be that that old familiar charm was emerging? I thought back to the rehearsal dinner for Megan's wedding. Of course, from the moment he started school in Arizona, Ned could be found in nothing but shorts, cool shades, and flip-flops—even in the dead of winter when he returned home to the snow and cold with his blond hair and perpetual tan. I will never forget the look on my mother's face when Ned appeared at the church for the rehearsal in knee-length khakis.

I was lucky to get him there at all, so I didn't argue. He'd spent a lot of time grumbling, and not very nicely, about the imposition of all the wedding commitments when he had to get ready to go back to school the day after. But once he was at the rehearsal dinner, he turned on the signature Ned smile and was the beau of the ball, chatting up this guest or that one. As I observed him, I saw that the secret to his charm was always turning the conversation back to focus on whomever he was talking to. "And how are *you*, Aunt Lynn?" I could hear him say. "How's Bob's new motorcycle?" Amazing how quickly he could go from being completely self-absorbed and communicating exclusively in surly grunts at home, to articulately humoring various grand-mothers, aunts, uncles, and out-of town friends over cocktails.

"Ellen," they would tell me after being enthralled by Ned, "what a wonderful boy you have there! So sharp! So articulate!" as Megan, standing nearby, mimed the universal gag sign. I certainly got my money's worth for the Dale Carnegie course.

THE THOUGHT of leaving our good friends and terrific staff at Mass General was daunting, but the doctors were telling me Ned needed rigorous physical and occupational therapy at a rehabilita-tion center. There were several right there in Boston. While we were weighing our local options, out of the blue, Ned and I were visited by the northeast representative of the Shepherd Center in Atlanta.

I was completely disinterested. "Atlanta? You've got to be kid-ding. Too far away" was my initial response. "I can't just pack up and leave everyone again. We need to be closer to home." Our fam-ily clergyman was aghast. "You can't take away his support system now. He needs to be surrounded by his family to give him strength." I certainly had a hard time disagreeing with him.

But as I learned more about Shepherd, I remembered suddenly—certainly I had selective listening at that particular moment, but it all now came rushing back—the second part of what that doctor in Arizona had told me about what he'd do if it were his son: First, get him home. Then get him to a spinal cord specialty hospital like Craig Hospital in Denver or the Shepherd Center in Atlanta as soon as he was stable. I began to take the pro-position a lot more seriously. Maybe it was Ned's best hope.

"Shepherd was founded by a couple whose son sustained a spinal cord injury in a surfing accident," the rep told us. "Our mission is to return catastrophically injured patients to the highest level of functioning possible, enabling them to continue their lives with hope, dignity, and independence."

It was everything I desperately wanted for Ned but couldn't begin to visualize.

I started the chessboard moving; arranging for transport, preparing my other kids for another long separation, and jumping through the insurance hoops.

"You did a great job getting all this together," the Shepherd rep told me. "One last thing before I can sign off on Ned's admission. We need to firm up a discharge plan."

"Discharge plan?" I echoed. "We haven't even gotten there yet."

"I know it seems odd." She smiled, but it was the Clipboard Lady smile, which I was being introduced to. Every medical facility has its Clipboard Lady, and there's no stopping her once she shifts into paperwork mode. "Our objective is to prepare Ned for the next step, whatever that may be. We can't do that if we don't have a long-range plan."

In the months since Ned's accident, I hadn't been able to think past the moment. We didn't even have the luxury of "one foot in front of the other." The next step for us was the next blink, the next breath. A long-range plan required either hope or resignation; I was terrified of the first, and the second was simply foreign to my nature—and Ned's.

I was suddenly overwhelmed by the *foreverness* of what had happened to him and to our family. One moment had redefined all the moments to come. We weren't talking about transportation arrangements or transitional care. We were talking about the rest of Ned's life. That left only one possible answer to her question.

I didn't believe it for a moment myself, but I said it with all the certainty I could: "We'll bring him home."

She glanced up from her clipboard. "How?"

"*Some*how," I told her, without a glimmer of a plan. "Somehow we'll bring him home."

4

Meanwhile, Back at the Monkey College . . .

I N THE LATE 1970S, HOPING TO IMPROVE THE LIVES OF DIS-abled veterans, researchers M. J. Willard and Judi Zazula set out on a mission to train capuchin monkeys to assist people with spinal cord injuries. Capuchins belong to the New World order of primates found in Central and South America. With a life span of thirty to forty years in captivity, these intelligent and agile monkeys were chosen for their perfect size (a compact six to eight pounds of body weight on a wiry frame less than two feet tall) and because of their teachable talent for manipulating objects and solving problems. With major support from the National Science Foundation, the Veterans Administration, and Paralyzed Veterans of America, Helping Hands placed its first service monkey with a paralyzed man in 1979, and the two remained friends for twenty-eight years.

About the time Ned wrapped up elementary school, Kasey advanced from foster care to Monkey College in Boston. Monkeys spend two to four years in Monkey College, learning tasks and developing bonds of trust and affection with their trainers. Ever the social butterfly, Kasey loved interacting with all the expert trainers and staff who worked with her over her first few years. As she progressed through college, her primary trainer/handler became Megan Talbert, now the executive director of Helping Hands.

Kasey's Monkey College training began with Phase One: "Cubicle." In a small, soundproof room, free of distractions, Kasey curiously eyed a toy familiar to anyone who's had a toddler around: a yellow post with a stack of plastic donuts in graduated sizes. Kasey's trainer placed a donut on the post. She did it again and then handed a third donut to Kasey, who played with it for a while but quickly learned to follow her trainer's example and place the donut on the post. The trainer would then ring a bell, praise Kasey mightily, and reward her with a lick of peanut butter.

Other toys followed: plastic cups and balls, bright plastic flowers and blocks, and eventually a wooden box with a light switch. The trainer flipped the switch.

"Kasey, do this?" she said.

Kasey flipped the switch and applauded wildly, happy that a well-trained human promptly offered another gooey little dollop of peanut butter. Kasey was ready for Phase Two: "B-Room."

The trainer sat in a wheelchair. Kasey examined every inch of it with great scientific interest and learned that if she hopped up on her trainer's lap and gently placed her trainer's hand on the joystick, they could zoom around the room together.

"Kasey, change?" The trainer tapped the outstretched tray on a CD player. "Kasey, change?"

Kasey turned the CD in her hands and nibbled the edge a bit before she positioned it to play and slid the door shut.

"Good job! Come get your treat."

New games were played, introducing more complicated manipulation of objects. Kasey learned to open and close a refrigerator, put a drink in a drink holder, and insert a straw. Using only positive reinforcement—never negative consequences or "discipline"—her trainer would refine each task with infinite patience. Kasey became adept at pushing buttons, shifting switches, and operating basic equipment, and she took up residence in the roomy cage that would become her palace and sanctuary.

Phase Three: "Apartment" was designed to return Kasey to the world in which she grew up: a human home.

There was a bed, a working TV, radio, refrigerator, and microwave. With plenty of time for cuddling and playing between tasks, Kasey learned to open food and drink containers, scratch an itch on her trainer's face with a soft cloth, and push reading glasses up on her nose.

"Kasey, can you open? Kasey, open?"

The trainer pointed with a little laser pen in her mouth and kept her hands still. Kasey deftly attached a magazine to a tilted rack, whisked open the cover, and flipped to the first page.

Monkeys have different levels of intelligence, just like humans, so a brighter monkey is able to master more complex tasks and assist an individual with a greater injury. Kasey was as bright as they come, and soon the search was on to find the perfect match. Her skills would be a godsend for any paralyzed individual, but it was her exuberant personality that made her different. She'd be able to handle a family home that sometimes resembled a circus tent.

Of course, we had no clue about any of this as we sat in Ned's hospital room at Mass General, watching a major storm brewing.

"RESCUE EFFORTS continue in the aftermath of Hurricane Katrina . . . much of the city of New Orleans under water . . . entire Gulf Coast paralyzed . . . emergency workers slowly making their way to the stranded . . ."

I glanced over, expecting to see Ned sleeping, but he was staring up at CNN's ongoing coverage of the disaster. There seemed to be a sad understanding in his eyes as he watched a replay of a helicopter swooping in to save a man from a rooftop. The guy had been badly injured by a falling tree when he went back to the Ninth Ward to get his dog, but as the waters rose, he heaved himself over to the edge of a roof and, after clinging to the rain gutter for hours, grabbed a can of spray paint bobbing by in the floodwater and wrote "HELP ME!" on the bare tar paper.

"Wow. What an incredible story," I said. "I mean, what are the odds? Stranded, clinging to a roof and a can of spray paint floats by?"

We could identify with the exhausted, displaced survivors on the screen. Tragedy had blown in and instantly upended their lives, just as it had ours. The seemingly random centimeters that separated the living and the dead sent a chill up my spine and took me back to what the doctors had told me during those first terrible days in Arizona some three months ago.

But here we were. Not only had Ned lived, he was breathing on his own. Maybe the only logical response to the word "impossible" is to shrug and say, "Stranger things have happened." Because impossible things—good and bad—keep happening all around us.

I'd worked through a lot of red tape to get Ned into the Shepherd Center in Atlanta. He was disinterested at first, but that changed when he saw a DVD with patients with injuries similar to his working out in the gym. The gym was Ned's natural habitat. He was more than ready to meet the challenge. I had all the administrative ducks in a row. Megan and Ron were preparing to move in with Maddie and Anna for the duration, and Jake was engrossed in his freshman year at Bentley. Unfortunately, with hospitals all over the Southeast either full up or out of commission, and doctors and staff being diverted to disaster relief centers because of the hurricane, Ned's bed at Shepherd disappeared. We were in a holding pattern; I was doing the MedFlight plate-spinning act again, trying to coordinate an available flight with an opening at Shepherd and a window of stability in Ned's condition.

We'd been in Boston for some seventy-eight days when it all finally came together.

"When will you be back, Mom?" Anna asked as I folded clothes into the small suitcase I was allowed in the cramped space at the back of the tiny airplane.

"Hard to say," I told her truthfully. "At least a few weeks."

"So I guess you won't be here for Back to School Night. To meet my new teachers."

"Maybe Megan can go," I offered.

"It's not the same, Mom." She shrugged and shook her head. "Whatever. It's okay."

No, it isn't, I thought. *It's hard.*

But there was no point in telling Anna what she already knew.

"You and Maddie are all set for school," I said instead. "Books, activities, all that. Megan's got the schedule, and your rides are all lined up. Don't worry. You're good to go."

"I'm not worried. It's just that . . . well, when you're gone . . . the dogs miss you."

I nudged her shoulder and said, "I miss them, too. A lot."

The next morning, Megan brought Maddie and Anna to the runway at Hanscom Field, and we huddled together in the cool September rain, holding umbrellas over Ned, who mouthed lopsided kisses to the girls as the medical staff hoisted him into the plane.

Tucked away on my little shelf in the back of the cabin, I tried to concentrate on Ned and what he needed in the here and now, but nagging doubts about our "discharge plan" were just under the surface of everything now. I was wide awake to the new reality of our lives and reluctant to get ahead of the hard facts.

Get-well cards said, "Miracles do happen!"

Doctors said, "Never, no way, no how."

Complete faith in either would be like overdriving my headlights. I wanted to believe what I'd told the case worker, but in my heart I was already looking at fallback positions. I could only deal with what I could see, and right now, I saw no way Ned could thrive—or even survive—outside an acute care facility. The truth was, I had been willing to say anything that would get him into the Shepherd Center.

So I got him in. And now we were on our way.

Walk through one door at a time, I told myself, *then look for a key to the next.* That was my strategy, and I was sticking to it.

5

Stranger Things
Have Happened

"HEY, Y'ALL! YOU MUST BE NED. AND THIS MUST BE MOM. Ellen, sugar, how are you?"

We had just arrived at the Shepherd Center in Buckhead, an upscale Atlanta suburb. The intake host greeted us with genuine Southern hospitality and a drawl as thick as molasses.

And she didn't bat an eye at the severity of Ned's condition. It was all in a day's work for the expert staff.

"Ned will spend today and tonight being evaluated, then we'll get him settled in his new room," our host explained before passing me along to the full staff who'd assembled for my orientation.

The information they provided covered Ned's various therapies and activities, lodging, as well as insurance, Social Security for the disabled—the mounds of paperwork that surround any catastrophe. A case manager, clipboard in hand, pressed me again about the discharge arrangements, but that was fine. I knew my lines. Every half hour or so, I was passed along to the next proficient staffer, who not only answered but anticipated my questions. Growing more impressed every step of the way, I felt like Dorothy being processed for her meeting with the great and powerful Oz.

Upstairs in the ICU, Ned was happily at the center of a swarm of physical, occupational, speech, and recreational therapists; an ear, nose, and throat specialist; a psychologist; and a team of physiatrists, who specialize in physical rehabilitation—all fluent in the language of *blink*. A soft collar replaced the body armor, and the assistive technology team rigged a call light he could activate by twitching his cheek.

For the first time since the accident, Ned was out of a hospital gown and in his own T-shirt and pajama pants, which had been on Shepherd's To Bring list. Shepherd is serious about preparing a patient for the real world, and the real world for Ned was a pair of Arizona Wildcats flannels with a Red Sox T-shirt. That's what he was wearing when I walked in. But seeing how huge they were on him was a jolting reminder of how emaciated he'd become after months of IVs and feeding tubes. Suddenly measured before my eyes was the difference between the robust 175-pound athlete he'd been before and the struggling 130-pound survivor he was now.

The next morning, I rented a car, grabbed a few groceries for my hotel room, and headed over to Shepherd to begin what I hoped would be a life-changing experience. And it was life-changing. Not just for Ned but for me, and even, we would discover, for the many friends and family members who came to visit while we were there.

Up to this point, the hospitals were all about saving his life; Shepherd was all about getting on with it. Ned's heavy-duty, seven-days-a-week schedule was nothing like the sedentary life he'd been living, and though it was a bit of a shock to both our systems, his attitude was generally *bring it*.

The first order of business was getting him out of bed and measured for a wheelchair, one that would precisely fit his body dimensions. I thought this was a good thing, the first sign that Ned could become mobile—even in a limited way—and I thought that he'd be looking forward to this, too. But the scowl on his face told me otherwise.

"Hey, what's wrong, Ned? This is going to be great. These people really know what they're doing here, and you're going to get an incredible chair," I said.

He turned his head away. Suddenly, I remembered.

"Oh. Gosh, Ned. I'm sorry—are you thinking about that guy who came to see you at Mass General?"

"That guy" was a nice elderly gentleman who had done a tour at the Shepherd Center and had been sent by the rep to give Ned a pep talk on Shepherd's wonders. The whole thing had backfired. Ned saw this older man show off the tilt feature of his wheelchair as if it were his personal space shuttle seat.

N O T M E, Ned had spelled out.

Who ever sees himself in a wheelchair? The whole experience was so not relevant to Ned's head at that moment in time that he blinked that he wouldn't go to Shepherd at all. It took me a week to get him back on track.

"Come on, Ned. You're getting the top-of-the-line, most technologically advanced wheelchair on the planet. You're going to start with this one here," the therapist told him, "then we'll order a custom-designed one for home."

Technologically advanced or not, custom designed or not—who imagines himself in a wheelchair?

Ned directed a pointed glance at an odd red and white apparatus snaking out from the head of the chair, then back to the therapist.

"It's called a sip-and-puff," he said. "You'll learn to use your breath to drive the chair by sipping and puffing on the device. Think Morse code, but instead of dots and dashes, tiny sips and puffs of air. Eventually, you'll be able to use that technique to turn the TV on and off, call the nurse—even use a computer someday."

"A computer?" I said. "Ned, that would be fantastic."

He shot me a look that said, *Settle down, Mom. One thing at a time.* But I couldn't help leaping at the possibility. Being able to use a computer would free his mind, even if he was confined to the wheelchair. He could communicate, even if he couldn't speak. It was a connection—possibly his only avenue—to the world outside.

We would later see the sip-and-puff at work with one of the other patients, a lovely man who used it to keep in touch with friends and family. But what seemed to come easily to this man would not come easily to Ned. He knew that mastering the sip-and-puff was the only thing separating him from human conversation, but week after frustrating week he couldn't make it work.

"Maybe he'd do better with eye gaze technology," an assistive tech staffer suggested sometime later. "Infrared light goes into the eye, senses where you're looking, and moves the cursor on the screen. You blink to type a letter or click on a link."

We tried a system from a company in Maryland. No go. Another system from a company in Arizona was more forgiving (and more expensive), but damage to Ned's optic nerves had left him with blurry vision at best and seeing everything in triplicate at worst. After a few more frustrating weeks, we had to accept that the computer was simply out of reach for the time being.

"We'll try again later," I promised, as I packed up the whole works to ship back.

Ned tried to muster a smile, but it was a huge blow.

. . .

MEANWHILE, Ned started going to a simulator room where he learned the painstaking process of using the puffer to drive his wheelchair. There was a lot to remember, and it was all he could do to summon enough air to make it work, but he kept trying. It was a struggle. Sometimes his pain and his eyesight were so bad that he had to retreat to the quiet of his room to regroup—totally frustrated and exhausted. There was a lot of bumper car–type action and there were some embarrassing collisions with doorways, walls, people, and service carts before he got the basic stop, go, and steering of his new chair down.

Dr. Marin, a young intern on rotation at Shepherd who had grown up in New England, was working to become a physiatrist, a rehabilitation specialist trained to treat pain and maximize function after catastrophic injuries. It meant a lot to Ned that Dr. Marin spent time just hanging out, bonding over the Red Sox and Georgia football. Apparently ESPN is like that universal translator they use at the UN; the communication challenge was nothing between these two Sox fans. It was heartening for Ned—and for me—to be with someone who recognized he was still a regular guy. What had mattered to Ned before mattered to him now. Everything that used to make him laugh was still funny. And of course, the Red Sox are forever.

"I want you to start visualizing movement," Dr. Marin told him. "Like arm curls. While you're lying in bed, *see* yourself doing that arm curl."

Ned gave him a quizzical expression.

"Visualization helps some SCI patients reconnect the brain to the limbs. Your brain still knows how to kick a soccer ball, right? See it in your mind's eye. Feel that feeling. Let's see if we can help your brain get that message to your body."

When Dr. Marin first said this, Ned and I just looked at him. What was he really saying—that imagining movement could create movement?

"Look," the doctor said, "Ned's spinal cord has been severely injured—his brain has been severely injured—but he can still remember inside his head that he moved. We've seen it happen before—if he 'sees' himself kicking his leg or moving his arm in a way that is familiar to his body, sometimes the brain will start to try to reconnect with the limbs—sending out signals. Maybe his arms or legs won't immediately feel those signals, but sometimes . . . they do."

It was worth a try. Anything was worth a try.

From the get-go, Ned charmed the nursing staff; they were wrapped around his little finger. I could argue with him all morning in that mother/son way. He'd snarl with his upper lip and give me eyebrow action I wouldn't care to put words to. But when Teryl, his favorite nurse, breezed in to get him into the chair, she got a million-dollar smile.

He spent his afternoons in the gym, tackling aggressive physical therapy or working out with his occupational therapist. We both went to lectures on wound care, the Americans with Disabilities Act (ADA), wheelchair vans, home accessibility needs. True to form, Ned took it all in, wide-eyed and attentive.

Recreational therapy (which wasn't nearly as much fun as it sounds) included trips to the mall, a park, the drugstore—everywhere he'd need to go in the "real world." But it put right in his face everything he was missing about his "normal" life as an independent twenty-two-year-old. Ned was used to going wherever he wanted to go, doing whatever he wanted to do. He hated being dependent on anyone for anything.

One outing took us to the Hartsfield Airport, where Delta flight crews were to educate us about taking commercial flights. Ned was suffering particularly fierce nerve pain that day; I could see it in his eyes. My heart ached for him, but I tried to be as encouraging as I could.

"Come on, Ned," I said, nudging. "It'll be good to get out."

He screwed his eyelids into a vehement double blink. *No!* I grabbed the alphabet card.

"Look, Ned, you need to try to move forward," I said.

I N P A I N. L E A V E M E A L O N E.

With serious lobbying from his therapists and nurses, we got him on board with the day's agenda, but the long, jostling bus ride and commotion inside the crowded airport made his nerve pain even worse. The harrowing experience of actually boarding a plane as a quadriplegic began with Teryl pushing his chair down the jetway, which was too narrow for his limited sip-and-puff capabilities. At the door of the plane, four Delta employees made the frightening transfer from his large power wheelchair to an "aisle chair" narrow enough to roll between the rows, then helped him through another awkward move to an aisle seat, where he was battened down with a thick chest strap so he wouldn't fall over.

"Come on, buddy. Here we go. You can do it," they coached, as if he had a choice about having four well-intentioned strangers heft him back and forth like a sack of meal.

Ned looked more anxious than annoyed, and I was feeling a little alarmed myself. Who were these people? What did they know about working with quadriplegics? By the time we got off the airplane, Ned was done with the whole adventure. Completely, visibly done. Teryl gave him meds to calm his nerves and help him cope with the pain. Even so, we couldn't wait for this "recreational therapy" to be over.

But what would a trip to the airport be without a bad meal?

The Shepherd staff herded all the patients, family, and attending aides over to the food court for lunch. For Ned, who had been living on formula through a feeding tube but still had a perfectly tuned sense of smell, it was torturous. Fast-food aromas filled the air: tacos, pizza, burgers, and fries. Everything he had been denied for months.

Damn it, I berated myself. How thoughtless could I be? I should have anticipated this, should have shielded him from all this somehow.

A busy traveler hurried by with a heaping tray of teriyaki beef, and Ned's eyes squeezed shut. When I saw the terrible anguish in his face, I had to look away myself.

Welcome to Ned's "real world."

ONE STEP FORWARD, two steps back.

Respiratory issues required suction to clear Ned's lungs. Nerve pain drove him out of the gym to his darkened room. A "swallow test" indicated that water went down to his lungs instead of into his esophagus, so the feeding tube would have to remain in place. He went daily to speech therapy, and he still couldn't utter a sound.

"There's an experimental electric shock treatment we could try," the therapist told him. "It seems to sometimes jump-start the ability to talk in spinal cord and brain injured patients."

Ned and I exchanged a glance, a quick nod. "We'll try it."

Not a spark of progress.

Ned's spirits lagged and began another downward spiral. He preferred the solitude of his room to the humiliation of having a respiratory nurse babysit him wherever he went. It was profoundly depressing for him to hear the other patients on his floor, most of whom were between sixteen and twenty-five, gathering at the nurse's station, ordering pizza and subs, cruising down to movie night in the rec room, and *talking* to one another. Ned wasn't able to engage in those simple, all-about-nothing conversations. He'd always been able to walk in the door, break the ice, and connect with anyone in the room. Now, without even the simplest connecting rituals of *hello* and *how are you,* he was unarmed and isolated. Where do you go after a smile and a nod if a smile and a nod are all you can offer? We forget, I think, the huge importance of small talk and how intensely lonely it is when we can't respond to others with so much as a penny's worth of our thoughts.

Fortunately, throughout our stay at Shepherd, a steady parade of friends and family rode in and out like the cavalry. Megan and Ron came down together. Maddie and Anna made a trip. Judy and Jane came and saved my sanity. Teddy returned from Europe and put his new life on hold so he could spend five weeks in Atlanta bolstering Ned's resolve.

"Hiya, buddy. Great digs."

Ned visibly lightened when Teddy strolled in. It was as if nothing had changed and they hadn't missed a beat in their friendship. And really, they hadn't. Soon Ned's friend Annie and Teddy's sister Heather showed up, and they took turns going to physical therapy and tagging along on recreational (or not) outings. On Halloween, teams of patients and therapists chose themes and made costumes for a parade, and Ned and Teddy spent all week in the art room working on their Pac-Man getups. Holding a paintbrush in his mouth, Ned decorated a Ms. Pac-Man for his wheelchair. The staff created a haunted house, and Teddy helped Ned throw a pie at his favorite therapist.

My sister Lynn came down from Cleveland to take over my listening and learning responsibilities so I could go home and spend a few days with the other kids. Lynn is Ned's godmother, and they've always been close. I did my best to prepare her, but I knew there was no way she'd fully grasp the reality of his condition until she was in the room with him. Seeing is believing, but some things are even bigger than that. She was devastated when she first saw him. We didn't have much time together—we'd overlapped trips as little as possible so I could maximize my precious time at home—but as she drove me to the airport that evening, I filled her in on everything that had happened so far during our brief but eventful stay at Shepherd.

"Oh, Ellen." She shook her head in disbelief. "How are you going to do this? You really think you can take care of him at home?"

"No," I said bluntly. "I don't. I was hoping he could stay here for a while. Or maybe we'd find another place closer to home for—for the long haul. But the case managers insisted on a discharge plan and they're not fooling around. They want specifics. They want *pictures.*"

"Oh, dear . . ."

"I'm meeting a contractor who specializes in handicap-accessible home improvements. I'll get everything in place and figure out the rest later. Including how to pay for it."

HOME WAS HEAVEN. I snuggled with my daughters and dogs, slept in my own bed, took a quick visit to Jake's football practice at college, which was fortunately just twenty minutes away, and began the enormous task of preparing a place for Ned to come back to. My timing was perfect.

"You're coming home for my Back to School Night? You mean it?" Anna had squealed when I called to tell her. Then there was silence.

"Anna? Anna? Are you there?" I said.

"That's great, Mom." But behind her leaden voice were years' worth of business trips and hospital vigils.

"I'll be there, Anna," I promised. I so didn't want to let her down yet again. And I didn't.

After I'd met her teachers and heard how well she was doing, another mom touched my elbow and tugged me aside in the hallway.

"I know what Anna's going through," she said. "My son Joe is having a rough year, too. Boys this age—you know how they zero in on a verbal punching bag for the semester." She bit her lip, and a tear slid down her face. "Anna's there for him . . . stands up for him. I just want you to know how special she is. He wouldn't have made it through middle school without her."

My Anna. I was so proud—and not at all surprised. But it made leaving home again all the harder. I was missing so much in the girls' lives, and Jake's freshman year, and I was putting so much on Megan's shoulders. As eager as I was to see Ned, I have to admit I didn't look forward to resuming the daily grind in Atlanta. On the flight back, I reset my internal alarm system and steeled my backbone for what lay ahead: the generic hotel room instead of the warmth of home; the sterile regimen of institutional life—even at an institution as wonderful as Shepherd—

instead of the open air and freedom to deal with each day as it came.

I'd always thought of myself as resilient, a do-what-needs-doing kind of person, but these months of managing so many challenges were taking their toll.

Susan was a new friend who was an old friend of an old friend, and one of the people who appeared out of the blue to adopt me and Ned when we arrived in Atlanta. Her ready smile, balloon "treatments," and willingness to do anything to help us were very welcome in our unfamiliar surroundings. When I got back from Boston, she picked me up at the airport looking like the cat who swallowed the canary.

"What's up?"

"Nothing." She stifled a smile. "Everything's fine."

"How's Ned?" I asked, heaving my suitcase into the trunk.

"He misses you."

"Okay . . ." I wasn't buying it.

Walking into Shepherd, I had the odd sensation that doctors, therapists, and staff—everyone including the floor sweepers was looking at me, smiling a little too warmly, whispering behind their hands. A nurse turned her head to wipe her eyes as I passed by.

"This just doesn't happen," I heard someone say.

I quickened my steps, practically running down the hall. I burst into Ned's room, a bevy of nurses and aides behind me. Ned and Teddy faced away from the door, working on the laptop.

"Ned?" I said. "Ned, I'm back."

"*Hi, Mom!*"

"Ned . . ." I stood frozen at the sound of his voice.

It was strained and atonal, like someone recovering from a bad case of laryngitis. But it was Ned all right. Teddy turned him to face me, and Ned lurched his left arm in a punchy half wave. I crossed to him and gripped his hand, astonished to feel a weak squeeze in return.

"*Ned.*"

Only vaguely aware of the tearful, joyful crowd that had gathered behind me to witness this huge event, I hugged Ned. Teddy hugged the nurses. The nurses hugged the therapists. Susan hugged everyone. Not a dry eye in the house.

"People with his level of injury . . ." Ned's occupational therapist dabbed her eyes. "They don't just start speaking and moving one day."

"You're one of Shepherd's miracles, Ned," said the nurse manager.

We immediately called my mom.

"Hi, Nonnie," he rasped. "This is Ned."

Her reaction—shrill as a flute—could be heard across the room.

"Got to call Jake," said Ned. "And girls."

And just about everyone else on the planet. Ned got a huge kick out of surprising people. He didn't sound like himself; his voice was gravelly and gritty, each syllable was labored, but everyone was amazed and elated when they realized it was him on the phone.

"I bet you've got a lot to say to me," I teased, thinking back over the aggravating weeks.

"Just you wait," he replied.

The next evening, we had a visit from one of the stars of *Murderball,* a documentary about quads playing rugby. Around the room, the Shepherd patients introduced themselves, sharing how and when they'd sustained their spinal cord injuries. Each story was more poignant than the last.

"I'm Amber. My car got sideswiped by a drunk driver."

"I'm Randy. I was hauling logs . . . lost my brakes and the truck rolled."

"I'm Ned," he said, when it was his turn. "I just . . . started talking . . . yesterday."

Everyone who could clap applauded like mad, and the whole room cheered wildly.

"I'm Jeannie. I was in a car accident on my way back to check on things after my house got destroyed in Hurricane Katrina."

"I'm Mark. I was in Katrina, too. Went back for my dog, but a tree fell . . ."

As he described the rooftop, the unlikely gift of spray paint, and the swooping helicopter, Ned and I traded astonished glances. *What are the odds?*

That just doesn't happen.

IN ORDER TO HAVE Ned released to me, I had to be completely trained to care for his respiratory health, manage his feeding tube, transfer him from bed to chair and chair to bed, give him a shower in a shower chair, and reposition him to avoid pressure wounds. I took courses, attended lectures, met one-on-one with doctors and nurse managers. At the end, I'd have to pass an extensive written test and clinical sessions where I'd be evaluated by nurses and therapists.

Meanwhile, Ned gave his all in PT and OT. His therapists introduced a wide range of possibilities: educational, intellectual, and physical activities; water and wheelchair sports; art classes. One day, we were visited by a team who trained assistive dogs for wheelchair-bound people. They brought a beautiful, impeccably trained black Lab.

"Ned, that's a great idea," I said after they'd gone, but Ned wasn't interested.

"We . . . have . . . dogs," he said flatly.

"Not like that, we don't! That dog just now was like a Green Beret. Guy and Bailey are like . . . like sorority rushers."

"Mom . . ." He gave me one of those back-down looks again.

"I know, but . . ." I paused as a hazy memory brushed the back of my mind. "Do you remember—a long time ago, didn't we see something about trained monkeys?"

"You mean, like for a circus or something?" one of the nurses asked who was getting him ready for OT.

"No, these were monkeys trained to assist people. Like an assistance dog."

"Seeing eye . . . monkeys?" he said skeptically.

"I'm serious. I think I saw it on . . . I don't know, *60 Minutes* or something."

He rolled his eyes, letting me know I was nuts, but when the occupational therapist came in, I asked her if she'd ever heard of such a thing.

"Trained monkeys? Not that I know of," she said.

"I guess it's kind of a farfetched idea," I sighed.

"Mom, you . . . could get . . . *flying* monkeys . . . *Wizard of Oz.* Maybe . . . Cowardly . . . Lion, too."

"Yeah, you're hilarious. Good night."

Back at the hotel, I sat down to check my email. Scrolling through my inbox, which was always filled with sustaining notes of encouragement from friends and family, I came to a message from Maddie and Anna's school. My breath caught in my throat.

"*Oh* . . ."

I closed my eyes, opened them wide, read the message again. The words were as unlikely—as divinely serendipitous—as a can of spray paint in a raging flood.

Dear Parents: You are invited to attend this Friday's assembly where Helping Hands: Monkey Helpers for the Disabled will be visiting.

6

Natural Habitats

M ADDIE AND ANNA CALLED ME FRIDAY AFTERNOON right after school.

"Tell me everything," I said.

"Mom, the monkey is so cute! Her name is Ayla, and she's super smart."

"Please, Mom, can we get a monkey? She did all these tricks and then Judi—"

"The Helping Hands person—she dropped something on the stage—"

"Ayla ran right over and brought it to her. It was so adorable."

"And then Ayla opened a water bottle, put a straw in, and held it up for Judi to drink."

"We *have* to get a monkey. Seriously, Mom. Please? She's so awesome. Can we?"

"Please, Mom. It would be so cool. It would be awesome. For *Ned*, I mean."

"Right! For Ned. Just think of all the stuff she could do for him."

"Hey, you don't have to convince me." I laughed.

I couldn't wait to badger Megan—who'd gone to the assembly with the girls—for the hard information.

"Did you talk to them?" I asked her. "What did they say? How was it?"

"It was kind of intense at first," Megan said. "Too close to home for Maddie. She had a hard time when they talked about people with spinal cord injuries. It's still pretty raw, especially to have it come up for discussion in front of all her friends like that."

I winced. "I should have thought of that."

"It's okay, Mom," Megan reassured me. "She had to leave for a few minutes, but she got her composure back, and afterward we went right over and got to see the monkey up close and personal. Mom, this monkey really is adorable—so intelligent and sweet. This really would be great for Ned."

I tried to collect my thoughts. "You know, when I saw this in a routine announcement of a school activity—Megan, I nearly jumped out of my skin. They just happen to be visiting Concord Middle School? This week? And I just happened to think of it out of the blue?"

"That is weird," she conceded. "At the very least, it's a huge coincidence."

"Coincidence, divine intervention, synchronicity—whatever it is, I'll take it." I allowed myself a smile. "Did you have a chance to tell them our story?"

"I did. I got everyone's contact info. I'm on it."

I breathed a grateful sigh. "That's my girl."

In addition to educating people about how monkeys can assist individuals who live with severe disabilities, the Helping Hands Spinal Cord Injury Prevention Program (SCIPP) is presented to thousands of school children and young adults across the country every year.

Skimming the Helping Hands website, I tried to remember what we did before the Internet.

The SCIPP program highlights spinal cord injury prevention, disability awareness, and human-animal bonding. This safety and prevention information is critical to children at an early age, because most spinal cord injuries occur between the ages of sixteen and twenty-six.

I clicked to a gallery of images and marveled at what the clever, dexterous little monkeys were capable of: putting a CD in a CD player, scratching an itch, turning a page—a thousand mundane tasks we take for granted. Until we can't.

I could just imagine the practical difference this would make in Ned's life, not to mention the companionship element. It killed me to think of Ned being so lonely, even with other people around.

I reminded myself to be pragmatic, not to leap ahead. Still, I couldn't wait to get to Shepherd in the morning and share all this with Ned.

He took it in, considering for a long moment. Mr. Cool.

"A monkey . . . instead of a dog," he finally said. "Maybe."

IN ANOTHER HOTEL in another time zone, Megan Talbert crawled into bed and clicked off the light. Kasey crawled under the covers, clinging to her trainer's leg like it was a tree trunk, and there she stayed until morning.

"At first I worried that she'd have a hard time breathing under there, but that's how she liked to sleep," Megan told me years later. "Kasey was an angel when we traveled. She was the first and only monkey I've ever traveled with that I wouldn't have to bring a separate carrier for her to sleep in because she was trustworthy enough to sleep in bed with me."

This made perfect sense to me. I've been through enough upheaval in my life to know that home is where your family is. A natural habitat is anywhere you feel safe being yourself.

After she graduated from Monkey College, Kasey was matched with a woman in Texas. She seemed to be settling in, but on the third day, something peculiar happened.

"She started getting strange blisters on her hands and feet," Megan said. "It looked like a contact reaction, so our first instinct was that Kasey had an allergy to something in or around her new home."

Helping Hands took Kasey back to Boston and tried again with a different monkey, who had the same rocky start but ended up living in the recipient's home for many years. The important discovery that came out of this was that emissions from an ionic air cleaner were to blame. (Now placement teams know to ask about these purifiers and unplug the unit when they enter a home.) Also on the upside: while Kasey waited to be matched with another recipient, she took on a role as a Helping Hands ambassador, traveling all over the United States, bewitching audiences at universities, corporate dinners, spinal cord injury prevention programs, and other events.

Kasey had found her calling.

She was the life of every party and particularly loved donor functions, where the ladies were sure to have nice jewelry. Kasey was all about bling. Fond of bracelets, necklaces, and earrings—the fancier, the better—she could deftly undo buckles, clasps, and latches. She wriggled her hand into the pockets of potential donors. Shirts, shorts, pants, jackets were all fair game. She was looking for treats, but she was so clever, so beautiful, and so socially competent that checkbooks were soon coming out of those pockets with needed funding for the growing programs at Helping Hands. People just felt *happy* around Kasey's winning personality. Before they knew it, they were wrapped around her little finger. (Sound familiar?)

All the wonderful qualities that made Kasey so *Kasey*—just like all the wonderful qualities that made Ned so *Ned*—had a flip side. Their tenacity had a stubborn streak. High-pitched enthusiasm was sometimes a setup for frustrating setbacks. Patience was a virtue they shared, but only when they felt like it. While neither of them was blindly obedient, both of them were motivated by a deep desire to do the right thing. And when it came to the people they loved, they both loved big.

Kasey and Ned also had a mischievous streak in common. That little bit of devil gets on a mother's nerves at times, but I always had to cover my mouth with my hand so Ned wouldn't see me laugh. He was never directly naughty, but he couldn't resist setting off little depth charges just to see what he could get away with. Kasey was the same way. Like Ned, she loved to get air, launching herself off a bookshelf the same way he used to sail over a homemade skateboard ramp. And then she'd turn and scoff at her startled audience with the same "What were you so worried about?" look I used to get from him. Imagine that playing out at a fancy luncheon or a formal fund-raising gala with champagne and chandeliers. Naturally, contributors found her irresistible.

During the years she traveled with Megan, Kasey became a regular at Talbert family functions, traveling home for holidays and long weekends, and this was where Kasey the Party Animal showed her softer side. Megan has a great picture of Kasey riding around in her mother's corduroy overalls on Thanksgiving.

"When my mother was recovering from major surgery," Megan told me, "I went home to visit and brought Kasey. We went to Mom's room, where Kasey very carefully and gently crawled up on the bed, sat on Mom's pillow, and began to groom her hair. Then Kasey curled up in a little ball and snuggled right in, the sweetest, most gentle little monkey she could be."

Megan said she saw for the first time that day the power of Kasey's instinctive love and sensitivity for someone who was in pain. She knew there was someone out there who needed Kasey more than the lecture circuit did.

NED, IN THE MEANTIME, was occupied with his own circuit. Now that he could move his arms a little and had started to wiggle the fingers on his left hand, the pros stepped up his therapy. When they talked about his long-term prognosis, they started using tentative words like "possibly" and "could be" instead of absolutes like "never" and "can't."

And after what seemed like an eternity without the basic pleasure of eating, Ned finally passed his swallow test.

"You did great," said the therapist. "Ready for a few bites of soft food."

"Awesome." Ned closed his eyes, relishing the thought, and I practically did a cartwheel on his behalf.

"Any requests?" I asked. "I'll bring you anything you're allowed to try."

"*Chef,*" he replied. Since he was a little boy, that's how he referred to Cream of Wheat with brown sugar.

"Okay . . . take it slow . . ." I carefully fed him his first spoonful of real food in almost six months. "How is it?"

"Good. It's good," said Ned. "I really . . . wanted . . . fettuccine . . . Alfredo . . . from Olive . . . Garden. But this is a good start."

A good start indeed. Things were looking up, I thought. Nevertheless, those months at Shepherd can be pretty much summed up by the old *Wide World of Sports* intro: "The thrill of victory and the agony of defeat." Our weekly break from the roller coaster was a wonderful nondenominational Sunday morning church service, a raucous hour of gospel music, healing testimonies, and revival tent enthusiasm.

"Praise the Lord!"

"Hallelujah!"

This boisterous form of worship was totally foreign to Ned, who was raised Catholic, and to me, the Presbyterian stoic, but it was uplifting. There was joy and gratitude for every small gain. For every setback, there was a community of understanding and support. The very air was filled with faith and hope. I couldn't help occasionally throwing out an inspired "amen" myself. When Lynn was standing in for me, she noticed that the service started at the same time as a Red Sox game and asked Ned if he wanted to skip church or miss the first several innings.

"I couldn't believe he said he wanted to go to *church,*" she told me later. "But it was everything I needed to hear, and more importantly, what Ned needed to hear."

It was what I needed to hear, too, but part of me missed the sturdy traditions and familiar music of my natural habitat. Full disclosure: I hadn't set foot in a Presbyterian church since I married my first Catholic. But I immediately accepted an invitation to attend a Presbyterian service one Sunday with the father and stepmother of a Boston friend. As much as I had benefited from services at Shepherd, the familiar hymns and long wooden pews felt like home.

Another sanctuary I found was the beautiful garden at Shepherd, an oasis in the middle of the bustling suburban complex. If I could get a nurse to bring Ned out, we would sit talking or just sit. More often, I found myself with other parents, sharing our stories, shoring one another up. It was humbling for me, the tragedy snob, to see so many families in such pain. Some people were completely alone in the world. Every time I got mired in how bad things were for Ned and our family, I'd listen to another parent's heartbreaking story, silently thanking God for our blessings.

It was December now. Ned had made significant progress at Shepherd, but nerve pain was holding him back.

He'd reached a plateau.

"It happens," the staff assured us. "SCI patients often make a burst of progress, then stay at that level for a while."

It didn't mean he'd be at a standstill forever, but for now no progress meant no insurance funding. Strange as it sounds, I was terrified to go home. Home was full of unknowns. We'd made friends and gotten familiar with the surroundings at Shepherd. Ned felt safe and comfortable there. I'd worked hard to learn everything I could and passed all the tests, but I felt completely unprepared to care for him alone.

I knew it was going to happen sooner or later, and unfortunately, it was sooner. The case manager showed up as I sat in the garden.

"Ellen, it's time to talk about Ned's discharge."

I hated that word, her infernal clipboard, the whole idea. I tried to stall.

"Please. We're not ready," I said. "If you could just give me a little more time to make the space workable and set up nursing care . . ."

But she was adamant. I had to face facts. I had to get my act in gear.

Ned was coming home.

7

No Place Like Home

CRISIS MODE DISTILLS LIFE TO ITS ANIMAL ELEMENTS. Niceties and convention fall away. Only the essentials remain: air, food, friendship. What matters most rises to the top: love, water, the will to find a way. I realized that over the long months of logistics and choices, setting priorities and making tough calls, the constant question I'd had to ask myself was: *What matters most?*

Sometimes it was about who was hurting most at any given moment. Other times it came down to which issue demanded my immediate attention. Always the answer stood out from the noise, unmistakable and urgent, and it was never about all that clutter I used to call important.

Our MedFlight out of Atlanta would be a little less complicated now that Ned was better stabilized, but his insurance didn't cover it, and I'd tapped out my credit card getting him to Shepherd. We'd learned the hard way that commercial flight wasn't an option, which left no options I could see until Bill, a childhood friend of mine from Cleveland, offered his own private jet.

There wasn't a moment of *oh, I couldn't possibly*. I'd gotten over that a long time ago. I gratefully accepted any and all help offered to me. And believe me, there'd been a lot.

"Bill, that would be a godsend. Thank you."

"Least I can do," he said. But of course it wasn't.

My wonderful friends aren't in the habit of doing the least they can do.

As I went around Ned's room, packing his things, I collected all the evidence of love and support, a thousand small kindnesses that meant the world. Someone had sent a Patriots rug for the floor, and the walls were covered with Red Sox signs, Celtics memorabilia, and a signed photo of UGA VII, the Georgia Bull-dogs mascot. Well-wishers had sent words of encouragement, and photos from far and wide plastered the bulletin board and mirror. Susan had set up a little Christmas tree in Ned's room, decorat-ing it with ornaments that sparkled with words like "Hope" and "Courage." Ned loved it so much we decided to take it back to Boston with us. The flight crew didn't bat an eye when we brought it on board.

Teryl came along to help settle Ned at home, and as she boarded she uttered the single word on everyone's mind: "*Sweet!*"

Bill's jet was quite an improvement over the previous tiny planes. For starters, it had a marble bathroom bigger than any at my house. The seats in the plane were enormous—big enough, it seemed, that Teryl, Ned, and I could all three fit in one. They were set up like a living room rather than a typical airplane cabin, and our personal flight attendant, a really lovely woman, plugged the little Christmas tree in right beside Ned so he could see it per-fectly. I settled in with a Bloody Mary, just because I could. The consummately professional crew secured Ned in a plush leather seat where he watched a DVD and dined first-class on specially prepared pureed potato soup and tomato juice in a crystal glass.

When we landed in Boston, an ambulance and a welcom-ing crowd were there, right on the tarmac. Everyone waved and cheered as our plane pulled up to the aviation building. The crew barely had the steps down before Maddie, Anna, Megan, and Judy bounded aboard to do some serious gawking.

Anna peeked inside the bathroom palace. "Mom, guess who we passed in the lounge."

"It was Steven Tyler!" Maddie stretched out on a leather lounger.

"Um, hello, girls. Remember me? And your brother, Ned?"

"Mom." Anna firmly set my priorities straight. "Steven. Tyler. From *Aerosmith*."

We were definitely home.

WITH ALL THE COMFORTS of the luxurious flight and happy homecoming, I'd started feeling a warm and fuzzy glow of *maybe this'll be okay*. Welcome signs, balloons, and the agency nurse I'd arranged for awaited us at the house. In addition to the outpouring of email, cards, and gifts Ned and I had received in Atlanta, there was an ongoing bucket brigade of help for the girls at home. The pantry was stocked, the kitchen floor swept clean, and the living room had been set up as our temporary M.A.S.H. unit.

I allowed myself to exhale.

Back home, amid the familiar chaos of dogs barking and teenagers vying for attention, I felt oddly soothed, almost comfortable.

"We'll get through this," I told Megan. "Ned's a fighter, and he's come so far. Really there's so much to be grateful for."

"There is," she eagerly concurred. "Really. It could be worse. Ned could have died."

"Yes. Or he could have been in a vegetative state."

"Or still off in Arizona or Atlanta. At least we're all in the same time zone now."

It was my friend Judy who brought me down to earth. "Your life is never going to be the same, Ellen. You've got to realize that."

She looked at me with love and compassion, but nevertheless, the bluntness of the remark took me aback.

"Well, that's— No. I don't believe that's true," I said. "Besides, I believe in counting my blessings."

Ned was home. We were surrounded by family, by friends— by wonderful, caring friends. Friends who loved us enough to be honest. All this instilled in me such a great sense of relief, I was able—for the moment—to comfortably deny the severity and for-everness of Ned's condition. I guess on some level I was frozen in a reality that no longer existed, a world in which this simply could not happen. Not to Ned. Not to us.

No, I kept thinking. *This can't be happening.*

My divorce had finally come through. I was on my own and happy. I'd even started to date. The girls and I were settling into a great new house. Megan was married to a wonderful guy. Jake was off to Bentley University, and Ned . . . well, Ned was *Ned.* A survivor. A thriver. He'd be okay. He always came out on top.

Despite everything, I guess I couldn't really take it in, much less accept it. Deep in my brain, that primal light switch that flips on the self-defense mechanism was stuck on the *everything's going to be all right* setting.

Denial is a powerful thing.

It didn't take long for reality to come crashing down.

As the EMTs lifted Ned from the stretcher onto the hospital bed, Guy and Bailey frisked and yapped, so delighted to see us.

So . . . so very delighted.

Within about seven minutes I was ready to tie their tongues together.

"Mom, shut them up," Ned groaned. "That barking sets off my nerve pain."

"Don't be crabby, Neddy. They're happy to see you," said Anna.

Ned curled his lip and slid a sneer the dogs' way, setting off another paroxysm of barking.

"Okay, Ellen," said Teryl. "I've given the agency nurse all the info, schedule for Ned's meds, all that. I guess I better head back to the airport." She turned to Ned.

"Hey, bud, you're gonna be good," she said.

"Yeah," he responded. "Keep out of trouble."

And with those few words, Teryl and Ned, two of the most levelheaded people on the planet, communicated a wealth of knowing and respect.

On her way out the door, Teryl slipped me a $20 bill.

"What's this for?" I asked, surprised.

"Ned's first trip to Olive Garden," she said. "Fettuccine Alfredo's on me."

My eyes welled with tears.

And then she was gone. The final link to our safe haven at Shepherd was out at the curb. Getting into Judy's car. Closing the door. Driving away.

I glanced over at Ned, and I could tell he was feeling as apprehensive as I was.

"Girls, come help me organize Ned's things." I motioned them to follow me to the hall closet that was now our pharmaceutical supply warehouse. "Tell me about everything I missed."

"Caroline's moving to Atlanta in May," said Anna.

"The place across the street from our old house is on the market," said Megan.

Maddie jumped in with "Christy has a new pony at the barn."

"That construction guy was here again today," Megan added. "He says you haven't paid him, and he was *not* happy."

"You should see all the food in the freezer," said Maddie. "We could feed a village in Africa."

"Okay . . ." I took a deep breath. "We'll miss Caroline! How much are they asking? I hope it's a good jumper. I'll worry about the construction guy later."

"I also heard back from the monkey person," said Megan.

"Fantastic!" She had our full attention. Maddie and Anna were completely on the monkey bus with me, so to speak. "What did they say? How do we get the ball rolling? Can we get the monkey right away or are we on a wait list?"

"Well . . ." she hedged. "I emailed, explained Ned's situation, said he'd be home this week. I requested an in-home visit as soon as possible."

"And?"

"You're not going to like this, Mom. She said they can't even begin the application process until he's been living at home for a year."

"*A year?*" I coughed. "As in . . . three hundred and sixty-five days?"

"That's what she said."

"Fifty-two weeks?"

"That's right."

"Twelve months?"

"You got it."

"No, that's no good," I said. "Ned needs this now. He's been so discouraged about the plateau in his progress. He needs something to keep him interested in life, motivated at PT, focused on something positive."

"I tried to tell her all that. She was adamant," said Megan. "Seriously."

NED'S NERVE PAIN escalated dramatically as the evening wore on. The agency nurse was solid-bodied and had a pleasant face. Her manner was professional but not unkind.

"I'm so glad you're here," I told her as she administered his late evening meds.

"Glad to help." She smiled. But then she gathered her things. "Have a good night."

"Wait—you mean—you're leaving? When does the other nurse get here?"

"The next nurse . . ." She puzzled over her paperwork for a moment. "There isn't an order for another nurse for the night. But I'll see you tomorrow."

I immediately called the agency.

"What do you mean?" I begged the dispatcher. "Of course we need a nurse tonight!"

"No, there's no other nurse coming," the woman assured me. "There must be some mix-up on your end."

Home Health Care Lesson #1: The mix-up is never the agency's fault.

Through the long night, I was wide awake and terrified, one eye on Ned, the other on the clock, telling myself, *I can do this. I know what to do.* I gave him his meds on schedule and mentally reviewed what I'd learned about repositioning him to avoid bed-sores. I don't know how a little five-foot someone like me, who shops the petite department and still has to have her pants tailored, brought forth two big, strapping men, but both my sons towered

above me by the time they were in junior high. Ned outweighed
me by a good thirty pounds, and I'm so short, it was almost impossible to get any leverage. But what could I do? At 1:30 and 5 A.M.,
I repositioned him, hefting as gently as I could, afraid of hurting
him or getting the feeding tube twisted. Both times he groaned
in agony.

"Oh, Ned . . . I'm so sorry. We have to do it."

"It's okay, Mom. We got it. It's okay."

This increasing nerve pain Ned had begun to experience
while at Shepherd had all the doctors and therapists scratching
their heads in bewilderment. So who was I to be entrusted with
the care of my severely disabled son as he lay there suffering? How
did they expect me to manage him in our living room with a
handful of rent-a-nurses?

It wasn't supposed to be like this.

I'd been trying to tell myself it would be okay. Ned would receive kind, proficient care from aides and nurses round the clock.
I'd be free to come and go as needed for work, for errands, for doing things with the girls. I'd even harbored a fleeting fantasy
about seeing my friends once in a while outside the context of tag-
team hospital room vigils. Clearly I was in major denial. This was
our cold, new reality.

By the time the nurse arrived in the morning, Ned was in in-
describable agony, I was dead on my feet, and the tension in the
house was palpable. He was miserable. The girls were heartsick
that he was miserable. I was miserable that the girls were heartsick, and everyone was heartsick that I was miserable. The over-
cast morning sky thickened to a heavy snowfall.

"Wow, it's really coming down out there," the nurse kept saying, nervously glancing toward the window.

By noon, the sky was dark, and blinding snow whipped up, down, and sideways.

"I need to get home to my kids before this gets any worse," she said, and then grabbed her coat and headed out the door without so much as a backward glance. Her meaning was clear: *I'm taking care of my kids. You take care of yours.*

The storm howled with increasing ferocity. The lights flickered occasionally, sometimes winking out completely and coming back on after fifteen or twenty torturous seconds. Talking calmly with the girls and keeping to Ned's stringent schedule, I fought to keep the fear out of my voice, but I kept thinking of all those people who'd been stranded without power during Katrina. What if the lights didn't come back on? How would I be able to clear Ned's lungs without the suctioning machine? What about the machine hooked to his feeding tube? Would anyone be able to get to us in the whiteout conditions? Why hadn't I thought of this before?

"I'm calling an ambulance," I told Ned. "Before this blizzard gets any worse. We need to get you back to Mass General where you're safe and they can do something about this pain."

"Yes. Do it." Ned heaved a huge sigh of relief. "Mom, don't feel bad. I know you tried hard to have everything perfect, but I'll be better off at the hospital. It's okay."

It was sweet of him to console me, but to be truthful, I suffered not an ounce of guilt over the prospect of sending my son away from home again. I was completely over my head and had no trouble admitting it.

Ned stayed at Mass General for three weeks trying new drugs and therapies, and the rest of the family practically moved in with him. Megan brought mashed potatoes from the restaurant across the street, and she and Ned shared the entire bowl, laughing and talking. Their relationship had always been the typical love-hate sibling rivalry. Six months earlier the thought of those two sharing *anything* would have been laughable, which made this scene all the more touching now. She fed him a bite, then she took a bite, and on and on until the whole bowl was devoured.

The medical team worked on Ned's wracking nerve pain. It was comforting to see him at the center of the coolly professional hive of white coats, and it brought home how truly, appallingly not ready I'd been to take care of him. I shuddered to think what Ned would have gone through had I been too proud to acknowledge I needed help—or too meek to demand it.

Home Health Care Lesson #2: Mother knows best . . . and knows when to call 911.

We decorated Ned's hospital room with a tiny tree and Christmas decorations, and piled his gifts around it. Little things like CDs and T-shirts. He couldn't make use of much else. Happy faces firmly in place, we went to Ned's room on Christmas Eve, pretending everything was merry and bright, but ghosts of Christmas past filled the room. Our family traditions were all about food and fun, games on TV, a festive round of house-to-house visits with our friends. We always ended the day reading "'Twas the Night Before Christmas," and I got everyone involved, reading each line and pointing to one of the kids to supply the last word. By the time they were out of elementary school, they all knew it by heart, so most of the confusion and fun happened when one or another of them got caught texting or dozing off and then there'd be no end of razzing.

Jake spent the evening with us at the hospital, then went off to visit friends. Megan and Ron went home, and the girls trudged up to bed. Standing in the silent living room–turned–hospital bivouac, I decided I wasn't about to let go of our small, important tradition.

"Girls! Get out of bed."

Sleepy groans could be heard overhead.

"Come on! We have to do 'The Night Before Christmas,'" I insisted. "We'll conference Jake and Megan in on the phone."

"You've gotta be kidding," Maddie harrumphed on her way down the stairs. "Mom, it's too late. I'm tired."

"We're doing it anyway," I grimly informed them. "It'll be *fun*."

Jake and Megan were less than thrilled to be interrupted while doing whatever people do at eleven o'clock on Christmas Eve, but I forged ahead, dragging everyone with me line by line.

"'Twas the night before . . ."

"Christmas," someone said as if it were a wake.

"And all through the . . ."

There was a long silence, a noticeable hole in the voices.

Again that realization of *foreverness* swept over me, and now it was starting to sink in with the rest of the family. I'd been living with it for a while, but the kids weren't used to it yet. Seeing Ned away from home on Christmas Eve—so dependent, so helpless, in that sterile white setting—had brought the painful reality into full, unobstructed view.

Your life will never be the same, Judy had said, but tradition allows us to pretend there's something unchangeable in a world that spins out of control. This little ritual left over from their childhood may have seemed silly and simple to my kids, but without that anchor, I didn't know where we might drift—or drift apart.

On Christmas morning, I went to the hospital.

"They want a discharge plan right after the holidays," I said. "As if a person gets to decide these things. It's all about insurance really. And what the doctor says."

"Which is what?" asked Ned.

"He wants you to go around the corner to Spaulding Rehabilitation Hospital. He decided you need more rehab before you go home."

I was grateful for that. It lifted the burden of having to say it myself.

"It's not a defeat," I told Ned. "Just a detour."

"You should probably get back," he said.

I nodded and touched his cheek. As I left his room, I glanced back in time to see him pick up his right hand to wave good-bye.

"Ned!" I rushed back to his bed. "Did you do that on purpose?"

"I've been visualizing those arm curls." He grinned. "All of a sudden, I actually brought up my arm. Watch. I think I can do it again."

And up it came. I crowed and clapped my hands together.

"Wonderful! Do it again, do it again."

But he couldn't. It went away completely after that, and I was the only person who'd seen it. We were both simultaneously thrilled and disappointed. The roller coaster ride continued.

"One step forward, two steps back," I sighed.

"Yeah, but then there's another step forward," Ned reminded me.

I squeezed his arm.

"Merry Christmas, Ned."

"Merry Christmas, Mom."

8

Help Wanted

PROGRESS. REAL PROGRESS. NED OUTGREW THE PUFFER and graduated to a joystick to drive his wheelchair. Slowly but surely, he was able to eat a few more soft foods. We introduced each new food as watchfully as I had when he was a baby, feeding him hot cereal, then some pureed fruit, adding a smashed banana, a few bits of cake, eventually going for the gusto with some mac and cheese after the doctors finally removed the feeding tube. His lung function and ability to productively cough grew stronger. Out came the trach.

In the late spring of 2006, almost a full year after his accident, Ned was ready to come home. I was ready, too. As ready as I'd ever be. I'd had five more months to observe the experts turn, feed, and care for him, and more importantly, I'd had that time to get my head around how all this was going to work. We brought Ned home without Aerosmith or ceremony, and he supervised as I unpacked his survival gear and sports paraphernalia in the living room.

"You know what this means," I said. "We can finally start the countdown on that helper monkey application."

Having Ned at home brought a host of new challenges, including the difficult task of finding, screening, interviewing, trying out, training, assimilating, and hopefully loving new nurses and personal care attendants, or PCAs as they're called. After more disastrous experiences with an agency, I decided to take charge and place ads on several employment sites: "Looking for NURSING/PHYSICAL THERAPY/OCCUPATIONAL THERAPY students or QUADRIPLEGIC-EXPERIENCED CNAs (Certified Nursing Assistants)."

> To: Ellen
> Subject: The answer to your prayers
>
> Good afternoon, Ellen! I saw your posting online for a Personal Care Attendant for your son, Ned. Has he found his perfect companion yet? Very selfishly, I am hoping he has not! I am desperate to stumble upon that someone who truly deserves and is in need of me. I simply would like to gratify my own need to give. I will be so bold as to say, if I had a loved one in need, I would pray for someone such as myself to take care of them! Hope to hear from you!

Delete. File under "Whack Job."

> To: Ellen
> Subject: At your service!
>
> I have no relevant training or experience, but I am a mom! I am not available during the time slots you require, and I have a bad back, so I cannot do any lifting or turning. BUT: I'd be happy to help out!

Delete. File under "Are You Serious?"

Being a PCA is an important job that requires specific education and care experience. Why, then, was I getting all these résumés from massage therapists and phlebotomists? Parking garage attendants, babysitters, and a steady stream of unskilled and frankly strange folks apparently figured, *Hey, what the heck?* Out of every twenty responses to our online ad, maybe ten were remotely qualified. The rest were people who seemed to have fallen through the cracks in life: the owner of a failing organic pet treat business, an unemployed piano tuner—I couldn't imagine what made them think they could handle the delicately balanced needs of a quadriplegic.

To: Ellen
Subject: No medical experience but I could double as personal chef!

Hi Ellen! I enjoy being outdoors, cooking, gardening, reading, writing, talking and exploring all that life has to offer.

What—no candlelight dinners and walks on the beach? Delete.

To: Ellen
Subject: Personal Care Attendant job

How much you gonna pay?

A fair question, but maybe not the best foot forward when one is applying for a position with the word "care" in the job description.

Delete. File under "Dogs Will Instantly Hate."

Guy and Bailey guarded Ned like a couple of centurions and were, as it turns out, pretty good judges of character. Guy—who actually started out as Jake's dog—was thrilled to have Ned home and watched over him like a little mother, up on her hind legs with her nose between her paws on the edge of his bed. When he was suffering, she'd hover there, offering little whimpers of support and driving him crazy.

"Mom! Get Guy out of here," he kept calling.

"Just ignore her," I called back, because there was nothing we could do to keep her away.

"Come on, Ned," Maddie pestered one afternoon. "Let Guy up. She's dying to see you."

He groused. "Maddie, that dog whines, cries, and pees everywhere. Why would I want her on top of me?"

Maddie picked Guy up and deposited her on the end of Ned's bed. Guy promptly belly-crawled right up to his face and started grooming him.

"Maddie!" Ned protested, but she took her brother's left hand and guided it gently along Guy's back, petting and patting.

Guy was in ecstasy, and Ned had to admit that it was nice to be able to feel, at least a little, how soft she was. There was no getting rid of Guy after that. Being with Ned was her job, and she didn't take kindly to interlopers, regardless of their résumés.

I, on the other hand, was always looking for the next prime candidate. Once I'd eliminated inappropriate respondents, I requested phone interviews. This cut the crowd in half. Half of that half wouldn't return my call. Half of the half who did didn't speak fluent English or couldn't work the hours we needed. I was left with a small handful of potential candidates, whom I invited to the house for a personal interview, and about half of those actually showed up. Of that last half handful, anyone who made it past the front door and survived the face-to-face interview with Guy and Bailey perched on the kitchen table staring them down, I figured might—just *might*—be a match for the Rogers-Sullivan-Kokos-Holsinger household.

"IT SAYS HERE you're about to finish nursing school, Charity."

The dogs and I eagle-eyed the pleasant, pretty girl at the kitchen table.

"Yes." She smiled without a hint of serial killer, shoplifter, or psycho. So far so good.

"So you're looking for a hospital job?" I asked.

"Eventually," she said. "Not sure when I'll get around to taking the boards."

"I see. Well, Charity . . . Ned requires round-the-clock care. Day shift is 8 A.M. to 6 P.M. I'm here full-time, but I need someone conscientious and dependable enough to care for him when I'm out getting things done. He tries hard to be as independent as he can, but he needs to be transferred from his bed to his wheelchair, given a bed bath, shaved, dressed, et cetera. You'd also be taking him to PT and reporting on his progress afterward."

Charity smiled and gave me a "no problem" nod.

"I cover evening hours with help from my kids. We also have a night shift, which is midnight to 8 A.M. If you are interested in that position, you would adjust his sleep apnea mask, reposition him when he's in pain, make sure he doesn't get dehydrated, and just be awake and vigilant in case of an emergency." Encouraged by another nod, I continued. "Vital signs have to be noted, and it's imperative that his meds are administered on a precise schedule, lest we wind up in the emergency room."

"Of course," said Charity.

"Basically, we're looking for an experienced caregiver who wants to be an invested, intelligent companion. That means talking with him, writing a note to his grandmother, working on a photo project for his friend Brie. That kind of thing."

In a perfect world, the nurse or aide would sit and discuss politics or engage in a postgame analysis of whatever Boston team was in contention, but that's where most applicants started looking a bit glassy-eyed. Sometimes, candidly, we felt desperate. If someone sounded nice on the phone, made it through the interview, and had any sort of past association with disabled people, I'd give her a chance to do a "trial day" with us.

Charity was looking good for a trial day. She didn't turn on her heel and walk away when she saw the dogs. (Been there.) She didn't show up for her interview in cutoffs and a "Yankees Suck!" T-shirt. (Been there, too.) And she hadn't attempted to float bogus references or tell me her previous employers had dropped off the face of the planet. (You'd be amazed.)

By 10:30 A.M. on trial day, I knew I'd struck platinum.

Charity was about Ned's age, knew her stuff, and clicked perfectly with the family. Sealing the deal: she was a serious Red Sox fan. Ned switched on the charm. "Oh, Charity, my face is burning with nerve pain. I know you're busy, but could you please get me a cool towel for my forehead?"

"Sure, Ned. No problem."

"Thanks, Charity. You're the best."

If he was talking to me, it was: "Mom! Cool towel. And this time wring it out better."

It was a luxury going off to get things done while they laughed and got acquainted like a couple of regular twenty-somethings. Which they were.

"Charity, are you into Jack Johnson?" asked Ned.

"Love him! We'll listen to that CD while we stretch. Anything good on TV today?"

"I like Discovery Health Channel. Nat Geo. That kinda thing. How about you?"

"I'm totally in love with the *Dog Whisperer* right now. We are so watching that, Ned," said Charity, reaching down to give Guy a nuzzle. "You might learn a few tricks we can use on these little monsters."

That's right. Even Guy and Bailey loved her. I came to feel as if she were another daughter. To this day, I wish I could clone a dozen full-time Charities—enough for day and night shifts and the rest to keep on call—but there was only one of her, so the search continued.

"You know what this reminds me of?" I told the kids at our regular Sunday dinner. "Trying to find nannies for you way back when."

In another life.

"Remember the one who didn't show up because she was in jail?" said Jake.

"Or that girl from the Czech Republic," said Maddie. "She left me and Anna in the car with the windows up."

"I liked the one who hid all the dirty dishes in her dresser," said Anna.

"Don't remind me." I shuddered, seeing the parade in my mind's eye: the Irish chain-smoker, the girl who didn't know how to open a can of tuna . . .

After twenty years of babysitters and nannies there was not a happier day in my life than the day I wrote the last check to a nanny. Finally, my kids were old enough to pretend they didn't need me.

Since leaving the corporate rat race and starting my own consulting firm, I had worked out of the house, so my schedule was flexible whenever they had to admit that Mom was still handy on occasion.

Now I was right back where I started.

One day, I opened the door to find a young girl with bright purple hair in a million braids. Her scrawny boyfriend slouched against an old beater of a car in the driveway.

"Rosa sent me," said the girl. "I hear you're desperate for help."

I was desperate enough to ask, "Have you had any experience?"

"No, but I graduated CNA school on Friday, and I can't wait to get started. Seriously. I'm ready to start. Right now."

I softened a bit at her eager smile. She was as desperate as I was. It took courage to come to a stranger's house and ring the doorbell, offering herself for work. With purple hair.

"We really need someone with experience," I said.

But I genuinely wished her good luck.

I WAS (and still am) an unapologetic autocrat when it comes to screening and training these people who work intimately with Ned and are woven into the fabric of our family. So I suppose I should have expected a vigorous shakedown from the Monkey College, but the huge packet of paperwork took me by surprise.

"You'd think I was applying for a job with the CIA," I said to Megan when she came over to help with the imposing stack of forms.

Helping Hands wanted to know everything about Ned, everything about our family, everything about our house—and our home. They wanted pictures of Ned in his wheelchair from the right, from the left, from the front. They wanted pictures of him in bed, from all angles, and they wanted a video that demonstrated his ability to talk and work his wheelchair.

Damn. Even though he'd graduated from the sip-and-puff and gained reasonable control over the joystick, Ned often ran his wheelchair into walls, doorways, medical equipment, even people.

"I can't see a damned thing," he told me. "There are two or three of everything I look at. I'm trying to steer this silly chair through the doorway, but I see three doorways. Which one am I supposed to aim for?"

We spent a lot of time at the renowned Massachusetts Eye and Ear Infirmary, where highly specialized neuro-opthalmologists tried to determine if there was anything that could be done to improve Ned's triple vision. Unfortunately, there was no surgical solution to the damaged optical and cranial nerves.

"But he's young," the doctors told me. "There's a chance his eyes and brain will eventually learn to compensate."

I wasn't sure what they meant by "compensate," and I wasn't sure what this would mean for Ned's monkey application, either. We'd figure that out after we mowed through the multiple questionnaires and the essays, including two from Ned.

"Number one," I said, settling in to take dictation. "Why do you feel you are a good candidate to receive a helper monkey?"

"Well . . ." Ned considered the question. "Mom, what are you typing? I didn't say anything yet."

"I put down 'Ned feels that he would be an excellent candidate for monkey assistance.' That's all."

"Just wait, would you?"

"Fine. I'm listening," I said, but as was usually the case when I should have been listening to him, my mind was moving on to my To Do list. Medical supply store, dog food, watermelon.

Conversation and communication was an ongoing frustration for Ned. When he first started speaking, I was so thankful and thrilled that I didn't realize until later—after we brought him home from Spaulding—how severely his speech was affected by the brain injury. It took him longer to get each word out, and with so little air passing through his larynx, there was little volume or inflection, which made it difficult for us to understand him. Ned had always had a lot to say, so it was beyond frustrating for him to constantly repeat himself, especially in a crowd, where everyone has to yell anyway. He ended up nodding and smiling a lot.

"I try so hard to talk as loudly and clearly as I can," he told me again and again, "but I can see from the person's face . . . I'm losing them. They nod when they shouldn't nod. They look away like they're hoping someone'll come to their rescue. It's really embarrassing."

Literally adding insult to injury, Ned's brain took longer to process information and visual stimuli than it had before. The complex plot of an action movie or TV show blew right by him. Books on tape were almost impossible because he had to relisten to so many paragraphs before he could move on. Forget about keeping up in a rapid-fire conversation with multiple people, which was the constant state of affairs at our house.

I ran 200 mph all the time, as so many of us do, multitasking an entire To Do list of errands, appointments, and domestic brushfires that needed stamping out. I'd ask, "Do you need anything at CVS?" But he'd be stuck on my last question: "What do you want for lunch?" And I'd be tapping my toe, trying not to lose my temper. This was a huge failing on my part. Adjusting *my* speed rather than expecting him to adjust his—it's something I still need to work on. *Am* working on.

But at that moment, I was working on this.

"Ned, what if we say something about how greatly you'd benefit from—"

"First, the nerve pain might . . . of intellectual . . . and stimulation that it . . . retreats."

"What was that? Say it again?"

He flared. "Mom, are you deaf? You have to listen more carefully."

"Just tell me how you feel about the monkey in terms of—"

"I'm trying to tell you . . . how I feel . . . and you're not hearing me."

"Okay. Fine."

I waited, twisting my rings.

"Maybe we should review that video one more time," I said after a long silence. "Do you want me to pull up that research file again? Because if the monkey—"

"*Mom.*"

"*Okay.* Sorry. I'm listening. Take your time."

After an hour or so, we came up with a brief, workmanlike essay:

First, Ned believes the intellectual and emotional stimulation the monkey would offer could potentially relieve some of the intense nerve pain that he suffers from. He has found that if his mind is stimulated, his pain retreats to the background.

Secondly, he believes the ongoing progress he has achieved with his motor skills over the last few months could actually be accelerated with the assistance of a monkey's help.

Finally, Ned completely recognizes that it will take patience, kindness, love, and compassion to foster a successful, long-term relationship between him and the monkey. He believes that it is a serious commitment but one which he is enthusiastic to make in order to benefit from the monkey's help.

The next night we tackled Essay Question #2: "What are your expectations?"

"Expect . . . ations . . ." Ned folded the word in half, thinking about it. "It could help with my hands . . . when they hurt . . . and adjust the bed up and down . . ."

"Good. That's good," I said, typing away.

Ned would like to work with his monkey on the following tasks:
- Stretch and massage his fingers
  (he has a lot of pain in his hands)
- Wipe his face with cloth
  (pain causes him to feel very hot)
- TV, radio, and CDs

"Do you think it could adjust my SCI bracelet?" asked Ned. "Yes—when it rubs. Good one." I kept typing.

- Adjust Spinal Cord Injury bracelet on his arm
  (it gets twisted)
- Hold books, cards, or magazines and turn pages
- Help guide his limited self-feeding and drinking

- Adjust covers
- Scratch itches

It struck me as a bit dry, but "expectations" was a dicey area for our family at the moment. Life had trained us to pray for the best and prepare for the worst. The difference between the two, for Ned, came down to these modestly realistic tasks—little things even a monkey could do.

So often I felt like I was caught in a parallel universe where every shimmer of possibility was just a prelude to getting the rug yanked out from under my feet. I thought if only I could wake up in the *right* world, where Ned was undamaged, I'd be back in the life we'd built and rebuilt. I'd get out of bed on the first day of the rest of my life, free to actually *have* a life.

I took hold of myself in those moments.

Head high. Shoulders squared. Do what needs doing.

Wanting that daydream to be real—needing to think it was possible, even remotely—I evolved an elaborate Golden Monkey Myth in my head. I suppose I let my imagination run away with itself. But who could blame me? Lately it had so few places to go. I tried to keep myself in check, but I just kept thinking how everything would be so much easier, so much happier, so much *right*er if we could just get that magical monkey in the house. That little guy would help Ned. It would be his friend and companion—maybe his best friend. They'd teach each other things, entertain each other, love each other. And maybe, just maybe, for the first time in over a year, Ned could feel that something had been added to his life rather than taken away.

If only . . .

9

What Doesn't Kill You . . .

I WAS DESPERATE TO MAKE A GOOD IMPRESSION ON HELPING Hands, present them with the perfect, easygoing Norman Rockwell family, the kind of people who never raised their voices or swore. The kind of people we definitely weren't most of the time. They wanted detailed information about our daily routine, as well as three glowing references—one of which had to be from a non-family-member caregiver willing to go on record about what nice folks we were. Unfortunately, our house was pretty much Grand Central Station 24/7: kids traipsing in and out at all hours, dogs walking on every surface. Everyone was *loud*. And not one of us was a candidate for sainthood.

This was going to be a challenge.

"Mom, can you go onto my computer and find those inspirational sayings and stuff I learned in Dale Carnegie? Let's find that and print it out so I can have it in front of me."

"Softball practice," Anna called on her way out the door. "See you later, Neddy."

"Remember, Anna," Ned called after her. "What doesn't kill you . . ."

"Makes you stronger." Anna impatiently finished the thought as she passed by. "Yes, Ned. I got that the first five hundred times you told me."

Despite everything he'd been through, Ned's personality had remained fundamentally intact. That's not always the case with brain injuries like his, so I celebrated a little every time I saw his same old mischievous smile or heard the *Ned*ness shining through his halting speech. He remembered every quote in that collection and hadn't lost a shred of his belief in them. He still lived for sports—watching games, listening to commentary and postmortems, talking about who was playing whom. Everything about his surroundings had changed, but inside he was still Ned. If anything, he was more Ned than ever.

"Frontal lobe injury often magnifies existing personality traits," an acquired brain injury doctor at the Shepherd Center had told me, and I watched that happen over the following year.

Stubborn became STUBBORN. When he got himself wrapped around a particular issue, Ned wouldn't quit. I applauded this in PT and OT, but it made us all a little crazy when it came to having every little thing the way he wanted it.

"Mom! My hips need to be moved about an inch to the left in my wheelchair."

"Mom! The fan is on too high."

"Mom! Turn the TV to channel seven and take down the volume by 16 percent."

All reasonable requests individually, but a little hard to take when fired off at regular intervals. Charity turned out to be a godsend. She knew how to baby Ned when he needed babying and how to deliver a well-tempered kick in the pants when he needed that.

"Oh, Ned?" she'd say sweetly. "How about a nice hot cup o' *get over yourself*."

We quickly learned that applying temporary solutions to our permanent situation was like trying to fix a flat tire with duct tape. The free medical ride service was the best way to show up late for PT and end up marooned at the hospital. We'd have to customize a special minivan with a ramp and a door tall enough for the high back on Ned's wheelchair. Ned's living room bivouac was no substitute for actual living quarters. We'd have to take the financial plunge and build an addition that gave him a space of his own: privacy and peace instead of teen club–meets–dog track, a properly equipped shower instead of the daily humiliation of a sponge bath.

Beyond the monetary challenge, these two major investments were a mental leap for all of us. This was our life now. The drastic physical change to our house literally brought home that reality.

Waiting for Helping Hands to make their decision was agonizing. I tried to nudge things along—diplomatically—and was told—diplomatically—that while my enthusiasm was appreciated, they'd learned that recipient families needed time to iron out the details of daily living.

So I kept ironing.

WE COULD make a reality show about life in our house: *Survivor: Elm Street*. If you failed to wipe up your own toast crumbs or pick up after yourself in the bathroom, you'd be immediately voted off the island. The winner would be the person who managed to get my undivided attention for more than sixty seconds.

The phone rang just as the UPS man entered the competition, risking his hearing (not to mention his ankles). Guy and Bailey made it as difficult as possible to deliver six hand-truck loads of boxes filled with medical supplies.

"Hello?"

"Hi, Ellen. This is Jill Siebeking from Helping Hands."

"Yes! Hello! I'm so happy to hear from you." (Cue the angel chorus.)

"Is this an okay time for you?" asked Jill.

"Absolutely. It's great. I just need one second."

"Sure. Go ahead."

I hastily scribbled my signature on the paperwork handed to me by the driver.

"Don't suppose you could put those in the garage for me, could you?" I asked hopefully.

The nice driver always did that. This was not the nice driver. He piled the boxes just inside the front door so no one could get in or out.

"Hi, Jill. I'm back. So sorry."

"No problem," said Jill. "We got your application packet and everything looks great."

"Really?" I tried not to sound as surprised as I was about the ice hockey. "That's—that's great. I was worried about the video because—"

There was a beep on my call waiting. Caller ID popped up: "MADDIE @ BOUTIQUE."

"Jill, I apologize. My daughter's calling from work. I need to just quickly check and make sure it's not an emergency."

"Sure. Go ahead."

I clicked over to the other line. "Maddie? Is everything okay?"

"Mom, you have to see this dress—"

"Maddie, I can't talk right now," I tried to tell her, but she was in an altered state, in deep desire of this magic dress she absolutely had to have. "Maddie? *Maddie.* I'll call you back."

I clicked back over to Jill. "Hi again. Sorry about that."

"Everything all right?" said Jill.

"Oh, yes. Everything's fine here. We're all just really fine. All the time. The thing is—about the video? We don't have a video camera, so we didn't include that, but I want you to know, I'd be more than happy to buy one if—"

"No, no. That's not necessary, Ellen. In fact, since you're only thirty minutes away from the Monkey College, I was thinking I'd stop by. Usually applicants are far away. It's great that we actually have the opportunity to visit your home and get to know you and Ned and the whole family."

"Yes. Great," I echoed, thinking, *Oh, God. How soon can I buy a new house and get the Dog Whisperer over here?* There was another plaintive beep from call waiting. Caller ID popped up: "ANNA CELL." "Excuse me, Jill. My other daughter. I'll be right back. So sorry."

As I clicked over to Anna, Guy and Bailey ambled into the kitchen, whining and yipping.

"Anna? Is everything okay?"

"Mom, where are you? Softball practice ended half an hour ago."

"Oh, Anna! I'm so sorry."

"You *forgot*," she cried, justifiably stricken. "You dumped me at softball practice and *forgot* about me."

"No, of course not. I'll be over in— Oh, wait. No, I won't. That Crabby Abby PCA didn't show up. I can't leave Ned."

"Great. So I guess I'll just live at school now. I'll just sleep on the softball field and eat out of the vending machines."

"Someone will be there shortly, Anna," I said without commenting on the drama. "Hang tight while I figure it out. I'm putting you on hold."

"Yeah, what else is new?"

Bailey whimpered, and I reached down to pat her as I clicked back to the other line.

"Jill, I am so sorry. It's not usually so—"

"Who are you talking to, Mom?"

"Maddie? Wait—how did you—"

"Did you get the picture I just sent you?" Maddie asked. "You have to come right now. We're about to close the boutique. Mom, I *need* this dress for prom."

"Fine! Get it. Whatever you want. I can't talk right now."

"Well . . . you don't expect me to *pay* for it, do you?"

"Maddie, I'll call you back. I'm busy."

"Mom!" Ned yelled from his room. "I need you to reposition me in my chair."

"Yes, Ned. Hang on. I'll be right there."

I speed dialed Megan, hoping to intercept her on her way home from work.

"Hi, Mo—"

"Anna! Softball! Monkey on the other line!"

"Awesome," said Megan. "I have nothing better to do. I'll just reroute my entire—"

"Thank you." I clicked back to the other line. "Anna?"

"No, actually this is Jill. Should I call you back?"

"No! No, everything's fine here. Everything's under control. Just one second."

"Mom!" Ned called. "Hurry it up. My hip is killing me."

"I'm on the phone. Hang on. Anna? Anna? Are you still there?"

"Where else would I be? Nobody cared enough to pick me up."

"I said I was sorry. Megan's on the way."

By the time I clicked back to Jill, Bailey had collapsed against my leg.

"Jill? Sorry about that. Um, what were we—*oh*. Visit. Yes! We would love to have you."

"Wonderful. How's the last week of August for you?"

"August . . ."

It sounded so far away—it was weeks and weeks away. *We're ready now,* I wanted to tell her. *Come Tuesday. Come tomorrow!*

"August is great," I said, calmly reaching for a roll of paper towels. "Jill, thanks so much for calling. I have to run, but let's email and set up a date for that visit."

We exchanged hurried but pleasant good-byes. I dropped onto a kitchen chair and shook my head in total exasperation. The rest of the evening was remarkably quiet. No one was speaking to me.

I WANTED everything perfect for Jill's visit. I had Ron take the dogs and pressed the girls into service spiffing up the house. Finally the doorbell rang.

"Places everybody."

Jill Siebeking, Helping Hands' occupational therapist and placement specialist, was a friendly, hip-looking woman, just a few years older than Ned. She showed us a slide show on her laptop—wonderful pictures taken at the Monkey College—and candidly spoke to him about what it was like to have a monkey. She asked a lot of questions, focusing intently on his answers.

"What were you studying in college?" she asked.

"I was getting my degree in communications and public relations before I had my accident," he said, batting those baby blues at her. "What about you, Jill?"

She was hooked.

The rest of Jill's visit didn't seem so much like an interview as a lively conversation between two kindred twenty-somethings at a local bar. While Ned was his most charming and engaging self, he was clear about why he wanted to become a monkey recipient.

"I think a monkey could help me regain some of my independence," he said seriously. "From what I understand, a monkey might help me make progress with everything from my mood to my motor skills and maybe distract me from the pain. I know it's going to be a lot of work. And it's already pretty crazy around here. But it might also help me feel less lonely and isolated. It would be nice to have someone to hang with."

The conversation went so well, we all lost track of the time, and Ron came back with the dogs while Jill was still there, but they were fine, and she was fine with them.

"Postgame analysis," Ned announced after she left.

We huddled. Big smiles all around.

"I think we did great," I said.

But then months went by. We continued adapting to our new lifestyle, but there were some seriously rough edges. It was hard for Ned to endure the daily grind of physical and occupational therapy through his pain. He and I were often at loggerheads. The girls and I seemed to have more than our usual share of disagreements. It was a challenge keeping everyone on an even keel, juggling all the complexities of caregiving with the girls' needs. And a hundred times a day, when I was trying to be three places at once, I wondered, *What's taking so long?*

Where was that monkey? We *needed* to get that monkey. The Golden Monkey Myth had taken on even greater proportions.

Finally in December, Helping Hands made another appointment with us.

"The brass from the Monkey College," I told Ned. "They're coming for a home visit."

"Okay." He nodded. "Let's not get ahead of ourselves. Don't be nervous."

But I couldn't help it. What if they changed their minds about us? What if this amazing possibility drifted out of our lives just as inexplicably as it had drifted in? What if . . . a lot of things?

Another dangerous place to go: *what if.*

All we could do at this point was put our best foot forward, and we were ready to do that. During Ned's last year we'd faced some massive readjustments, not the least of which was the new addition to the house. It began with the contractor, Brian, and me at my kitchen table with blank pieces of paper and the dogs vying, as always, for my attention.

"I want this room to be really special for Ned—spacious, bright, welcoming," I said, but ever the pragmatist, I added, "but let's not forget the 'future buyer.' Let's design everything so that Ned *and* the next owner are going to love what we've done." (Another one of those denial moments, surely.) Drawings were drawn; handicapped-accessible consultants were consulted. We stood inside imagining. We stood outside imagining. We tried to see what Ned would see when he was in his bed, when he was in the shower, when he looked out the window.

The project gave me a whole new purpose, a reason to be energized, hopeful, and excited. The fact that the girls were at best indifferent, and at the worst annoyed that such major doings were now occupying my every non-Ned waking minute, mattered not. The fact that Ned saw this as yet another one of my "getting

ahead of myself" interludes was completely ignored. The fact that
I couldn't get into my own driveway and had to park three blocks
away was lost on me. I was on a mission to make this the best room
anyone could ever have.

As the autumn leaves were falling, we were getting close, so
very close, to having a real room for Ned. Brian arrived early one
morning and pulled me outside into the yard.

"Look, Ellen, I had this idea last night—what about a terrace
with a stone wall right outside Ned's room? With a graded path
leading out to the front of the house? His own entrance? A space
for him to enjoy the outdoors? For all of you? A grill? A table and
chairs? What do you think?"

The dollar signs were chinka-chinking in my head, but wow—
was he right. I could see it, feel it, smell the spring air—and so
would Ned.

"Let's go," I said, and I never looked back. By the first snowfall, it was a space with floors and a ceiling and a perfect non-
handicapped-looking walkway for his wheelchair, along with a
matching one leading to the main front door. There was still a lot
of finishing work to be done, but the heavy construction dust was
beginning to settle, and I could clearly see how far we'd come.

It hadn't killed us. We were stronger.

10

Monkey in the House

"WHAT'S A HOME VISIT?" ASKED ANNA.

"It's a nice way of saying they want to make sure we aren't serial killers," I said.

"Or vagrants or animal beaters," Ned added.

I'd have felt better about the inspection if we'd been able to finish off the new addition to the house. Unfortunately, on the big day, despite the best efforts of the contractor and his crew, Ned was still installed in the living room, and our customary state of chaos was in full swing. Fortunately, we had Charity on board that day, and Maddie and Anna were so eager to have this fantastic new "pet" in the house, they were doing everything they could to help make it happen.

We Rogers-Sullivan-Kokos-Holsingers are not a mopey lot. We're not the kind to wring our hands or wallow in our sorrows. I'm proud of the way my gang of hard-striving overachievers makes bouncing back a way of life. But we've never been particularly quiet about it. I've been told it can be a bit overwhelming for the uninitiated.

"I want us all on our best behavior," I told the whole crew. "Anna, those dogs are officially banished for the day. Maddie, get in here and help me tidy up." (And by "tidy up," of course, I meant "tear around and shove things into drawers.") As Anna herded Guy and Bailey out back, I took a deep breath and opened the front door.

"Jill! It's so nice to see you again." We hadn't seen her since her first interview in August.

"Hello, Ellen," she said with a warm hug. "This is Megan Talbert, Helping Hands' executive director."

Megan greeted us all warmly, and I invited them in with apologies for the mess.

"No problem," said Jill. "We can see you're in rebuilding mode."

I smiled. *You have no idea.*

"Ellen, you have a lovely home," Megan said.

"Thank you. Would you like the nickel tour?"

"Absolutely." It was friendly. All guest, no gestapo.

We walked through the family room filled with framed photos, travel souvenirs, and the usual artifacts of a growing family. We peeked into my office, which was stacked a mile high with paperwork.

"Before we moved Ned into the living room here, it was furnished with my grandparents' things," I said. "Antiques, a beautiful old Steinway grand. I'm looking forward to getting all that out of storage when we get Ned's addition finished."

"No doubt," Jill said. "How's that coming?"

"Come see for yourself." I guided them to the work-in-progress. "As you can see, there's ample space, lots of natural light, his own access out onto the patio."

"And this will be finished when?"

"Good question!" I laughed. "Honestly, it's like herding cats to get anybody—" I stopped myself, thinking that might not be the answer she was looking for. "Soon," I said. "Very soon."

Apparently convinced we weren't complete derelicts, Megan and Jill settled comfortably in our family room for what I thought was going to be a pleasant chat. There was small talk. *How was your Thanksgiving? Great, thanks. How was yours?* That sort of thing.

"So, Ned . . ." Megan leaned down and nonchalantly unzipped her backpack. "I hear you're a huge Patriots fan."

"Yup." He grinned. "I think we might even . . . *Whoa!*"

Ned rasped a sharp gasp of surprise. Out of Megan's backpack sprang a silky, sweet-faced little monkey.

"*Monkey!*" Maddie and Anna cried out.

All I could find was "*Oh . . . wow.*" She was as pretty and as perfect as I'd imagined.

"This is Kasey," said Megan, her voice full of love and pride and the tremendous kick she got out of our reaction.

"She's adorable!" Anna cried in delight.

"And so *tiny,*" Maddie added.

"About five pounds. The perfect size for her job."

Kasey leapt up onto Ned's shoulder, her eyes bright and curious as she surveyed the room and sized everyone up. She leaned into the side of Ned's neck, settling in just under his jaw, and a look of pure pleasure and gladness came into his eyes.

"She's beautiful," he said softly.

Cameras were grabbed. Lots of oohing and aahing went on. We were instantly, completely captivated.

"I never thought I'd use the word 'elegant' to describe a monkey," I said. "But she really is elegant, isn't she? *Regal,* even."

But Kasey had apparently had enough of the fashion show. She jumped up on the bar, attempted to open a bottle of soda, and dove into a dish of cashews left over from Thanksgiving. Then she launched herself over to the coffee table, where she paged through a few issues of *People* magazine. Finding nothing of interest there, she darted up on top of the sofa, pulled back the curtains so she could see out the window, and finally returned to Ned's shoulder, leaving us all breathless.

All this in about five seconds flat.

I didn't say so out loud, but I was relieved to note that Megan had her on a slender leash.

"*Phew*," Ned breathed. "What a whirlwind. She's like the Tasmanian Devil."

Kasey explored Ned's nose for a moment, then bounded over to Maddie's shoulder and checked out her necklace.

"Oh, she's so sweet," Maddie cooed, and I could see Anna dying for her turn.

"Can I hold her?" Anna started to ask, but before she could get the words out, Kasey was on her shoulder, then on mine, then Ned's again.

"Kasey isn't one to be held," said Megan. "Especially when she's meeting people for the first time. Let her come to you."

Ned beamed from ear to ear as Kasey gave his neck a brief nuzzle, searched his pants pockets, and checked out his SCI bracelet. The air in the room seemed lighter, full of oxygen and joy. It was simply not possible to look at that funny little face without experiencing a giddy, giggly feeling of pure monkeyshine happiness.

"Okay." I laughed. "We're officially in love."

"The feeling seems mutual," said Megan, coaxing Kasey back into her pack.

Ned's face fell. "She can't stay?"

"She'll be back," Megan assured him. "We'll move her in and start training soon. How's December 18?"

"Works for me," I said. "What do you think, Ned?"

"I think she liked me." He smiled shyly. "Do you think she liked me?"

"Definitely," said Megan. "We'll see you again soon."

For days after Jill and Megan's visit, the girls and I were buzzing with anticipation.

"I call feeding her first," said Maddie.

"I call . . . everything else!" said Anna.

"How great is it going to be to have a little monkey? My friends can't wait to come over and play with her!" Anna said, and we all giggled at the thought, each imagining this monkey becoming our personal best friend—noting as an afterthought that she'd also be a marvelous service animal for Ned. I'll admit, I was the worst of the bunch, imagining Kasey to be the answer to all our prayers, singing Kasey's praises to anyone who'd listen.

"This'll change everything," I told my own Megan. "I feel like we're really going to turn a corner now."

I couldn't wait to call Jake. "When you come home for Christmas, you'll meet the new addition to the family. The monkey's coming!"

As usual, Ned had the healthiest attitude of all of us.

"Geez, Mom," he chided me, "you're getting way ahead of yourself with this monkey thing. Let's just be patient and see how it goes."

Ned was looking forward to Kasey's arrival as much as any of us—probably more—but he took his typically measured approach.

"Let's just maintain . . . see how things develop," he said. "I'm ready to give it a shot, but it's not a good idea to get all attached to the idea until we know if it's going to work out."

But I was incapable of any such restraint.

"It'll be great," I told him.

"Mom, we don't really know what's involved. Like . . . feeding her . . . cleaning up."

"Ned, I've had five kids, multiple dogs, a pony or two—not to mention the assorted high school and college boyfriends and girl-friends." I shrugged. "How difficult could a monkey be?"

"A MONKEY?" said the contractor. "You're asking me to put the rush on for a *monkey*?"

I wasn't asking. I was begging. And I *really* don't beg. I'd been reduced to it by a four-month parade of carpenters, electricians, plumbers, painters, kids tripping over equipment and one another, dogs barking themselves inside out every time the door opened. We were all getting a little uptight. Not to mention that a few key pieces of the puzzle were still missing: a physical therapy mat, an electric Hoyer lift built into the new room's higher ceiling, a desk and bathroom sink at wheelchair roll-up level.

The contractor rolled his eyes, but he had a crew working at the crack of dawn.

"I'm not sure it'll all be done by the eighteenth," I told Jill, "but I think we need to just get the monkey into the house, and the room will eventually come together."

Jill considered it for a moment before she said, "I'm okay with that. Let's set up that date to bring Kasey over and start training the family."

A few days later, Jill came with all the paraphernalia we'd need to take care of Kasey, including the makings of a monkey cage. A few days after that, she returned with Megan, Kit (a staff member training to become a placement expert), and the Queen Bee herself.

"Kasey's here!" The girls were beside themselves with excitement, but I was afraid that Kasey's entourage would see all this
chaos and take off faster than a speeding bullet. "I'm so sorry for
the mess—the noise—" I said.

Megan smiled and said something else I had no hope of hearing. The house was bustling with construction activity. Intermit-
tent hammering and manly conversation could be heard over the
rev of a power drill and the whining rip of a band saw, not to
mention the dogs yapping and leaping. I tried for a friendly meet-
and-greet, but it was impossible to hold a polite conversation over
the fray.

"Maddie, grab Guy."

I scooped up Bailey and tried to muffle her yapping against
my shirt, appreciating even in the moment that it's really saying
something when you're worried that your home is too crazy for a
monkey to live in. We hustled the pups upstairs and chucked
them in my bedroom, but bounding down the stairs to rejoin the
trainers, I narrowly missed stepping in a small "present" left by
one of the hyperexcited dogs.

Ned remained characteristically relaxed. Mr. Cool. But Charity was working that day and didn't try to hide her excitement.

"I can't wait to meet the newest member of Team Ned," she
said when I made the introductions all around.

"It's great that you're here," said Megan. "Let's get started."

First on the agenda: getting the cage set up. The structure was
a lot bigger than I'd imagined—six feet tall, three by three feet
wide and deep. Grating on the front, sides, and all the way around
the top allowed for a basically unobstructed view of the room.
Underneath the grated floor was a large tray lined with "chux"

pads. (We'd soon learn what *that* was all about.) It didn't exactly match the drapes, but otherwise it seemed to fit right in.

"This is her bedroom," said Megan, indicating a shelf high in one corner. "She'll go up there to snooze, relax, get a better view of whatever is going on."

She opened the carrier and out popped Kasey, looking even more beautiful than before. Her eyes darted around the crowd, as if she was taking a head count. She wore one of those tiny size-zero diapers they use for preemies and a woven fabric harness (actually a modified dog collar) under and around her middle. Attached to the harness was a short leash, and Kasey delicately held the end of it in the air with her beautiful tail so as not to let the leash get caught in anything. Megan attached a four- to five-foot tether to the metal ring on the tip of Kasey's short leash, and quick as a wink, Kasey was perched on Megan's shoulder, looking at us inquisitively.

What are you all staring at? Her face was mesmerizing, one precious expression after another. Her eyes shone with intelligence, affection, and fun. She gracefully hopped to Ned's shoulder, then Maddie's, then Anna's.

"She looks so wise," Ned marveled.

"How old is Kasey?" asked Anna.

"Almost twenty-one," said Megan.

"Just what we need," I said dryly. "Another twenty-something female in the mix."

"How does that translate to—you know, like dog years or whatever?" Maddie asked.

"That's about forty-two in human age. Capuchins live thirty-five to forty years in captivity, so she's in her prime." Megan strolled

around as she spoke, allowing Kasey to check out her new surroundings.

"I read online that she has the intellect of a human three-
year-old," said Charity.

"That's right. Plus Kasey has a great deal of experience with a
variety of social situations and people. That's why we think she's
going to be perfect for you, Ned. And for your family."

I'd barely had time to consider whether that was a compli-
ment or a commentary on our chaotic household, when all of a
sudden—*thwap!*—Kasey flew off the kitchen counter and attached herself to Megan's leg like a burr.

What was that about a flying monkey? I wanted to ask Ned.

"Kasey is full of surprises," Megan said, as she attempted to
walk stiff-legged into Ned's room.

"It's like we saw on *Animal Planet*," said Anna. "The mommy
monkey walking around doing her thing with her baby clinging on."

But I was thinking about how I loved traveling that way myself when I was little, riding on my dad's shoe, latched tight to his
leg. He'd pretend to ignore me, striding back and forth, swinging
me along as I shrieked with laughter. When I saw Kasey riding
along on Megan's calf, the sudden memory made me smile.

"Time to get started," Megan declared, and Kasey leapt back
up to her trainer's shoulder, instantly at attention.

Monkey Boot Camp had begun.

11

Learning Curve

"BONDING IS THE KEY TO EVERYTHING," MEGAN SAID. Kasey trilled and nuzzled her neck, just to confirm that opinion before she set off exploring again.

"We're good buddies. She knows she can depend on me for everything she needs. But she also knows I mean business when I bust out my Monkey Police voice. An essential part of the bonding process is learning who's who in the hierarchy."

"The connection between the two of you is amazing," I said. "The trust and respect are plain to see."

As our first training day commenced, I was intrigued at Megan's uncanny understanding of Kasey's complex vocabulary. Every squawk, whistle, warble, and trill of Kasey's was nuanced with inflection, tone, and volume. *Lots* of volume, we soon discovered, sometimes accompanied by back flips and airplane zooms.

Standing next to the open cage door, Megan removed Kasey's diaper.

"Oh," I said. "She doesn't, um . . ."

Megan read my mind. "No worries. We'll get to that later. Kasey, cage?"

The specific upward inflection in her voice made it sound more like an invitation than a command. Still, Kasey wasn't convinced. At first, she stayed put on Megan's shoulder, evaluating the situation.

"Every monkey has a different personality," Megan said, "and Kasey's particularly social. Usually when she finds herself in a room full of interesting people, someone's bound to have treats, so she's a bit reluctant to go in."

But after a moment, she deferred to the "Monkey Police." With one last look around, she hopped inside. Megan closed and secured the door.

"A combination lock?" It seemed a bit much.

"You can't imagine how clever monkeys can be." Megan spoke with the sage voice of experience. "Given the opportunity to observe and enough time to noodle on it, they can open *anything*."

Kasey confirmed this with a curt *purrrup,* then scrambled up to her bedroom, happy to be back in her familiar castle with all her favorite things.

"She has several polar fleece blankies she likes to snuggle with," said Megan. "You'll rotate those daily. She also has her favorite toys."

These were a black pleather coin purse, which Kasey zipped open and shut, a plastic Baby Einstein bath book called *Mimi's Toes* (about a monkey in the bathtub), and a little unit with chubby beads that slid around on a roller coaster—a miniature version of that toy that you see in every pediatrician's office.

"This enclosure is an exact replica of the one she's lived in her whole life," said Megan. "The cage is her refuge, especially her bedroom. That's her sanctuary where she feels at home."

Kasey *pip-pipped* softly, zipping and unzipping her purse.

"Soon the most interesting thing in her life will be you, Ned. She'll focus all her attention on you. Once she's learned that you're 'her guy' and it's her job to take care of you, she'll be enthralled with every little thing in your day. And she'll love to have you focus on her. After all, she's *Kasey*. She thrives on undivided attention."

She's not the only one, I thought.

MENU

BREAKFAST: 7 A.M. *Two heaping tablespoons of old-fashioned 100% oats, sprinkled with cinnamon, served warm, add 1 squirt of fish oil*

MORNING SNACK: 9:30 A.M. *⅓ cup veggies (plain broccoli, cauliflower, green beans, green pepper, etc.)*

LUNCH: 12:00 P.M. *Four pieces 5049 Monkey Chow, moistened*

AFTERNOON SNACK: 2:30 P.M. *⅛ Red Delicious apple and ¼ adult chewable vitamin*

DINNER: 5:00 P.M. *Four pieces 5049 Monkey Chow, moistened*

NIGHTTIME SNACK: 7 P.M. *One plain chicken wing (halved) or equivalent piece of chicken or turkey*

BEDTIME: 9 P.M. *Unsalted nuts (3 pistachios or 3 peanuts or 3 almonds or 3 cashews or 1 walnut)*

EXTRA TREATS (FOR BATH TIME, NAILS, ETC.) *Natural-style no-salt peanut butter, cucumber, hummus, tabbouleh*

"Kasey's diet has to be followed to a tee," Kit said. "Every day without fail. I can't impress on you how important this is. Capuchin monkeys can become diabetic if given an improper diet. Kasey needs *these* specific foods and vitamins at *these* specific times. She can have reward treats—peanut butter, cucumber, hummus, or tabbouleh—and *nothing else.*"

I followed along, smiling and nodding in what I hoped were the appropriate places.

Unfortunately, I had reached the end of my attention span. I'd absorbed a lot of information that day, but some of the seemingly minor details were being sorted and tossed into my mind's construction Dumpster.

"Monkey Chow is the mainstay of Kasey's diet," Kit said. "The perfect balance of protein, carbs, and other nutrients. I've made enough for dinner tonight and left some dry chow for a few days, and you'll be getting a twenty-five-pound bag that'll last about six months. Keep that bag sealed tight and stored in the garage. Dogs go crazy for Monkey Chow."

I nodded. Blankies. *Mimi's Toes.* Monkey Chow. So far, so good.

"Monkeys can be picky," Kit continued, "and Kasey likes her chow a certain way . . ."

The Monkey Chow looked like large, dry dog biscuits, each nugget the size and shape of a fat cocktail weenie. I was sure it was the one idiot-proof item on the menu. Toss the monkey a few biscuits and off you go, just like the dogs, right?

No such luck.

I tuned in again as Kit said something about adding "just so much water," medium-sized Tupperware container, shaken not stirred . . .

"Wait, wait," I said. "How much is 'just so much' and . . . what was that last part?"

"Making Chow for picky monkeys is a bit of an art form," Kit said, "but once you've done it a few times, it's easy."

Picky monkeys, indeed. I didn't go to that much fuss cooking dinner for my family.

While I was in monkey culinary school, Jill was outfitting Ned's wheelchair with a handy treat dispenser so he could offer Kasey a dollop of natural no-salt peanut butter on his finger.

"The treats help train Kasey to come to you and do tasks," Jill told Ned. "Everything she does for you should be followed by a peanut butter reward."

"Okay . . . I'm trying. It's just . . ." Ned's hand was still pretty much immobile. He shook his head, discouraged.

"Relax. We'll tweak the position until it's right where you need it."

Jill worked patiently within the limited dexterity of his left index finger until he could bend it enough to grab some peanut butter.

"Excellent." Jill squeezed his shoulder.

"I'll keep at it. We'll get there," he said, practical but determined. "Cesar Millan—you know, the Dog Whisperer? He says, 'An animal is like a mirror. They reflect your energy right back at you.'"

Jill nodded. "This is one of the many ways Kasey's going to be therapeutic for you, Ned. Not just emotionally, but physically. Over time, the exercise of giving her the peanut butter treats may help you gain mobility and strength in this hand."

I couldn't help it; my mind immediately leapt ahead to images of Kasey helping Ned regain full use of his left hand. Maybe his right hand, too. She'd keep him company, cuddle with him every evening, trill him to sleep. He'd lose himself and all his pain watching her play. And maybe someday, he'd—

"Let's start with the basics." Megan's no-nonsense tone brought me back into the room. "First and foremost, Kasey is a service animal, highly trained to assist with specific tasks. Always use a positive, encouraging tone. Monkey College is all about positive re-inforcement, never negative feedback, so scolding or yelling at her won't do any good. If Kasey does something wrong—say she grabs something she shouldn't have—just say, "*Uh-uh.*" If the tone is suf-ficiently firm, she'll drop it. She might screech a little, but monkeys know when they've misbehaved, and they feel terribly guilty about it. She has a mind of her own, but she genuinely wants to do the right thing."

Megan undid the combination lock. Kasey immediately knew what was up.

"Kasey is 'cage trained'—the diaper is only used when you're out of the house—so every time you get her out of the cage, you ask her to potty." Megan made eye contact with Kasey and said, "Kasey, potty?"

Kasey didn't bat an eyelash—and didn't potty onto the chux pads lining the tray below, or anywhere else.

"Kasey, potty?" Megan repeated, with the same result.

"Maybe she doesn't have to go," Anna suggested.

"Monkeys have fast metabolisms. What goes in comes out. Quickly. And quite often." Again there was that sage voice of experience. "You have to be persistent. If she sees that treat dis-penser waiting for her, she'll do her thing."

Which she was now doing, managing even that task with sur-prising panache.

"Does she ever, um . . . I mean, is it true . . ." Maddie stepped up to ask the question that had crossed everyone's mind. "Do they throw poop at people?"

"That's a myth." Megan shook her head. "There are a lot of misconceptions about monkeys. Good potty, Kasey! Good potty!"

We all joined the celebration, then it was back to business.

"Down the road a ways, once Kasey feels at home and you've monkey-proofed the room, she'll be able to just come out when you, and someday you, Ned, open the cage door. But until then, for training purposes and her own safety, we'll be getting her out of her cage with her long tether. Watch carefully, Ellen. You're going to do this in a few days." Megan stood in front of the cage. "Kasey, leash?"

In half a moment, Kasey was there with the end of her short leash in her hand. Megan opened the door, Kasey politely handed it over, Megan clicked the longer tether to the leash, and Kasey jumped lightly onto Megan's shoulder.

"See? Easy."

"Sure," I said, though it actually seemed . . . *too* easy.

"Good. On to something a little more challenging. Ned, start by asking Kasey to 'come, sit' on your lap."

"Kasey," Ned said eagerly. "Come sit?"

She shot him a blasé look and didn't budge, like a strikeout at a singles bar.

"Try it with peanut butter on your finger," said Megan.

He scooped up a dollop. "Kasey, come sit?"

That did the trick. Kasey flashed to Ned's lap, greedily licked off the peanut butter. But she was back on Megan's shoulder quick as a wink. Ned couldn't mask his disappointment.

"That's it? She's not going to stay on my lap or my shoulder?"

"Right now, she's all about doing her job—especially since I'm here. She'll come around," Megan reassured him. "It'll take time and patience—for both of you. Meanwhile, learning the basic tasks takes repetition, so let's try it a few more times."

Ned nodded tightly. By the time he and Kasey had practiced the task to Megan's satisfaction, he was worn out and riding waves of nerve pain triggered by the commotion. Time to call it a day. With Kasey comfortably settled in her cage, Megan prepared to leave us.

"Don't worry about Kasey. She's fine. She'll be curious tonight, watching everything that's going on. She'll probably watch a little TV with you. Kasey loves watching TV."

"She came to the right place, right, Ned?" I said it lightly, but it was the best news I'd heard all day. Television was Ned's only way to the outside world. Channel surfing between sports and news helped break his isolation and kept him connected to the big picture. Now he had a companion in front of the set: a small thing of huge importance.

"Do you think she'll like it here?" Ned asked. "I want her to feel at home and be happy."

"That's really sweet of you, Ned. Some applicants are totally focused on 'What can the monkey do for me?' Kasey's got so much love to give, but she needs to feel loved in return. So it's nice to see that you're concerned for her happiness. That means a lot." Megan smiled and patted his shoulder. "She's had a long day, so don't be surprised if she goes up to her bedroom and crawls into those blankies. Monkeys at the college are out cold by nine and sleep till eight the next morning."

Kasey stretched and *twurred* languorously, as if to say, *I need my beauty rest. What of it?*

That evening, as predicted, she perched on her bedroom shelf, watching intently as we transferred Ned from his wheelchair to his bed. She seemed particularly fascinated with the workings of the cranky old mechanical lift. This thing took up a huge amount of real estate in the living room and looked like it came from the same medieval torture chamber as the halo. I always held my breath when I saw Ned suspended in it; it looked ready to topple at any moment. Kasey seemed to have the same reaction.

I heard a muffled yapping upstairs and glanced at my watch.

"Uh-oh. I forgot!" I said to Anna. "Better release the hounds."

Moments later Guy and Bailey barreled down the stairs with several hours of pent-up energy to burn.

"They destroyed the inside of your bedroom door," Anna informed me.

The new state of affairs in the living room brought them up short. Their house had been invaded by strangers. There was a giant monolith in the living room. And Ned's attention had been hijacked by something even smaller and noisier than two ambitiously barky little dogs. That last development put them over the top. Panting and whining, they scuttled and sniffed around the base of the cage.

"*SKEEEEEEEEEK!*"

Kasey suddenly plummeted from her bedroom all the way to the grated floor, shaking the entire structure. Guy and Bailey yelped and fled, tails between their legs.

"Poor little girls!" Anna ran to their rescue, kissing and stroking them, giving Kasey the evil eye. "Don't worry. *I* still love you."

"Mom!" Ned called. "Those dogs are scaring Kasey. Do something!"

"Fine," I sighed. "I'll talk to Megan about it tomorrow."

I positioned Kasey's cage so she could keep one eye on Ned and the other on the TV, then went to get her chow. The semi-spongy texture struck me as pretty unappealing, but Kasey peeped and pinwheeled with joy as soon as she saw it coming.

"Wow." Ned laughed. "Dinner and a show."

After she had eaten her chow, Kasey settled down with her little plastic book, studiously turning the pages as if she were reading *War and Peace* instead of *Mimi's Toes*.

"Reading *aloud*," said Ned. "Geez, she's noisy. I wish I could understand what she's saying."

"Me, too." I leaned closer to study her nimble little fingers and sweet, funny face.

"I think we made a pretty good start today, Mom."

"Me, too, Ned."

It was so good to hear him talking about something other than his pain. That in itself felt like a precious step forward.

I turned out the light and whispered, "Good night, you two."

THE NEXT MORNING Kasey was sitting up in her bedroom with the covers still over her head.

"A little early for you, eh?" I joked.

Ned laughed. Oh, that was good to see.

"Let me go get your chow. I made it fresh for you—I got up extra early," I crowed. "Just the way you like it." I didn't know what was worse. The fact that I was talking to a monkey like she was my sixth child, or that I was proud of my first attempt at making Monkey Chow.

I went to get Kasey's chow and looked forward to the same cartwheels of joy she'd given me last night. No such luck. She picked up the chow and it disintegrated into a mealy mush. She upended her bowl with a disgusted "*hmph!*"

Ned fretted. "Mom, you didn't do it right. She's hungry. You have to—"

"Yes. I know. I got it. Keep your pants on."

Back in the kitchen, I ran the chow-making video in my head. Scoop. Add water. Seal. Flip. Wait thirty seconds. Flip. Wait twenty minutes.

"Mom?" Ned called. "I think she's really hungry."

"Okay . . . um . . ."

I stared at the kitchen clock to make it go faster while Kasey paced and circled in her cage, complaining loudly. After fifteen minutes or so, I gave the chow a good shake and put it in her dish. It was still a bit . . . al dente. Actually, it was hard as rocks, but I thought Kasey might be hungry enough to just do a quick crunch and munch.

No.

She examined each nugget with disdain and looked me dead in the eye as she dropped the nuggets one by one through the grate in the bottom of the cage. Then she shrieked at Guy and Bailey, who scarfed down the chow like a couple of scavenging dingos.

"I know!" I said before Ned could open his mouth. "I know."

So I tried again. *This much water . . . Tupperware container . . . Shaken not stirred.* Somehow, with German precision and meticulous timing, I managed a batch of soufflé-perfect chow. Kasey devoured it appreciatively and climbed to her bedroom.

Third time's the charm.

"THOSE DOGS ARE A PROBLEM," Ned told Megan when she arrived for Day Two of boot camp. "Last night when Guy and Bailey came in, Kasey pounced and screamed, shaking her cage like she was terrified."

"Oh, believe me," Megan laughed, "Kasey's not scared of those two. She did that to intimidate the dogs and chase them away."

"Poor doggies." Maddie sprang to their defense. "Why'd she scare them like that?"

"Monkeys are extremely hierarchical. They have a very specific social structure. In Kasey's mind, right now I'm at the top of that hierarchy, but in time it'll transfer to Ned, with your mom right up there, too. Then Kasey. And then, um . . ."

Maddie folded her arms in front of her. "You've got to be kidding."

"Sorry. As far as Kasey's concerned, everyone else is beneath her in the social strata. Dogs are the lowest of the lower life forms. She's making sure they know that."

"So you're saying . . . Anna and I are somewhere between a *monkey* and the *dogs*?"

"In Kasey's world," Megan nodded, "that's the way it works."

No doubt about it. We were all living in Kasey's world now.

"Is it always going to be like that?" I asked.

"Kasey and the dogs will eventually come to terms," said Megan. "They may never be best friends, but everyone is soon going to know her place."

"Great."

Maddie excused herself politely, clearly as displeased as Guy and Bailey about the new family totem pole. I wasn't sure how I felt about it myself, but I didn't want Ned to see my concern.

"Let's start with scratching an itch," Megan said, producing the "itch pad"—like a loofah, only softer. "Itching is one of her favorite tasks. Give it a try, Ned."

"Kasey, itch?"

With the words hardly out of his mouth, Kasey plucked the itch pad from the container, ran up Ned's arm, and vigorously itched his head.

"Good girl!" Megan exclaimed. "Kasey loves itching. And she loves to hear how good she is. Always praise her."

"Good monkey, Kasey," Ned said warmly, and Kasey scurried to his lap and devoured the PB reward, which he had ready and waiting. She bounced back to Megan's shoulder. Ned repeated the command. Kasey complied again.

"Good, Kasey!" I laughed out loud because—well, come on. A monkey itching Ned's head? How cute is that?

"Mom. Please." Mr. Cool levied his measured response. "Megan, this might seem like a strange question, but is Kasey doing this just for the peanut butter? I mean, it's like we're bribing her. Will she ever come to me because she wants to?"

"Rewards for performing tasks—that's how the monkey helpers learn," said Megan. "A trained service animal is happiest when she knows what her job is and knows she's doing it well. The rewards help Kasey stay clear on that. She'll eventually begin to see you as her protector—her guy—and when she knows she can trust you, she'll want to come to you."

"Okay," he said. But he looked a bit dejected.

"Ellen, let's give Ned a break while you and I do bath and nails," said Megan. "You have a great sink in the kitchen. I'll get it set up."

"Set up . . ." My eyes strayed to that great sink. In my beautiful kitchen. Which was now a monkey's personal day spa. "Okay. Great."

Megan attached a carabiner lock—the kind rock climbers use—with a cable tie around the faucet. That should have told me something: the high locks-to-monkey ratio.

"Kasey likes a good hot soak," said Megan, running the tap water over her hand. "Add a healthy squirt of baby shampoo, check the temperature, and fill it up almost to the top."

When the sink was close to overflowing with suds and bubbles, Megan went to Ned's room and returned with Kasey on her shoulder. Kasey glanced around the kitchen, clucking warily.

"She doesn't look too enthusiastic about bath time," I said.

"Not to worry. The clucking signals caution. Kasey's just scoping out her new territory. Once she's sized everyone up, she'll be fine."

Kasey jumped into the sink, clapping at the bubbles, and we laughed when she looked up with a sudsy white beard.

"Does it ever wear off?" I asked. "I mean, how ridiculously *cute* she is?"

"No. Fortunately for her, it doesn't."

Megan deftly attached the ring on the end of the short leash to the lock on the faucet. *Piece of cake,* I thought as she gently wiped Kasey's face and body with a washcloth. *I've bathed a lot of squirming kids in my day.*

"You might want to stand back," said Megan, but before I could move, Kasey was up on the counter, shaking water everywhere.

"I wouldn't have guessed a five-pound monkey could absorb as much water as a woolly mammoth," I said, dabbing my face with a dishcloth. Apparently, she can.

"Have a nice soft towel ready," said Megan.

She wrapped the soggy little Kasey into a fresh bundle, but Kasey had no patience for that. A moment later, she was fluffing and preening on Megan's shoulder. Blond and bouffant, she was gorgeous, and she knew it.

Time for a mani-pedi.

"A monkey's nails grow incredibly fast," Megan cautioned. "It's important to keep them clipped. They can be sharp if they get too long."

Kasey sat quietly on her lap, presenting one hand, then the other, her right foot, then her left. Megan snipped them with a regular nail clipper—*et voilà!*—done in a minute. She made it look easy, but truthfully, I was anxious. I'd hated clipping my kids' nails. I was always afraid I'd accidentally cut their fingertips—which I did, of course.

Later that evening, Ned's friend Annie came over and Kasey was a shameless flirt. She'd cock her head and sort of smile at Annie, and when Annie cocked her head and smiled back, Kasey coyly turned her head the other way. *Yes, I know. I'm the fairest of them all.*

"She's so cute," Annie crooned. "Oh, I've always wanted a monkey."

That monkey was everything I had envisioned: such an incredible distraction for Ned, and his friends were enchanted. The phone was already ringing off the hook with excited monkey lovers wanting to hear every detail. People would be lining up at the door to visit Ned and his incredible monkey—this was going to be great.

Ned seemed to let his guard down a little, allowing himself to relax. I passed by his room later and saw him watching Kasey as she pushed beads around her little roller coaster. For Ned, this was better than television—and a whole lot better than staring at the walls. The way he was smiling warmed my heart. But after a while, Kasey abandoned her toys, ambling round and round in her cage.

"Why do you think she does that?" Ned asked.

I shook my head. "I really don't know."

"I wish she felt more at home."

"In time, Ned," I assured him. "In time."

12

Fa la la la la

THIS YEAR, I WASN'T SO MUCH HOPING FOR A HAPPY HOLI-day as insisting on one. Yes, we were living in a construction zone, with Ned and everyone else unsettled and agitated, but at least we weren't in the hospital. There would be no repeat of the plodding blue Christmas we'd had last year. Control freak that I am, I approached the season in business manager mode. I decided to orchestrate this holiday the same way I'd wrangled any of a thousand projects during my many years as a marketing executive: setting clear goals, organizing for success, and rallying human—and, in our case, animal—resources.

"We *will* have a good Christmas," I announced.

There would be peace, joy, and merriment if it killed us. My first action item? Delegate as many action items as possible.

"Ron, find us the perfect tree."

"Jake, you'll pull ornaments and help set up the tree as soon as you get home."

"Teddy, you know where I keep the old Christmas lights? Dig those out and string up the trees and bushes."

"Megan, pick up wine and beer on your way home from work."

"Anna and Maddie, get all your stuff out of the family room to make room for presents."

I'd shopped online for the customary seven gifts and seven stocking stuffers for each of the five kids plus Ron, using a spreadsheet to ensure the *same exact amount*—not a dollar more or less—was spent on each of them. I efficiently prepared everyone's favorite Christmas Eve appetizers ahead of time. No need to cook a big, elaborate dinner; after opening a few gifts on Christmas Eve, we'd make our annual rounds to friends' parties, feasting on substantial fare cooked (blissfully) by someone else.

That was the Official Holiday Plan.

In my dreams.

In reality, as I worked my way down a list trying to find PCAs for the holiday shifts, I had about as much luck as Mary and Joseph finding room at the inn. My meticulously plotted preparations were fragmented between making Monkey Chow, hauling paint cans to the garage, chasing Guy and Bailey away from Kasey's cage, and getting Ned ready for training sessions with Megan.

"Okay, Ellen," she said the third day. "Your turn to take Kasey out of her cage. Ready?"

"Ready as I'll ever be."

I was nervous. I didn't want to make a mistake and have Ned—or Megan—lose confidence in me.

"Before you take Kasey out," said Megan, "make sure all the doors are closed. Monkeys are extremely suspicious about what they *can't* see. And let's keep the dogs—and actually the girls—out for now. Less distractions."

With the dogs and girls banished and the doors secured, she positioned me at the cage. Ned looked at me expectantly, treat dispenser fully loaded, ready for action.

"Go for it, Mom."

"Okay." I took a deep breath. "Kasey, potty?"

She totally ignored me.

Megan nudged. "Again."

"Kasey, potty?"

Success.

Here was another one of those surreal moments: getting a thrill out of monkey poop. We raised the chorus of potty appreciation, and Megan handed me the long tether.

"Excellent. Now stand with your body directly in front of the door, just in case she decides to leap out."

"Leap out?" The thought had never crossed my mind.

"Okay, Ellen. Now do just like I did yesterday."

"Kasey, leash?" I said, but she circled her cage and returned to her toys without a glance in my direction. "Kasey, leash?"

No dice.

"Try it again," Megan encouraged. "With monkeys, it's all about respect. It takes time to build that relationship."

"Kasey, leash?" I tried to keep the frustration out of my voice. "*Kasey*. Leash?"

Kasey picked up her leash and dangled it just beyond my reach. She knew precisely what she was doing.

"Reach in," Megan coached quietly. "Attach the tether to the harness."

Easier said than done. The opening wasn't all that big, and neither am I. Straining on tiptoes, I was finally able to snap the tether onto the harness ring. Kasey amicably hopped out and jumped onto my shoulder.

"Well! Hello there." I'll admit it: I was smug. "See, Ned? This monkey business isn't so hard, after all."

"Right, Mom." He rolled his eyes. "Kasey, come sit?"

Kasey dove for the peanut butter, stayed in Ned's lap for about a nanosecond, then romped over to Megan. We spent the long session repeating Kasey's basic tasks over and over again—fetching the remote, popping CDs in the CD player, scratching Ned's nose. Every time Kasey scrambled up his arm or hopped onto his lap, I watched his face light up. And I watched his expression fall every time she zipped back to her preferred perch on Megan's shoulder. He enjoyed working with Kasey, but I'm not sure he was sold on the idea that he'd ever really be "her guy."

"Mom?" Maddie tapped on the door. "It's getting late. We need to leave for town."

"Oh, Mads, that party—I forgot." I glanced at my watch, then at Ned, who was looking a bit haggard. "I'm sorry. We're about to wrap this up, then I'll drive you."

Maddie didn't say anything, but she closed the door a bit too firmly.

Mom, car? Mom, fetch?

"Sounds like a good time to call it a day," said Megan.

"Sorry. We're all a little on edge."

"Not to worry," said Megan. "Kasey's going to love Christmas here. There's a lot going on, people coming and going. To Kasey, that's entertainment. She always has a great time with my family for the holidays. Mom and Dad absolutely adore her, and she . . . she'll be missed."

"Is it hard for you to part with her?" I asked, but the answer was clear.

"It is hard," she admitted, blinking back tears. "Kasey and I came into each other's lives over . . . oh, gosh—I guess it's been eight years. We're very close. I'll miss her, and I'm sure she'll miss me, too. But working makes her happy. And I know how important she'll be to Ned when she's bonded with him."

"You really think that'll happen?" he asked.

"I really do, Ned." Megan cleared her throat. "That's what it's all about."

'TWAS THE NIGHT BEFORE CHRISTMAS, and all through the house, all the creatures were stirring, not to mention bickering, barking, whining, complaining, clucking, chirping, peeping, and squawking. Kasey ranged back and forth in her cage, clucking and trilling at Ned, who kept calling me in to translate, as if my guess was any better than his. I slumped into a chair, my fingers raw from miles of Scotch tape and curly ribbon. There wasn't a prayer of getting a nurse for Christmas Eve, so I was looking at a long night ahead.

"She's trying to tell me something, Mom. What do you think she wants?"

"I fed her exactly the right amount at the right time, Ned. I praised her in a positive tone when she pottied. I turned her cage for an optimal view of the TV. What more could she want?"

"Just hang out for a while," said Ned. "Help me figure it out."

"Eck eck." Kasey zipped her purse and waved it at me. "Kreeeeeeeee!"

It was as if we'd adopted a three-year-old from Chechnya. She was really cute, but neither of us could understand a word the other was saying. And culturally, let's face it, we were worlds apart.

"Mom, don't let those dogs—"

Too late. Guy and Bailey were in. Kasey *skreeked* and pounced, making them nuts. If the door was shut, Ned was isolated from the rest of the family. If the door was open, the dog and monkey show left him wincing with nerve pain. So we went back and forth—door open, door closed, door open, door closed—all day. And now Maddie and Anna were going at it.

"Anna, those are *my* jeans!"

"Then why were they in *my* closet?"

"Skraaaaaaaaaaaaaaak!" Kasey pounced to the side of her cage, shaking the grill.

"Yikes," I said. "*That* I understand."

"Knock it off, girls," Ned shouted. "You're scaring the monkey."

"It's our house, Ned," Maddie shouted right back.

"Kasey's not the boss of me," Anna added.

"SKREEEEEEEEEEK!" Kasey vehemently disagreed.

After a brief stare-down, the girls turned on their heels and set out to find a new place to carry on their argument, and Kasey went back to her toys.

"We'd better have Megan talk to them," said Ned. "They have to get used to Kasey being here."

Like they've had to get used to everything else?

I couldn't blame the girls for being on edge. Long before Kasey arrived, they'd been feeling like they were at the bottom of the heap. The vast majority of my time, energy, and waking thoughts were occupied by Ned's care. Meanwhile, Maddie and Anna hustled rides, packed their own lunches, and missed out on many of the regular happenings of regular girls. Now a screeching monkey was putting them in their place. All they wanted was a little upbeat Christmas spirit among sane, normal company. There wasn't much of either at our house.

Then Jake arrived, and new hope breezed in with a gust of cold air. "Jake's home!" Maddie danced down the stairs to greet him.

"I'll be back," I told Ned, hoping to catch Son #2 at the door, but by the time I'd made my way through the maze, Jake was plopped in front of the TV. He stood up to give me a hug that was more like a body bump, then sat right down again.

"It looks like a bomb went off in here," he said. "Where are you going to hang the stockings?"

I looked around at the construction remnants cluttering the kitchen and family room. Hospital equipment was shoved up against the living room mantel where we used to hang our stockings.

"Come on, Mom, Megan and Ron are here!" Anna called from the doorway. "We need to get rolling."

The girls weren't the only ones counting the minutes till they could get out of the house. A sad thought, but I have to say I shared it myself. But first, the Official Plan called for our annual sibling-to-sibling gift exchange and a light repast of carrots and curry dip, deviled eggs, and cheese puffs. We moved Kasey's cage over by the family room so she could join the fun, and her loud skacking and clucking dominated the conversation.

"Geez." Anna covered her ears with her hands. "She sounds like a big bird."

"A big, annoying bird," said Maddie. "Mom, make her be quiet."

"Why don't *you* be quiet?" said Ned.

"Why don't *you* just—"

Jake cut in. "Come on, you guys, knock it off."

"Skkaaaaaaaaaaaaack!"

I wasn't sure if Kasey felt left out and wanted to be closer or felt overwhelmed by the commotion and wanted to be farther away. Whatever she was going on about, I realized, for my own sanity she needed to go back into Ned's temporary quarters in the living room.

"She'll have some peace and quiet," I told Ned, "and we can get back to the festivities."

He shook his head. "I'm out of steam. I'll go in with Kasey."

"But, Ned . . ."

"Mom. I need to go to bed," he said, slowly and softly, but with conviction. "*Now.*"

"Mom," said Megan. "Ron and I'll get Ned settled and stay here. You take the kids and make the rounds."

"But I planned . . . I wanted everyone to be . . ."

"Mom." Anna and Maddie were looking at me like a couple of inmates up for parole.

"Thanks, guys," I said. "That's really thoughtful of you."

As I roamed from home to home with Jake and the girls, Christmas was everywhere but inside me. Our friends' homes were so beautiful, fun-filled, joyous—so completely uncomplicated. It made us feel all the more fragmented and depressed. Returning home, I said good night to Ron and Megan and Jake, who was off to meet up with some friends, and went in to reposition Ned.

After I cleaned Kasey's cage and did the dishes, it was time to play Santa—usually one of my favorite times of the whole year. With everyone tucked in bed, I used to get a glass of wine and turn on Christmas music. I enjoyed filling the family room with piles and piles of presents for my kids. This year, exhausted, I dragged the boxes and bags to the tree. I looked around at the chaos and realized that I'd never figured out where to hang the stockings. Finally, I gave up and just laid them on the floor. It was the best I could do.

'Twas the night before Christmas . . .

I'd forgotten all about it. But I couldn't bear the idea of cobbling together another conference call. I picked up the book and put it away, unread for the first time ever . . . *ever*.

With a deep sigh, I set my watch for 1:30 A.M., when it would be time to turn Ned and tend to his medications. Then I'd be able to lie down for a few more hours before it was time to be up and at it again.

Get over it, Ellen. It's Christmas. Ho ho ho, damn it!

There was absolutely no benefit to being a big humbug.

I recalibrated my holiday attitude and rang in Christmas morning with a deliberately positive spin. The kids must have had the same idea. Everyone was happy and excited as we sat gathered around the coffee table, carols blaring, presents piled high, and our favorite Christmas breakfast: Sara Lee frozen Butter Streusel Coffee Cake, served directly from the tin, container to mouth. Only the best for my bunch.

Our special system for gift opening has been in place for years—absolutely necessary with so many kids and fourteen times that many presents. I had tracked everything I got for everyone on my elaborate spreadsheet and marked every gift with a special code, right down to the smallest stocking stuffers, like funny notepads and pencils. This way I could make sure everyone opened the same level gift at the same time, and if two people had similar gifts, they'd be opened simultaneously to maintain maximum surprise value. (I cling to the belief that someday, when they are parents, my children will worship me for this.)

"Stocking stuffers first. Then bigger presents," I reminded them.

We passed and presented across the coffee table, and for a while, there was that Christmas morning feeling of living inside a snow globe. Our circle became a pleasant flurry of happy voices and scattered paper and ribbons.

"Ned! Open this one from me."

"Here, Anna. Merry Christmas, Megan!"

"Merry Christmas, Ron."

"Jake, thank you! I love it!"

"Maddie and Anna," I said, "open those green boxes at the same time."

I'd gotten them each five pairs of brightly colored cotton undies from Victoria's Secret. Just what they'd wanted. Martha Stewart I am not, but I'd taken a lot of time making every package as pretty as possible, and as everyone ripped into their carefully chosen and gaily wrapped gifts, I sat thinking, *Am I good? Oh, yes. I am good.*

"Mom!" Maddie shrieked, and not a merry Christmas morning "just what I wanted" shriek either. My beautiful little fashion plate looked up, wounded.

"Large? You got me size *large*?"

"Oh, no . . . Maddie, I—"

"And Anna gets *extra small*?" Incensed—with a capital P—she grabbed Anna's package and brandished it at me. "How could you be so insensitive, Mom? How *could* you?"

In Maddie's self-assessment, her derriere is significantly smaller than her sister's. It's not. But there you have it. Serious insult upon injury.

"Mads, I'm sorry. I must have accidentally clicked the wrong size when I ordered. We'll exchange them. It's not a big deal."

"Obviously not to *you*."

She stomped upstairs, both dogs yipping in solidarity behind her. Kasey chimed in with strident cawing and squawking. A major princess prance was officially in progress.

"Could she be any more annoying?" Jake grumbled.

"Maddie or the monkey?" said Ned.

"Take your pick."

"We don't need everyone weighing in on Maddie's behavior," I told them, but everyone did, and "annoying" was the most common assessment because, according to family tradition, they couldn't proceed with opening the rest of their presents until she returned. *Poof.* The modicum of joy we'd managed to scrape together completely vanished.

"I'll go talk to her," Megan said.

She followed Maddie upstairs. There was a brief exchange of voices. A door slammed.

"That sounds like it went well," Jake said. Always levelheaded, he took a turn reasoning with Maddie, but returned a moment later. "Let's just open our stuff. I'm done with the drama queen."

I looked at Ron with the haggard desperation of a night nurse.

"I'll see what I can do," he sighed. Bless his heart, he worked some kind of solicitous brother-in-law mojo and returned shortly with a reticent, red-eyed Maddie in tow.

She slid me a glare that said, *I am so not speaking to you.*

I offered a smile that said, *I know.*

It wasn't about her. Everything was just so not right. Ned tried valiantly to participate in our Christmas traditions despite punishing nerve pain brought on by the chaos, but I could see he needed to get back to bed. The family festivities were over. The day was a disaster.

Later that evening, I sat in Ned's room and helped him open the last of the same sort of well-intentioned presents he'd received in the hospital a year before. Kasey observed his every move, chuckling and peeping at the colorful paper.

"We should have gotten a present for Kasey," he said.

"Sure. One more kid to get seven gifts and seven stocking stuffers for."

There was a lovely, peaceful moment, as Ned watched Kasey watching him. He smiled at her, and she offered him a soft *purrup*.

"Megan was right," he mused. "She does love to watch me."

Clang!

Ned and I about jumped out of our skin. Kasey had suddenly pounced to the front of her cage and now shook her water bottle at me. She looked purposefully at Ned, gave the bottle another vigorous throttle in my direction, then hopped up to her shelf, casually waiting for room service like it was the Ritz.

"Mom, didn't you refill her water when you changed her papers?"

"With all the goings-on . . . shoot. I'll get it."

When I came back with the refill, I discovered the fresh papers had been graced with even fresher pee and poop.

Terrific.

This was crazy. Exhausting. I'd asked for it—and the girls had begged for it—but now we were realizing this was not the super-cool "pet" we had imagined. She was a serious service animal with an elaborate diet, inflexible hierarchy, and a whole lot of self-determination. As I began to grasp how much work Kasey would actually be, I couldn't help but wonder, *What on earth was I thinking?* Instead of making life easier, she'd brought a whole new level of complexity to our already chaotic existence.

This monkey was supposed to make everything merry and bright.

Apparently, Kasey didn't get the memo.

13

Queen of the Jungle

I T WAS THE DAY AFTER CHRISTMAS AND NED WAS WAITING to pepper Megan with questions.

"Kasey still goes ballistic every time the dogs are around," he told her.

"She's the same way with Maddie and Anna," I added.

"Sounds like hierarchy issues," said Megan. "Kasey's establishing her place in the pecking order at your house."

"Hmm." I took that in for a moment. If anyone understands pecking order, it's teenage girls, so maybe there was some hope here.

"Monkeys constantly take note of whom they can rely on to care for and protect them," Megan said. "They want to know who's got their back—and who doesn't."

"The girls are nice to her. Just trying to make friends."

"Kasey needs to know that there are creatures above her in the hierarchy and some below her as well. It can take a helper monkey up to six months to figure out who's who in a big, noisy family like yours."

"And in the meantime . . . what?" I asked tentatively. "She'll keep screaming at them?"

"Pretty much." Megan nodded.

"Great."

"Once she figures out her ranking and makes sure everyone else knows theirs, she can feel completely safe, and that's a big step forward in the bonding process."

"Okay," Ned said, but he looked worried.

"It's not as complicated as it sounds. But you'll have to be patient. Give Kasey time to observe without pushing her to interact too much."

Kasey punctuated the advice with a curt *hmph*.

"Rather than expecting her to adjust to yours," Megan said, "try to adjust to her perspective and respect her position. You'll soon see which situations trigger a big vocal response."

"Is there anything I can do to help her relax and feel more comfortable?" Ned asked.

"What if . . ." Megan thought it over. "How about you and Kasey sort of gang up on the dogs?"

"Like how?"

"When Kasey screeches at them, instead of trying to calm her down, jump right in there. Say, 'Go get 'em, Kasey!'"

"I could be into that," Ned said, with a slow grin.

"Show her you're on her side," Megan said. "More importantly, show her you know the dogs are way lower than her in the hierarchy."

"That works for Guy and Bailey, but what about Maddie and Anna?" I asked.

"This might be hard for them to swallow," said Megan, "but Maddie and Anna need to back off until she's developed strong, secure bonds with you and Ned."

"And by back off, you mean . . ."

"They should leave her be. Ignore her."

"Ignore a monkey in the living room?" I said.

"Precisely," said Megan.

"How are they supposed to do that?" Ned asked.

"Especially when they were so excited about having her," I said. "They just want to be involved."

"Well, here's an important role they can play," said Megan. "Kasey needs people below her in the hierarchy. Maddie and Anna could help by agreeing to be those people."

Ned huffed. "Yeah, right. They'll love that."

So now it was my job to explain the complexities of monkey psychology to my highly sensitive overachievers, quashing their happy imaginings of big monkey fun. There was a conversation I couldn't wait to have. Meanwhile, we had to get back to basic training.

"It's good that you're not in the wheelchair today, Ned. Since you spend so much time in bed, Kasey needs to be familiar with that." Megan stepped away from the cage. "I'll move to the other side of the room so Kasey's not tempted to retreat to me. Ellen, let's have you get her out and take her to Ned's bed."

We performed the potty-leash-door ritual, and Kasey reluctantly hopped to my shoulder, eyeing Megan the whole time. I crossed to Ned's bed and dropped my shoulder, encouraging her to jump down next to him, which she did—for about half a second. Without the lure of the treat dispenser, she wasn't so keen on going someplace new.

"Ellen, try dipping Ned's finger in the peanut butter jar," said Megan after a few more tries. That worked for the three seconds it took Kasey to lick his finger clean.

"I don't want to make her do anything she doesn't want to do," Ned said. "I mean, if she doesn't want to come to me . . ."

"Monkeys are creatures of habit," Megan said. "Anything unfamiliar is cause for concern. She'll want to check it out."

True to form, Kasey crept behind Ned's chair, checking between the wheels with a suspicious *cluck kit ker cluck*. Up on tiptoes, she furrowed her eyebrows and tipped her ear toward the distant sound of the dogs in the yard.

"Reassure her that you're here for her, Ned. Even when she's in the cage and feeling safe," said Megan. "When she learns you're her 'dad'—her protector—she'll turn to you to feel calmed. Establishing this relationship is key. She *wants* to have someone at the top of her hierarchy. It's her nature. We need to help her understand that this someone is you."

"That makes sense." He nodded firmly. "Maybe we could work on that when—"

"Ka-caw!" Kasey interrupted, crowing like a grackle. "Caw! Caw!"

"Okay, like *that*," said Ned. "Sometimes she makes that noise all through dinner and we can't figure out what the heck she's trying to tell us."

Megan laughed. "Kasey's a diva. She wants your attention. If she feels left out of the conversation, she'll let you know."

Ned rushed to reassure her. "I'm here for you, Kasey. It's okay."

Singularly unimpressed, Kasey turned away with another duchess "hmph."

"If she gets too vocal about the dogs or a new aide or whatever . . . just turn her cage around," said Megan. "Give her a short time-out. She'll quiet down when she realizes tantrums are a waste of energy."

"Ah. Of course," I said. Time-out was a technique with which I'd had plenty of experience.

"She's so fascinating," said Ned. "I wish she wanted to hang out with me more, but no matter what she's doing, I can't stop looking at her."

Neither could I.

Squawking, screeching, and pecking order complaints aside, I was enchanted by this beautiful creature. Nor could Ned get enough—watching her, learning about her, working through the training exercises. He was benefiting from the distraction, if nothing else. But a question nagged at the back of both our minds: would it really be worth all this effort? "Congratulations," Megan said, as she gathered her things to go. "You've graduated to phone support."

"Phone support," I repeated, holding on to the notion as if it were a guy wire.

"How does that work exactly?" Ned wanted to know.

"Calls will be scheduled daily at first," said Megan. "One of the trained staff members at the Monkey College will check up on Kasey, see how you're doing, and coach you through new tasks when you're ready. And of course, feel free to call the support line with any questions."

"When will we see you again?" asked Ned.

"I'll be back in a few weeks to help you advance to some new tasks." Megan smiled and said, "Ned, you're incredible. You guys are going to be a great team."

Ned's expression was guarded, but he said, "Thanks, Megan. For everything."

"Yes, thank you, Megan," I said. "You've been terrific. Hey, we were wondering . . . would you mind—I know it is a little strange—but would you mind if we called you Megan Monkey? We've started to call you that amongst ourselves—you know, to distinguish you from our Megan. . . . Would it be okay?"

Megan *Monkey* laughed and said, "Sure—I'd be honored." Megan went to Kasey's cage, Kasey came to the edge of her bedroom shelf, and the two shared a long, connected look. The room suddenly seemed full of the significance of this moment of passage, for Megan and Kasey, for Ned and me. All four of us were stepping into the unknown, searching for our next new place in the world.

"Bye, Kasey," Megan said wistfully. "I'll miss you."

Kasey purred softly in answer.

"You take good care of Ned."

I silently seconded that. *Yes. Please.*

MEGAN MONKEY hadn't been out the door for an hour when the barking, screeching, clucking, quarreling Battle Royale broke out in the living room.

"Skeeeeeeeeeeeeee!"

"Go get 'em, Kasey!" Ned's voice was barely audible above the fray. "Get those doggies. Tell those girls who's boss."

"Shut up, Ned," said Maddie. "She is not either!"

"Skraaaaaaaaaaaaaaaaack!"

"It's all right, Kasey. I'm here for you. Come on, Kasey. It's okay."

"It is not *okay,* Ned." Anna was close to angry tears. "She's terrorizing the dogs and making everything miserable."

"Oh, suck it up. You girls are almost as spoiled as Guy and Bailey."

"*We're* spoiled?" Maddie dove in. "That's a good one! When was the last time anybody got any attention around here besides you and that little—"

"Okay, that's enough." I stepped between Kasey's cage and the angry mob.

"Crack-ack-rrrrack," Kasey scolded over my shoulder.

"Mom, Ned keeps telling Kasey—"

"I know, Anna. Please, help me get the dogs out of here."

"Cruck-uck-rrrruck . . ."

"Mom, you have to explain to them—"

"Ned, butt out. I'll take care of it."

"SKAAAAAAAAAAAAAAAAAACK!"

"*Enough.*"

Surprisingly, there was a moment of silence. Even Kasey looked abashed and hopped up to her bedroom.

"Ned, *stop.* Kasey, *quiet.* Dogs, *out.* Girls . . . we have to talk."

Maddie and Anna each scooped a dog under one arm and followed me as far from Kasey World as we could get.

"Look, I know the monkey is annoying," I said. "And I know it seems like I'm always doing something for someone other than you, but you have a really important part in this equation. Kasey needs to see herself in the middle of the totem pole. Ned and I are above her, and the two of you are—"

"We're down with the dogs."

"No, of course you're not. We're just asking you to pretend you are. Just go along with the hierarchy thing until Kasey gets used to living here. The good news is, all you have to do for now is ignore her. And if you can't ignore her, then you have to just . . . play second banana." There. I'd said it.

"And get treated like dirt," Maddie corrected me, "by a monkey."

"That, too, yes, and I don't blame you for being unhappy about it, but Kasey needs to establish herself in the hierarchy."

As disappointed as they were, when it came right down to it, my kids were one for all and all for one. Those grand sibling-on-sibling battles actually brought a little bit of normalcy back to Ned's life, and most of the time, the girls were sweetly compassionate, always ducking in the door to offer him a drink of water or just say, "Hey, bud."

I knew they'd go for it when I said, "Can you think of it as helping Ned?"

"Fine," said Maddie.

"Whatever," said Anna. "I guess having a monkey isn't as fun as it sounded."

Amen to that.

The next morning was our first trainer-free attempt at taking Kasey out of her cage. She was pretty disinterested when I made the potty suggestion. I looked over my shoulder at Ned. He smiled eagerly. I tried again, giving it a little more team spirit.

"Kasey, potty?"

She didn't even turn her head in my direction.

"Let me try, Mom." Ned rolled up to her cage so she couldn't miss seeing the treat dispenser, then commanded like the almighty protector, "Kasey, potty!"

She tipped her head, vaguely acknowledging his presence, then went back to playing with her coin purse. Ned and I looked at each other, stumped.

"Maybe we should try it again later," said Ned.

But I dug in. "I say let's just keep asking her until she does it."

I can be stubborn, too, when I want to be. Monkey stubborn. I was not going to let her shanghai the training session I had planned. After another dozen or so attempts, I suggested a new tactic.

"Okay, let's just ignore her. That used to work with . . . with one of you kids."

"Which one? Not me."

"Never mind," I said. "Pretend we're just talking amongst ourselves and—"

"Hey, look."

Mission accomplished. We praised her to the rafters, and I strategically positioned myself in front of the cage, nervously running through the procedure in my head.

Doors closed: check.

Tether in hand: check.

Body blocking door: check.

"Kasey, leash?" Check. *Okay, we can do this.*

I unlocked the lock. I carefully slid the latch.

Whoosh! A blast of golden fur whipped my face, and using my shoulder as a launching pad, she was in orbit. NASA would have been jealous.

"Br . . . !" In other words: *So long, sucker!*

"Mom!" Ned barked. "Mom, don't let her get—"

Too late. She was up on top of her cage, looking down on me. I stood drop-jawed, the tether dangling uselessly in my hands.

"Okay—okay—oh, my God—okay . . ." I searched my brain for Megan Monkey's voice. "She said monkeys always seek the highest spot when they feel in danger."

Yes. That was right. A remnant of instinct from the jungle, where the greatest threats are large animals on the ground.

"Great," said Ned. "Now how do we get her down?"

From the top of the six-foot cage, Kasey deftly leapt over my head to the drapes, tiptoed across the dowel, and did a fire pole slide down the side of the curtain.

"Mom, quick! Get the tether on her!"

"I'm trying!"

When she stopped off at a side table filled with pictures and mementos, I expected everything to go flying, but Kasey carefully picked her way through the memorabilia, sniffing a knickknack here, inspecting a photo there. She paused to admire herself in the mirror hanging on the wall and the next moment was back on top of her cage, zipping back and forth, *cluck-cluck-cluck*ing low in her throat.

Ned fretted. "Oh, geez . . . she sounds scared."

"She sounds *guilty,* Ned. She knows exactly what she's doing."

Kasey held the end of her harness leash tightly with the tip of her tail, teasing it just out of my grabbing reach. If I moved to the left and tried to snatch it, she'd dash to the right.

"Man, she's really got your number," said Ned.

There was no use denying it. I'd been outsmarted. And outpaced. In the next three seconds, Kasey took a flying leap from the top of her cage to Ned's bedside table, rustled something, and flew back over our heads to her high-altitude perch atop the cage, where she sat warbling a little tune with broadly faked innocence. *Doo dee doo dee doo. What? Who, me?*

"Ned . . . what's that in her hand?" I angled for a better view. "Oh, no . . . are those—"

"*Gummy worms.*"

"What? No, she—where the heck did she get those?"

The tiny glutton had a thick, sticky worm tucked under each arm, one in each hand and each foot, two stuffed under her chin, and her cheeks were bulging.

"Mom, we have to get them away from her."

"I know, okay?"

"Seriously! She'll get sick from the sugar."

"You're not helping, Ned."

After the elaborate care I'd taken following the persnickety Chez Kasey menu, our very first time without the trainer, Kasey was about to OD on sugar. She'd be in diabetic shock, I'd die of embarrassment, and Ned would be banished from the monkey recipient universe forever.

I ran for the phone, punched in the number for phone support, and set it to speakerphone so I could continue the chase.

"Loose monkey!" I yelled when the trainer answered. "Loose monkey with gummy worms!"

"Okay, Ellen, let's stay calm."

The voice on the speakerphone was cool as a cucumber. Obviously, this was not her first call from a panic-stricken newbie.

"I'm going to walk you through getting Kasey to drop the candy and get back into her cage, all right?"

"Yes. Good. I'm ready. I'm—I'm—I got it."

Looking down at me from the top of her cage, Kasey continued processing the wad of gummy worms stuffing her face, her expression a mix of shame, triumph, and sugar-induced ecstasy. I didn't know whether to laugh or cry.

"We're going to get her to 'trade up' by offering something she'll want more than she wants the candy. You have peanut butter handy?"

"Got it."

I dipped my finger in the treat dispenser on the side of Ned's wheelchair and offered it up to Her Majesty. She glanced at it disdainfully, smacking her lips with gummy goodness. I couldn't believe she wasn't going for it. Pure, unadulterated bribery had always worked on my kids. Kasey, not so much.

Ned chastised me. "Mom, did you pay any attention at all when Megan Monkey was training you? You should have expected this."

"Yes. Thank you, Ned. That's helpful," I hissed, dipping a bigger dollop of peanut butter. "Kasey, look! Look, Kasey! Yummy!"

"Cluck," said Kasey. Not buying it. Not even tempted.

"Mom, you have to do something!"

"That didn't work," I told Ms. Phone Support, trying to keep the panic out of my voice. "What do we do now?"

"Okay," she said seriously. "We're going to have to go for the one thing she loves more than candy—more than any other treat. Ellen, this should only be used in serious situations, but I think we're there. Get the Reddi-wip."

"The Reddi-wip . . ."

Reddi-wip was the red phone. The briefcase handcuffed to your wrist.

"Spray some in a small cup or on a spoon," instructed the voice on the other end of the phone. "Put it inside her cage, preferably up in her bedroom—and get ready."

I ducked out of the room and slammed the door behind me, leaning against it for a split second, thinking, *What an idiot I am! What could have possibly made me think I could do this?*

"Mom, hurry!" Ned called from the other side of the door, and I could hear Kasey *cluck-cluck*ing at him.

I tore to the fridge, seized the Reddi-wip—thank God we had some—and oh-so-carefully eased through the door back into Ned's room. Kasey's eyes grew wide when she saw the bright red can. *Now we're talkin'.*

"Look, Kasey . . . Reddi-Wip . . . mmmmmm . . ."

I pointed the spray tip into a medicine cup and filled the room with that unmistakable seductive sound. Stretching as far inside her cage as I could, I set the cup next to her blankies on her bedroom shelf and slowly withdrew, keeping my hand on the door.

"Kasey. Cage?"

"Pip . . . pip . . ."

She didn't budge from the top of her cage, but she shivered with yearning, still clutching the gummies. I could see the struggle in her face: *Oh, the rubbery gummy goodness . . . oh, the dreamy dairy delight . . .*

"Come on, Kasey," Ned said softly. "Come on, girl."

She assessed the situation a moment longer, computing her little cost/benefit analysis. Having assured herself that there was no way she was keeping both, she dropped the remaining gummy worms and scampered inside to get to that treat of treats.

"She's in!" cried Ned.

I slammed the door shut, double locked it, grabbed up the stray gummy worms, and sank to the floor, finally able to exhale.

"Skee! Skee! Skee!" Kasey shrieked, stricken with remorse she was not about to bear alone. Clutching one hand to her heart, she pointed at me with the other. *Temptress! Bungler! You made me do it! You! You! YOU!*

Later I learned not to fall for her blame game, but at that moment, I felt completely humiliated and guilty as sin.

"Everything okay over there?" asked the support person.

"Yes. We're good." I thanked her and hung up the phone. "Well. That was fun."

Ned was not happy.

He scolded me. "Mom, it's your job to handle her. You totally screwed up."

"I'm sorry. I feel terrible. I promise I'll—"

"Now I can't practice with her today. And if she'd eaten all that sugar—"

"*Hey.* Wait a minute." I plucked a paper bag from its hiding place on the nightstand. "I don't recall gummy worms being one of the main food groups on *your* menu, either. Exactly where did these come from? And how did she know they were there?"

"From the candy store in town," he said sheepishly. "Anna got them for me."

"Skee kack kack." Kasey corroborated Ned's story.

"Geez, Megan Monkey wasn't kidding," he said, deftly changing the subject. "Kasey remembers everything. Who'd think a monkey would even know what a gummy worm is?"

The next morning, before we made a second attempt, I conducted a thorough search of the room, confiscating a half-eaten bag of M&M's, a Snickers bar, and some sour watermelon candies.

"Are you harboring anything else she might have seen?" I asked Ned, and he shook his head.

We'd learned that Kasey modestly preferred to be ignored while she did her potty business, but after that, I didn't take my eyes off her for a millisecond. I shoved my body fully in front of the door and stuck my arm right into her cage.

"Kasey," I said as sweetly as I could through gritted teeth. "Leash?"

She handed me the short leash with a polite *purrup* and posed a nice vogue while I snapped on the long tether. Maybe she felt guilty about the gummy incident. Or maybe she took pity on me, the bungling neophyte. Who cares? I was thrilled.

14

Room for Hope

A FTER MONTHS OF SAWING, BANGING, POWER DRILLING, and the steady march of construction workers, Ned's totally handicapped-accessible room was finally completed just after the New Year, a beautifully clean slate freshly painted warm blue and desert tan.

"This is awesome," he said at the doorway of his own wheelchair-navigable bathroom. "I can't wait to take a real shower."

Such an achingly simple pleasure, and he'd gone so long without it.

No more sponge bathing. No more camping out in the living/hospital room. Ned would be spending a good 80 percent of his day here; instead of a living room, he'd have a room where he could actually have a life. Now there was plenty of space for his new physical therapy mat, a desk, a few comfy chairs for visitors, and Kasey's six-foot domicile, of course. In this pleasant, private space, Ned's rest would be more restful. Kasey could wheel and whoop to her heart's content and not drive the rest of us crazy. Perhaps the two of them could now settle into the relationship we'd hoped for.

Ned was the undisputed king of his castle. He had it all planned out.

"I want all my Red Sox 2004 World Series pictures there. Patriots posters over here."

It was good to see him pointing with his left hand, which seemed to be gaining strength. Following his direction, I posted innumerable inspirational signs.

"COURAGE"
"HOPE"
"BELIEVE"

"All those pictures motivate me," he said. "I want to see them from wherever I am."

We installed lots of shelves and bookcases, with plenty of room for all Ned's stuff from before and after the accident, plus pictures of family and friends. There were places of honor for his first home-run ball, a signed copy of Tedy Bruschi's book *Never Give Up,* a picture of Ned and legendary University of Arizona basketball coach Lute Olson, the little jade dragons from Singapore, and other special mementos.

"This is really *my* room," he said proudly. "Everything's geared to inspire me—keep me positive."

Ned had named all his post-accident fundamentals. He'd christened his wheelchair "Storm Trooper." The ramp van became "Big Mama." He dubbed his new overhead lift "The Hawk."

"Welcome to the Room of Hope," he greeted friends at the door of his new digs.

He said it with a disarming grin, a bit hammy at times but always sincere. He was keenly aware of the initial awkwardness some people felt when they saw him in his wheelchair. So many people had zero idea what to do. Go in for a hug? Offer an awkward handshake? In time, Ned was able to thrust his hand forward, avoiding embarrassment on both sides, but at this time, that expansive welcome was the best he could offer. He'd named his new space in earnest, wanting guests to be inspired by how far he'd come. Long before his accident, he'd taken to the idea that he could motivate and mentor others. Ned was beginning to see that this was still possible, even if it wasn't going to happen exactly as planned.

"Let's get Kasey out and see what she thinks," he suggested on move-in day.

We removed anything that might lead her into temptation—no small task, since we were still unpacking boxes and putting things away—and Kasey clucked with cautious curiosity as I took her out. Ned rolled right up to her cage with the peanut butter dispenser in plain view.

"Kasey, come sit?"

No way. She ambled to the top of her cage.

"Come sit," Ned commanded again, but Kasey couldn't be bothered. Busy taking in the 360 from her lookout tower, she darted from one corner to the other, looking out the big windows and double glass door onto the terrace. She pounced and made loud, guttural sounds at a squirrel sitting on the stone wall. When Kasey spotted the dogs in the yard, she pulled back her eyebrows and smiled. Everything about her expression gloated. *I'm in Ned's room—and you're not!*

"Kasey, come sit?" Ned persisted, but she stayed on top of her cage, and after a while the invitation wore thin. Discouraged, he turned and wheeled to his desk. "I was really looking forward to working with her today."

"We've only had her two weeks," I said gently. "Now she's in a new room, having to get acclimated pretty much all over again."

"I know, but . . . still."

Kasey shimmied down the side of her cage, scooted behind it, and after a brief recon to see if the coast was clear, pooped on the brand-new floor.

"Okay. Enough acclimating for today." I put her back in her cage, fairly certain that this first accident would not be her last.

"We need to find exactly the right spot for her cage," said Ned. "I want her close enough so I can talk to her and reassure her. And she needs to see her two favorite things at the same time: me and the TV."

It was hard to say which she loved more. She kept an eagle eye on Ned, but she was hooked on TV. If there was violence or screaming in the program, Kasey would protest loudly, but she was instantly interested in shows with people talking, like the evening news.

"She even has favorite anchors," Ned observed.

"It really seems like she does," I agreed. "I've noticed how she flirts with Brian Williams, giving him this sideways come hither look."

"She likes Diane Sawyer, too," said Ned. "Gives her kind of a Mona Lisa smile."

"I think Fox News is her favorite."

"Yeah, except for—uh-oh. Here comes the lady with the impossibly white teeth. Kasey can't stand her."

She confirmed this, pouncing to the side of her cage with a leery shriek. She arched her back, her hair bristling.

"See?" Ned nodded toward the TV. "Kasey does that every time she comes on."

Unfortunately, the perfect location for Kasey's penthouse wasn't easy to pin down. After the girls came home from school, I went to make dinner and . . .

"*Skraawk! Ka-ka-SKRAWK!*"

"Mom," Ned yelled, "she can't see you and it's driving her crazy. Turn her cage."

"Good thing this thing is on wheels." I tilted it for a full view of kitchen activities just outside Ned's door. "How's this, Kasey?"

She continued to cluck and warble.

With the construction noise gone, I thought we'd finally get some peace in the house. But in the absence of the symphony of power tools, everyone seemed louder than before, competing to be heard.

Kasey hummed noisily as she played with her toys and cranked up the commentary on her new surroundings. Much of her meaning was completely lost on us, but a lot was unmistakable. Her facial expressions were incredibly human. (Or maybe human facial expressions are incredibly primal.) She left little room for doubt when she disapproved of some actor on *Days of Our Lives* or was on guard about a stranger entering the room. Waggling her eyebrows, she'd look them up and down. *This is Ned's place. State your business or hit the road.*

Ned, God bless him, had a new, prominent forum, with his room adjacent to the kitchen and less than twenty feet from my office. And he was still within earshot of the family room, so he now had a platform from which to voice his every waking thought. He was able to call my attention to all his terribly important (*ahem*) issues and didn't hesitate to include me in the special request loop, whether there was an aide present or not.

"Mom, Kasey's cage needs to be turned just a few inches to the right."

"Mom! The dogs are eating Kasey's chow!"

Ned would lasso me from anything and everything I was involved in all day. I loved him to death, but I have to admit I
missed being able to put him off with the old "Oh, I didn't hear
you calling me" excuse. There was nowhere to hide. Meanwhile,
the dogs were preaching, the TV was yapping, newbie aides were
asking questions, the girls were coming and going with friends
and boyfriends in tow, and the beat goes on.

One weekend after Ned moved into his new room, my mother
came from Ohio to visit. Let me say this about my mother: she's
in her late eighties and spryer than I am. Totally independent, she
drives herself and provides rides to people who need help, reads
everything and anything, makes jars and jars of jams and jelly,
runs up and down stairs like a twenty-year-old, and follows her
Indians and Browns religiously.

When I picked her up at the airport, she came trotting out the
baggage-level door, pulling an astoundingly large suitcase behind
her and lugging a carry-on over each shoulder. This is a petite
woman—smaller than me—but before I could get around to the
back of the car, she'd thrown open the trunk and tossed the lug-
gage in as if it were feather pillows. Several bystanders waiting for
their rides nodded appreciatively.

"Impressive!" one of them declared. She really is.

"Nonnie!" The grand chorus greeted her at the door with hugs
and tail-wagging.

"Maddie! Anna!" Nonnie hugged them and bent to give the
dogs their due diligence. "Where's Jake?"

"On his way home from school," said Anna. "He'll be here in
a sec."

"Ned!" Nonnie yelled as he came rolling up to the front door.
"Am I glad to see you!" she crowed. It was the first time she had

seen him since his accident, but she didn't show even a little shock. She's a Presbyterian stoic of the highest order. Ned beamed at her and waved his arm around to show off its ever growing strength.

"Come see my new room—and meet Kasey," he bragged.

Then it was Jake's turn.

"Hi, Nonnie!" Jake threw his big arms around her and answered all the standard "what have you been up to" questions, before lugging her bags to her room.

Soon Megan and Ron arrived. More hugs and hellos all around. The kids were immediately involved in rowdy conversation, and with so many people coming and going, the volume rose on the dogs and monkey show, but Nonnie settled in, remarkably unfazed by all the racket, sewing a button on Anna's jacket at the kitchen table.

That afternoon, in the midst of all the cacophony, I developed a bit of a headache. Well, it wasn't really a headache, more like a serious drilling feeling in my head, with a shrill ringing in my ears. I tried to ignore it, hoping it would go away, but no such luck. It was higher in pitch than a dentist's drill, with the same wincing effect. It was driving me crazy, ruining an otherwise lovely day.

"Mom, what is that noise?" Ned yelled out to me. "It's piercing my eardrums."

"You hear it, too?"

And then the girls called from upstairs: "Mom! Mom! What's that horrible sound?"

At least I wasn't going crazy. Not yet, anyway.

As I searched for the source, Kasey screeched and the dogs spun in circles. Was it Ned's alarm? Batteries in the smoke detector? Bats in the belfry? I spotted Guy barking ferociously at an empty living room chair and went to investigate. There it was. Nonnie's hearing aid, squealing at top volume.

I tapped her on the shoulder and dropped the hearing aid in her palm.

"Oh," she sniffed. "That silly old thing."

She sheepishly tucked it back in her ear.

No wonder my mother had looked so serene. She couldn't hear a blessed thing!

15

Stocks and Bonds

'D BONDED WITH MY CHILDREN WHEN THEY WERE BORN. We bonded with our dogs the second we brought them home. The bonds of friendship were sometimes the only thing kite-stringing me to my sanity through all this. But as I watched Ned and Kasey struggle to figure out what they were to each other, I realized I'd taken this word for granted.

Here was a tiny creature whose nature was to withhold trust and respect. Her instinct for self-preservation told her to protect herself until she knew who was who in the hierarchy. The leader of the pack had to earn that position; there were no shortcuts. On the flip side, I had Ned, who'd never been one to dive headfirst emotionally into any relationship. He was always sociable and friendly, but he was cautious about extending himself. He was true blue to the end, and his close friends were rock solid, but they were a select few.

Thrusting Ned and Kasey together—*Okay, you two, ready, set, bond!*—was like trying to build a cathedral out of popsicle sticks. Small steps forward were almost always followed by noisy stumbles back.

On the upside, Kasey provided Ned with endless visual stimulation (and offered a pretty good show for the rest of us). Even when she wasn't doing much—playing quietly with her toys, reading her little plastic book—he watched her with endless fascination. Whenever I approached with the chow, Kasey did snazzy flips off her bedroom shelf and flew around her cage like an airplane. Oh, it was good to hear Ned laugh.

"Mom, hurry!" he called. "She's doing somersaults! You've got to see this. It's better than *SNL*."

Checking in on them in the evening, I'd find them in front of the TV, watching each other out of the corners of their eyes. I was happy to see them so engrossed.

"Look at her up in her bedroom with her blankets," he said. "It's like her own personal skybox."

Even in her less entertaining moments, Ned enjoyed just looking at her, but most of the time, she was entertaining and then some.

At bath time she did De Niro: *You talkin' to me?*

Fluffed and fancy after the spa, she was Gloria Swanson: *Ready for my close-up.*

Browsing her plastic book, she chilled like Paris Hilton: *Hey, I read.*

Very nice. Adorable. They were interested in each other, that was clear. They kept each other company. But on the downside, we'd been taking Kasey out of her cage day after day, and she still acted like Ned was nothing but a boulder she had to climb over to get her peanut butter.

"This is normal," Megan Monkey told us. "It takes time to build the relationship."

How much time? I was afraid to ask.

"Ned," said Megan Monkey, "it might help Kasey loosen up if you talk to her even when she's in her cage. Tell her what a good girl she is. Get her used to hearing your voice. Move your working hand and arm around as much as possible, so she gets familiar with the way you move."

"She gets startled when my right hand or arm spasms," said Ned, "but I can't help it."

"That's okay. She's watching and internalizing what she sees."

"But most of the time . . . well, she pretty much ignores me."

"Oh, believe me, Ned," Megan said seriously, "Kasey's sizing you up all the time. Figuring you out. She has to do it in her own way."

"So I'm supposed to . . . what? Sometimes she's not even interested in her treats."

"Hey, two can play at that game. If she's not paying attention to you, pay no attention to her. Play hard to get. Kasey isn't one to just dive into a relationship, but she's not happy if she's not the center of your undivided attention."

"How could she not be?" I said. "She's constantly peeping, clucking, shrieking—one minute she sounds like a baby bird, the next minute you'd think someone's swinging on a rusty gate."

"Seriously," said Ned. "We keep wishing we had a Monkey-to-English dictionary."

"That peeping is a happy sound," said Megan, and I saw relief in Ned's face. "The bird sounds are just her way of making her presence known."

"What about that throaty Donald Duck impression?" asked Ned. "She does that when snow or icicles fall off the roof."

"That's fear. Different from the screeching. That's disapproval."

"That makes sense." Ned and I exchanged a knowing nod.

This was Kasey's usual response to the dogs, who'd discovered that Ned's new room had a handy exit to the terrace and were forever scratching on one side or the other, wanting to be let in or out. Maddie and Anna had risen to the occasion, following Megan Monkey's advice and staying out of Kasey's way, but Kasey had plenty of high-pitched scolding on reserve for any sisterly spats that erupted within earshot.

"What you've got there," Megan said, "is a big, bad case of sibling rivalry. Kasey's competing for attention, just like the rest of the kids."

There it was, whether I liked it or not.

Megan assured me all this would eventually work itself out, but I knew the score. Sibling rivalry never ends; it merely takes on new, more subtle incarnations. My kids started competing the moment they learned how to cry.

"Why does *she* get a new iPod?"

"How come you didn't let *me* go to that dance when I was a junior?"

When Kasey wanted my attention, she started with a soft trill and quickly ramped up to the clanging of the food bowl, slapping the side of her cage with her hand, and stuffing her blankies out through the food opening. My children escalated much the same way.

"Mom . . . Hey, Mom? Hey, *MOM!*"

What I couldn't say in our frequent support calls or during Megan Monkey's occasional training visits was that I'd seriously underestimated everything about having this monkey. As it was before, my hands were full caring for Ned and trying to be a parent to my other children. Perhaps my great expectations were a little overboard, but I'd have appreciated it if the helper monkey was a little more inclined to actually be helpful. We'd had Kasey for only a few weeks, but I was no longer convinced there would be some huge payoff for all this effort. So far, there hadn't been much reward.

Every day, I painstakingly attended to this monkey's laundry list of needs—the elaborate feeding requirements; the necessary time investment to carefully take her out of her cage, set up the treats on Ned's wheelchair, and work with her on specific tasks; and the nebulous ongoing issue of bonding.

And of course all that cage shifting was at once urgently important to Ned while simultaneously ridiculously silly to me. I'd be cooking dinner, on the phone, reviewing the girls' outfit choices, checking supplies in the garage, and I'd hear, "Mom, can you pull Kasey's cage up? Mom, can you move her cage a little more to the right so that she can see the TV better? Mom [or Mom!] I can't see her face. Turn the cage."

This was particularly irksome late at night when I was only nanoseconds from stepping out of Ned's room, shutting the door on that part of my life, and stealing a few minutes for myself—maybe sleep. Maybe email. Maybe that book I'd been trying to read for the past month.

But getting Ned all set for bed took about an hour—what with his meds, the apnea mask, the pillow positioning, one—no, two blankets, notes to the overnight nurse—and yes, positioning Kasey's cage.

"Okay, Ned, I think I've got everything right." He wouldn't be able to talk with the apnea mask on, so he'd give me the thumbs up or down sign. "Pillows? Clock? Radio? Blankets? Themostat? Cage?"

Thus I started the cage shift tango. I pushed it two inches to the left. He waved me to move it more to the right—he wanted it closer to the bed. Now he was waving it farther to the left. I was meanwhile dreaming of sitting, sleeping, reading, or maybe—NOTHING. I'd been getting pretty testy about this particular "task" since it seemed so incredibly unimportant to me (seriously, they're both going to be asleep in about thirty seconds), but one night, I took the Vanna pose—holding my arms out and elegantly moving myself and the cage one direction and then the other. "Would you like to buy a vowel, Ned?" After seeing him laugh through the mask, I Vanna-ed every night.

The small things Kasey did to help Ned would have taken me a fraction of the time and frustration of doing the thousand small— and not so small—things I had to do almost every hour to help Ned take care of Kasey. I kept waiting for some breakthrough, some sign of connection between Kasey and Ned, but it wasn't happening.

Anna and Maddie were doing their best to abide by the Rules According to Kasey, but this was still their home and they were tired of taking a backseat to her feeding schedule, her cage cleaning, her screaming hierarchical mandates. If they said a cross word to me, Kasey screeched and yelled at them from Ned's room. *How dare you talk to Mommy like that?* They were constantly cast as Guy and Bailey's defenders, with Ned egging Kasey on.

"We'll get 'em, Kasey, we'll get those mean doggies!"

Kasey trilled appreciatively. The dogs practically tied themselves in knots.

"Mom! Ned's telling Kasey to be mean to the dogs!"

"Mom! Manage the girls. They're upsetting Kasey!"

Ron and Megan would walk in on scenes like this and say, "Gee, this is fun," and promptly turn around and leave.

There were times I dearly wished I could follow them right out the door.

IN THE MIDDLE OF ALL THAT, Ned rededicated himself to his rehab (God bless him), resuming physical and occupational therapy sessions two times a week at Spaulding. He never canceled unless he was suffering serious nerve pain.

"I hate the ride," he confessed, "but I still look forward to it. Before Christmas, I was making serious progress on the mat. I want to keep going with that."

One day I walked in to find him sitting on the side of our mat with the help of Charity, but essentially holding himself up, balancing his upper body almost completely alone. I froze at the door, taken aback. It was so good to see him—just *him*—without the sarcophagus of the mechanical railed bed or the machinery of the wheelchair.

"Hi, Ellen." Charity smiled at my startled look. "He couldn't wait to show you his first sitting balance."

Ned grinned. "How do ya like that, huh?"

"I um . . . I like that . . . a lot."

"I'm getting stronger, Mom. I can feel it."

The occupational therapist had him working both arms to strengthen his shoulders and increase the dexterity of his left hand. It wasn't all home runs, of course. Spasms or nerve pain often got in the way, and on those days, he and Charity came home down in the dumps. One of his exercises was not unlike a game Kasey had played in Monkey College: picking up quarters and putting them in a container. The difference being, it was much harder for Ned.

"Last time I picked up ten in just a few seconds," he lamented one afternoon. "Today, I could hardly get any."

"Oh, shush. You're doing great." Charity pooh-poohed what he considered his failures. "Both therapists are really pleased with how much strength and dexterity you're gaining."

"Yeah," Ned said bitterly. "Impressive."

"Oh, come on. When we first started going to the gym, your legs and arms were strapped to the pedals and handlebars, so the bike did pretty much all the work. Today, you held the handlebar with your left hand—and you *pushed* it. You actually pedaled the bike on your own with your left foot. That's amazing, Ned. Don't sell yourself short."

"I guess." He lightened somewhat. "It's just . . . it's like I'm on a treadmill and can't keep up. Sometimes I feel like I'm going to fall off."

"When I go to the gym," I said teasingly, "you always tell me, 'Get out there and sweat, Mom. No pain, no gain.'"

"What doesn't kill you . . ." He shrugged and smiled. "Guess you know the rest."

"Yup." I squeezed his shoulder. "Time to get Kasey out."

Monkey Support had suggested I tether her to her cage—next to Ned, yet comfortably close to her "safe place"—but as usual, Kasey didn't want to go to him. She jumped out of her skin at every spasm in his hand and took flight every time he moved his wheelchair.

"Kasey, come sit?" he coaxed.

She gobbled her peanut butter and nipped back up to the top of the cage.

"Kasey, itch?"

She gave his nose a perfunctory dab, licked his finger, and took off.

We called for monkey therapy.

"Ned," said Megan Monkey, "let's have you participate in whatever ways you can with Kasey's care."

"*Yes.*" Ned lit up.

"She'll see you become a more integral part of her life. And it might actually be great OT for you, Ned."

"I'd really like that," he said. "I miss having stuff to do, you know? Responsibility. People think it would be so great not having to do anything all day, but it's not. It feels lousy to be so dependent on everyone."

"I hear you," Megan Monkey said. "If you take on some of the responsibility for Kasey's care, that would help your mom out."

"That would be awesome," said Ned. "I'd feel like I was getting back at least a little bit of self-reliance."

"What do you think, Ellen. Is there a way Ned could feed Kasey on his own?"

I wasn't sure how we'd swing it, but his enthusiasm made me feel lighter.

"Absolutely," I said. "We'll start with breakfast."

The next morning, I prepared Kasey's oatmeal and Ned's toast and brought them to his room, then moved her cage right up next to the left side of his bed.

"Good morning, Kasey," he said soothingly. "Hungry?"

She tried to give him a casual coo.

"It's oatmeal time."

That put her over the edge. Tossing decorum to the wind, she airplaned once around the cage and did a giddy little jig in place as Ned brought the small oatmeal container near the food opening. Ned struggled to get it close enough to her. His movements were awkward and agonizingly glacial. Kasey's eyes were big with *breakfast breakfast breakfast,* and little droplets of drool dripped from the corners of her mouth. But she waited.

I couldn't believe what I was seeing.

If I'd done a slow-motion serve like that, she'd have been grasping and scolding. I bit my bottom lip, forcing myself to keep quiet.

Another inch or two.

So close.

With the fierce focus of a weight lifter, Ned willed his hand just far enough for her to reach it, and when she could reach it, she gently helped him bring it just a little bit closer.

"Peep!"

She thanked him politely, scooped up a handful of oatmeal, and hopped up on her bedroom shelf, thoroughly enjoying her breakfast as Ned ate his toast.

"Here's a pretty contented scene," I observed. "We'll try this again tomorrow."

The next day—and the next day and the day after that—Kasey was ever patient with Ned, gently helping him guide the plastic container through the slot. She never grabbed or squawked, and each time, Ned's grasp and placement of the container improved the tiniest bit.

"How's it going this morning, Kasey?" he'd ask.

"Peep pip."

"Yeah, me, too."

They bantered back and forth through breakfast, and we repeated this exchange as often as we could for Kasey's other six meals of the day. (She ate sort of like a hobbit: "breakfast, second breakfast, elevensies," and so forth.) If Ned was up in his chair, I'd place the container of apples, chow, or green beans in his lap, and he'd roll to the cage to repeat the process he'd been working at from his bed. Ever so gently taking the container, Kasey would peep pleasant thanks, and the dinner conversation would commence.

"I'm developing a whole new respect for Kasey," said Ned. "I think she actually understands what I can and can't do. How do you know so much, huh, Kasey? Smart monkey."

"Now that you two are regular dining companions," I said, "maybe she'll be willing to sit on your lap."

"Maybe," Ned said. He was noncommittal.

So was Kasey. She sat on top of his shoes.

Ned scooped up a dollop of peanut butter. "Kasey, come sit?"

She scrambled up his legs, lapped her treat, and hopped up to the top of her cage.

Day by day, with growing respect for Kasey's intelligence and sensitivity, Ned worked to earn her trust. Come sit. Itch. Fetch. Every day for weeks. Some days it was discouraging, but little by little, Kasey spent a bit less time at his feet and lingered an extra moment or two over her peanut butter. One day, she actually bypassed his feet and jumped right onto his lap.

"Mom, did you see that?" Ned kept his voice at a hush.

Scoping out the situation, eyes darting back and forth, Kasey seemed suspicious, poised to launch right back to her cage. Ned scooped another dollop of peanut butter. She greedily licked up the bonus treat. Then she bolted. Eat and run seemed to be Kasey's modus operandi.

When Ned was in bed, I'd place a piece of walnut between two fingers on his left hand, though he didn't have much sensation or control. At first, Kasey would sit at the end of the bed, on top of his feet. She'd run up, grab the treat, and immediately return to the end of the bed. If a sudden spasm twitched Ned's hand and startled her, she'd skitter back to her cage. But if Ned dropped the walnut, Kasey would show remarkable self-control. Her tiny fingers would curl into a tight ball and she would eye that walnut. It would take every ounce of willpower for Kasey to hold herself back, but she wasn't about to disregard Ned by snatching it unfairly away. She didn't move, but she kept her eye on that glorious walnut while I picked it up and placed it in his fingers again; she waited to lunge for it until he said, "Okay, Kasey. Come and get it."

One day she sat on his knees.

Several days later, she sat on his belly.

Ned was impressed with her self-control but wanted her to come closer, so I tried putting the walnut next to his face. Kasey just turned her back.

"We see a flash of trust," I told Megan Monkey. "Then it disappears."

"It's like in OT," Ned said wearily. "I can do something all of a sudden—raise my hand or move my thumb—and then it's like . . . gone."

"Have your mom put the walnut pieces in your mouth," she suggested. "See what Kasey makes of that."

This unconventional suggestion worked . . . sort of. Kasey seemed to appreciate the gesture, but she still scampered back to his feet as soon as she'd scavenged her treasure.

"So, we've had her about a month now," Ned remarked on his birthday in January. He was more than a little disappointed at the glacial pace of their connection. He wasn't the only one. I was waiting not so patiently for the magic of the Golden Monkey Myth to kick in. Not to mention that, quite apart from all the work of the day-to-day feeding and tilting of that darn cage, it was always Mommy versus Kasey in the bath/nail wars—and the diva had the upper hand.

I was a less than professional monkey aesthetician and I took full blame for Kasey's anxiety around our grooming routines. I had gotten soap in her eyes and water up her nose more than once, and I had accidentally made her nails bleed when I used toenail clippers. My incompetence in this department would have caused any reasonable person (or monkey) to be anxiety-ridden during bath time. Kasey was anything but reasonable.

As soon as she suspected the upcoming trauma, she'd cower in the farthest reaches of her cage with her back turned to me. I would open the door and ask for her leash, but she'd simply glare at me as if to say, *You've got to be kidding!* This gave me no choice but to resort to bribes. I'd have to go out to the kitchen, get a medicine cupful of hummus, and then stand at the cage door trying to entice her. Even with this lure, she'd hold back. I'd stick the little cup into the cage and wave it in front of her nose. "Come on, Kasey," I'd coax her. "I'll be really careful! I promise!" Begging. Could this really be me?

I was so reluctant to put both of us through the bath and nails ordeal that I avoided it for long periods of time. As a result, her nails got to look like fierce talons, and she carried a powerful monkey odor with her at all times. Megan Monkey caught wind of this—literally—when she came to visit. She wasn't pleased.

"This is your job," she said firmly. "Kasey knows perfectly well how to behave during bath and nail time. She's got your number and she's taking advantage of you. Toughen up and get it done."

Dutifully reprimanded, I dug into the job with new resolve. Kasey wasn't going to make a monkey out of me. I devised a plan of action:

1. Change into a short-sleeve shirt and full-length apron. This is a water sport.
2. Fetch monkey bath towel, washcloth, new harness, and personal towel *without Kasey seeing me do this*.

3. Fill kitchen sink with water and baby shampoo.
   Hot—really hot.

4. Take off any personal jewelry that Kasey may be able
   to remove and, hence, fling into the garbage disposal.

5. Eliminate words such as "bath time," "tubby," and
   "B-A-T-H" from vocabulary.

6. Clear off all kitchen counters within ten feet of the
   kitchen sink. (Kasey can spot even the tiniest leftover
   dinner remains from thirty feet and will not hesitate
   to leap out of the sink to get them.)

7. Prepare bribe.

8. Order girls to vacate the premises. This saves lots of
   sibling rivalry issues—on both sides.

9. Drag dogs outside so Kasey won't pounce on them.

Bribe in hand, I got Kasey out, all the while reminding myself that she had a strong scent, that I was doing the right thing, for her and everyone else.

At the approach to the kitchen sink, Kasey usually clucked while looking suspiciously for the dogs and the girls. I attached her to the carabiner lock that the trainers had installed on the faucet. She jumped in and looked up at me with this heartrending expression, as if to say, *How can you do this to me?*

But the victim act didn't last long. Trying to seem nonchalant, she started playing with the water. She clapped her hands in the soapsuds. She washed her face and played with her little bath toys. I scrubbed her all over with the washcloth while she used one foot to hold my right hand off and one of her hands to prevent my left from taking over. The clucking was incessant, but it soon became apparent: she was enjoying herself. She looked over to the kitchen window, saw the dogs outside, and, standing up in the sink, dripping sudsy water everywhere, leaned out to give them a triumphant, gloating stare and victory growl.

I turned on the faucet spray to rinse her off. She jumped up onto the faucet and turned the water off as I pushed her back in the tub. I turned it back on. She jumped up and turned it off. I turned it on again. I grabbed her harness tightly so that I could finally spray the shampoo off her. Fortunately, this fun time was almost over.

Keeping her nails trimmed was much more trying. After my monkey therapy, I switched to a nail file (actually, emery boards were best—who knew?) rather than clippers to keep her nails trim. When the ordeal was over, Kasey galloped back into her cage and dove under her blankies. Exhausted and anxiety-ridden myself, I sought refuge in my nap because it was too early for wine.

VALENTINE'S DAY came and went. Still no love connection. Ned was trying his best, bribing Kasey with treats, taking her side against the dogs, indulging her in her favorite TV shows, but he was disappointed. He wasn't the only one.

One day after a grueling round of OT at Spaulding, Ned was tired and frustrated by his lack of progress at the gym. Even Charity's rah-rah spirit was subdued.

"How did it go?" I asked.

"Great," said Ned. But everything about the set of his jaw said, *It sucked.*

I looked quizzically at Charity, and she said, "Long drive. Long day. You know."

"Right . . . well . . . Ned, do you want to work with Kasey for a while?"

"Sure," he said, but again there was that jaw.

Kasey was aloof and distant. No amount of coaxing brought her next to him for more than the moment it took to nab the bribes.

"Just put her back," Ned said after a while. "I'm done for the day."

I started to offer some lame comfort, but Kasey shrieked and pounced on the top of her cage. She'd heard the girls bickering in the kitchen.

"Skaaaaaaaaaaaaaaack!" she screamed at them, rattling the roof, and Ned winced with a sudden stab of nerve pain.

"It's okay, Kasey, I'm—"

"Skee skee skee! AAACK!"

"Wow. Okay. Simmer down, will you?" And then he reprimanded me. "Mom, don't put off her bath again. Kasey really smells."

"Hey! Don't use that word out loud! Thanks a bunch, Ned—now she'll never get out for me," I grumbled. I could already see that I was going to get absolutely nothing done that evening—other than wait on this "service animal." I opened the cage door, and Kasey bolted up to her bedroom, slapped the side of her cage, and cawed like she expected me to serve high tea.

"Yes, I know, Your Highness," I told her. "But right now, I'm taking care of Ned. Do you mind?"

Ned turned his chair away, waiting, disheartened, for the lift. "I need to get in bed" was all he could muster.

I felt like I was watching him take two steps back without getting even one tiny step forward. Maybe this monkey thing wasn't such a great idea after all. Ned was trying so hard, but here he sat, dejected and in pain. And I'd set him up for it.

I couldn't bring myself to say it out loud, but I had to consider the possibility: maybe Kasey needed to go back.

16

With Friends Like This . . .

"IT'S THE OLDEST POOL IN CONCORD," THE REALTOR HAD IN-formed me when we were house hunting, as if that was some-thing to write home about.

For reasons I'll never understand, the monstrosity that occu-pies a good share of our backyard was constructed with steeply slanted sides and a garish portrait of Mickey Mouse at the bot-tom. It cost a small fortune to put water in it every spring. The first year, when it was freshly painted—that Mickey Mouse thing really needed to go—and being filled, I came home to find the water man gone, the safety gate open, and Guy thrashing in about three feet of water at the bottom of the pool.

"Guy," I called and coaxed. "Come on, girl! You can do it!"

But she couldn't get her footing. Struggling, whimpering, and yipping with frustration and cold, she made one desperate attempt after another, but it was no use.

"Okay, hang on. It's okay, puppy."

I tried to fish her out, stretching farther and farther over the slippery slope and . . . you guessed it. The next moment I was thrashing in the ice-cold water in my business suit and heels.

I managed to find my feet and chuck the dog up onto dry land, but I couldn't get out. No matter how frantically I clawed, how me-thodically I crawled—it was too steep, too slick. I'd make a little progress, lose my grip, and skid back to the bottom on raw hands and knees. There was no use shouting: no one was going to come to my rescue. By the time I was able to grasp the dangling water hose and pull myself out, I was panic-stricken, bleeding, and humiliated, shaking with cold and fatigue. It made a good story for dinner parties (back when I went to dinner parties), but I never forgot that feeling.

I was feeling it now.

EVERY MORNING at 10:30 A.M. on the dot, Kasey started banging her food bowl on the side of her cage.

Clang! Clang! "Skrrrraaaaaaaaaaack!" *Clang-a-rang!*

It was like a fire alarm inside my head. After two months with the Divine Miss K, I'd learned that the longer I delayed serving up her snack, the louder and more obnoxious she became. I hustled out the beans, hoping to spare Ned some nerve pain.

Ninety minutes later, she'd be banging the bowl again, demanding lunch.

"Hoop hoop!" she called.

"I need a monkey fast-food place," I told my sister Lynn when she came to visit.

She laughed. "Burger King Kong?"

"More like Hairy Queen."

Lynn had last seen Ned when he was still at Shepherd and couldn't even squeeze her hand, never mind move or talk. She was thrilled to see him offer her husband Bob a purposeful handshake. As they made small talk, Ned spoke up, shrugged his shoulders, made a broad gesture with his hand.

"I'm so proud of you, Ned," Lynn said, sincerely. "You've made such huge steps forward."

"Yeah, I guess I have," he replied, and I watched as it dawned on him.

Lynn's objectivity was an unexpected gift. We'd gotten lost in the weeds somewhere along the way, so bogged down by the daily grind that we weren't always able to see the big picture. It took someone who hadn't seen Ned for a while to point out the tremendous progress he'd made.

"We can't wait to meet Kasey," she said, not three minutes in the door. "You're going to bring her out to visit, aren't you?"

"Oh. Sure. It's just—she's never been out of her cage with anyone but immediate family and the trainer, so um . . ." I wasn't sure how to finish the thought. *Don't be offended if she hisses like a reticulated python? Be ready to snap a quick picture before she zooms up the drapes? Pretend not to notice she wants nothing whatsoever to do with Ned?*

"We're so fascinated hearing about all the things she does for Ned," said Lynn. "We want to see her in action."

I glanced apprehensively toward the cage.

"Pweet," said Kasey.

I had no clue what that meant. Probably something to the effect of: *as if.* I certainly wasn't counting on her strutting any of her helper monkey stuff, especially since Ned had now moved into bed, with no treat dispenser. At the very least, Bob and Lynn expected some sort of companion-like behavior. I was afraid we all were going to be mightily disappointed.

Approaching the cage, I gave Kasey a deep, meaningful look.

She came to attention. I swear, she nodded as she handed me her leash.

Kasey reporting for duty.

It was as if she understood how intense this moment was for me, as if she knew that I had built her up to such a degree to family and friends that I was terrified they would see that it was hardly working. Worse, that it was failing big-time.

I snapped on the long tether, and she darted out. Barely touching my shoulder, she bolted to the end of the bed, galloped directly to Ned's shoulder, and snuggled into his neck.

"How cute!" Lynn and Bob exclaimed. "So sweet. Look how she loves Ned."

Ned and I exchanged astonished glances.

"Pip pip purrup."

Kasey gave her man an affectionate nuzzle, then sauntered over to inventory Lynn's jewelry and even allowed Lynn to stroke her back for a few minutes. My sister was beside herself. Kasey basked in the petting and praises. I sat there in a daze, caught between the undertow of doubt and anxiety I'd been feeling and the monk-tastic scene around me. This small snapshot of what Kasey could be (when she wanted to be) dangled a cruel and tantalizing carrot in front of us. If Kasey had to go back now, it would be even more devastating for Ned.

That night, long after Lynn and Bob left, Ned and I still couldn't get over it.

"What the heck was that about?" he wondered.

"I don't know, but it was quite a performance," I said. "No walnuts, no peanut butter . . ."

"What was different?"

"Skee kit." Kasey sounded smug. *Just doing my job.*

"Do you think she'll do it again?" asked Ned.

"Who knows?" I opened my hands, nonplussed. "Let's hope."

She didn't.

Not the next night or the night after that or the following week.

"What happened?" Ned asked Megan Monkey. "I don't get it."

"Ned, I'm thrilled Kasey came to you when your aunt and uncle were there," she said. "It means she trusts you to take care of her. Believe me, I've known Kasey a long time, and she's a very social monkey, but she won't act like the social butterfly unless she's developed strong ties with the people at the top of her hierarchy—which she obviously has now."

"So even though it hasn't happened again . . . this is good?"

"Very good," she said. "Keep doing what you're doing."

OUR THIRD MONTH with Kasey, it did feel like our hard work was paying off. She seemed to look forward to her bonding time with Ned almost as much as she looked forward to her green beans. Every day at 1:00 sharp, she was circling her cage in a frenzy, squawking and cawing toward the kitchen, calling for me to get the lead out.

"I think this is my favorite time of day," Ned told me.

He rolled close to the cage, comforting her while I quickly Kasey-proofed the place: dogs outside, doors closed, plus a quick room and body check to make sure there wasn't a stray breakfast bit, breath mint, or candy wrapper lying around. The moment she was out, her first priority was a thorough security detail: looking under Ned's chair, creeping under his bed, crawling into his pillowcase, hoping for crumbs and on guard for monsters.

"Good job, Kasey." Ned readied the treat dispenser. "Spotting any intruders?"

She gave him a sharp cluck. *We're 10-26 here. Checking perimeters.*

Up on tiptoes, she peered over the windowsill, pulling back the curtains to see what the dogs were up to.

"She certainly is thorough," I said, once she was satisfied the coast was clear.

"Kasey, come sit?" said Ned, and she did. Definitely an improvement.

After the usual fetch and scratch exercises, she lingered on Ned's lap, and he willed himself to keep his left hand steady enough to pet her. She popped over to my lap, rifled my pants pockets, had my watch off my wrist faster than I could check the second hand, and popped back over to Ned.

"Hooah." She presented it to him with great aplomb.

"Thanks, Kasey." Ned laughed. "Just what I always wanted."

She lay down in his lap and let him pet her, which we were allowed to do on her terms. No amount of cajoling, coaxing, or dangling toys would entice her. When she'd had enough, she held his hand back with her foot, gripping his wrist with her long, elegant toes.

"For such a little monkey, she sure has huge feet," Ned commented.

"She does that in the tubby when I try to wash her face," I said. "I'm just beginning to appreciate her talented feet. And I wish my toes were as beautiful and aristocratic as hers are. I wonder if she'd like to have them painted."

"Please." Ned rolled his eyes, examining Kasey's dexterous digits. "When I was little, I used to wish I had opposable thumbs on my feet like a monkey. How cool would that be? Same gripping capability as hands."

"Ned, with your personality plus opposable thumbs on your feet . . ." I shook my head. "One of us would not have made it past your fifth birthday."

I thought I'd done a good search-and-destroy before letting her out, but Kasey suddenly spotted a bottle of water on the book-case. In about two seconds flat, she was up there with the bottle between her feet. She unscrewed the cap, reached inside for the straw, chugged a good quaff, screwed the cap back on, and shim-mied back down to Ned's lap without so much as tipping over a knickknack.

"Kit kit kit." She smiled up at him. *Oh, yeah. That hit the spot.*

Ned summed it up perfectly: "Never underestimate a mon-key's intelligence. Or her feet."

And then . . . "Uh-oh . . . I think she spotted George."

George was a sizable stuffed monkey in a surgical mask and scrubs. Ned's Nana, Ted's mother, who is in her late nineties, had laid eyes on it during a charity auction at her assisted living cen-ter and blew the other bidders out of the water. This was back when we were waiting for Helping Hands to make the place-ment decision, so it meant a lot to Ned when Nana sent George with a note that said with great certainty, "It's a good omen. Meant to be."

Kasey's reaction to George wasn't quite as warm. When I moved George onto the bed so she could get a closer look, she made a deep, throaty sound.

Do ya feel lucky? Well? Do ya, punk?

In a lightning-fast one-two knockout combination, she nailed him down with one foot, whipped off his surgical mask, and punched him in the mouth, sending him flying. Ned and I howled with laughter as Kasey did a victory lap over the covers.

"Mom, let me hold his leg," said Ned. "Come on, Kasey! You can take him!"

She glared at George, squaring off like a sumo wrestler.

"Get him, Kasey! That's right. It's you and me, girl!"

Ned was laughing, but he kept encouraging her, letting her know where his loyalties were. Kasey was into it now, boxing George's ears, delivering a bim-bam left hook like the Million Dollar Baby. While she worked George over, Ned held his leg tight enough to keep him in the fight. And I noticed how the game was working the muscles in Ned's hand.

So that was a good day.

The next day, Kasey was her old standoffish self. That's how the weeks went by. She'd trust us only so far, then retreat back into herself.

"Maybe she catches herself 'giving herself up' and needs to give us the cold shoulder," I speculated. "Just to remind us who we're dealing with."

"Maybe. So we return the favor like Megan Monkey said. Pretend to ignore her."

He rolled up to his desk. I strolled along the shelves, whistling an absent tune. We looked the other way. We watched TV. We talked among ourselves.

"How 'bout them Sox?" said Ned.

Before I could answer, Kasey was wrapped around his neck.

She was so skittish, the smallest unfamiliar sound or sudden movement sent her scampering to Ned's lap, then back to the top of her cage. Anything different in Ned's room—a new picture frame, a pillow out of place—was enough to unsettle her. If a new item showed up on Ned's nightstand, she eyed it off and on for days, cluck-clucking suspiciously.

With the fetching and itching down cold, I thought Kasey and Ned might be up for a new challenge. I went to the educational toy store in town, thinking that would be a likely resource for toys that didn't have tiny components she could choke on, nothing toxic or painted she might gnaw on.

As I browsed the "Age 3 and Under" area, a salesperson stepped over and asked, "Are you shopping for a little boy or a little girl?"

I briefly considered telling him, but "monkey" didn't quite conjure that Queen of Sheba meets Little Miss Broadway personality.

"A little girl," I said. "And I think I see exactly what we need."

I picked up a bright pink purse with big, soft handles and flower appliqués.

It was so Kasey.

Inside were plastic keys, a credit card, and pretend lipstick and cell phone. Best of all, there was a Velcro closure and—icing on the cake—a little mirror.

"What more could a little girl want?" said the salesman.

Especially a little girl with opposable thumbs on her feet and a penchant for admiring herself. Kasey eyed the purse the second I walked in the room.

"How does she know it's for her?" I wondered when she peeped with excitement.

"I don't know," Ned said. "Doesn't go with your outfit, I guess."

I set the purse in his lap, preparing to take her out. Kasey, in the meantime, danced like a shopaholic on Rodeo Drive.

"Hang on, Kasey." Ned laughed. "Mom, let's give it to her before she explodes."

In a flash, she was in his lap and rapturous with love at first sight. No bonding process needed between Kasey and her new treasure. She admired herself in the mirror and punched a few buttons on the cell phone, but all that went by the wayside when she discovered the plastic lipstick. She scrambled up to Ned's shoulder, itched his head with the lipstick, then scrambled down to his lap and put it in his hand. He rewarded her with peanut butter and warm praise.

"Okay, Kasey. Can you put your toys in your purse?"

She gave him a sideways look, and then—*she did it.*

She put the toys in her purse. Ned and I were both blown away.

"Mom," he whispered. "Are you seeing this?"

"I'm seeing . . . not sure I'm believing."

"Kasey, can I have a toy?" Ned asked.

She promptly took the cell phone out and placed it in his hand. For the rest of their playtime, they went back and forth.

"It's like she took it on herself to make up a new game," said Ned. "She's sort of combining itch and fetch."

There were other games, too.

Kasey just loved to write. We'd discovered this by accident a while back, when she had taken to jotting her own personal opinions at walnut time on Ned's med sheet beside his bed. So next to "Two Tylenol: 2:00 pm," Kasey would add her own observations.

One time, we took Kasey with us to meet one of Ned's doctors who had been asking to meet her. After being let out of her carrying case—really, a small dog carrier—Kasey jumped from Ned's lap right onto the doctor's desk, grabbed a pen, and wrote vigorously on Ned's chart. Once satisfied with her handiwork, she picked up the doctor's iced tea bottle and took a quick swig before diving into the trash can to retrieve a discarded bag of chips. Clutching the bag to her chest, she tore back to Ned's lap, where she reached into the bag and devoured every last crumb. Fortunately, the doctor thought all of this was wonderful—especially when Kasey then went and curled up in her lap.

On this one day, after dragging a pad of paper to Ned's lap, she held a pencil in two hands and used her feet to hold the paper securely in place. She dragged the pencil—the correct end, mind you—and wrote until she was "done" with that page and then turned it over to get to a clean one. Then she handed Ned the pencil. Actually, she slapped the pencil a few times on the pad to get Ned's attention, and then slapped it on the palm of his left hand. "Oh, I see," said Ned. "You want me to write first." So he did, and then returned the pencil to Kasey for her turn. It was, as they say, a win-win situation: Ned got great occupational therapy, Kasey got to express herself, and I got to watch the most entertaining show around.

We had another unlikely discovery. One evening, Maddie casually tossed a soft mini soccer ball in Kasey's direction and she expertly snatched the ball out of the air.

"Kasey, throw it back! Throw it back!" we all encouraged her.

Hmph, *Not me*, and took the ball to Ned. Ned handed it back to Maddie. This time, Kasey stood on her hind legs and waved her hands over her head as if to say, *Right here! Right here!* A monkey who loves to play catch—who would have ever thought?

She also began to anticipate walnut time every night at nine. As soon as she heard me getting the vitamin jar and walnut container in the kitchen, she'd start preening.

Ned egged her on. "Fluff up, Kasey. Fluff up, girl."

She fluffed and preened and poofed herself all over with her hands and feet.

"She's getting herself dolled up to come out," Ned decided one evening.

When I entered with the coveted treats, she did a last-minute fluff followed by a somersault-flip combo off the bedroom shelf, practically shoving her harness leash at me.

"Boy, have we come a long way," I said.

Kasey peeped and pinwheeled. *Walnuts walnuts walnuts!*

It was all I could do to hang on to her harness before she bolted to Ned's shoulder.

First she searched for dinner crumbs on Ned's shirt, then she took a moment to rummage through his wheelchair backpack.

She tiptoed gracefully around his desk in search of forgotten goodies. After a quick leaf through a recent issue of *National Geographic,* she hopped back to Ned. All this gave me just enough time to place Kasey's vitamin between his fingers. Both Ned and Kasey were so intensely focused—he on keeping his hand steady, she on holding herself back—the air between them was charged with shared energy. Kasey balled her hands into tiny fists and waited until Ned said, "Come and get it, Kasey."

He never had to tell her twice.

After the vitamin came her beloved walnut. Poised and drooling on Ned's chest, she waited for me to tuck the walnut in his mouth. Sometimes he teased her by clamping his mouth shut tight. Using both hands and a foot, she pried it open, which was easier when he couldn't stop laughing.

One afternoon in late March, Ned's friend Brie came to visit. Kasey was out; Ned was in his chair. When Kasey heard company coming, she scaled the side of her cage, up to the top, scoping out the changed game plan.

"Ned!" Brie burst in and ran to give him a kiss and hug. "It's so good to see you."

Before she could get her arms around him, Kasey launched off her rooftop and flew to Ned's shoulder. She grabbed on to his neck with both arms and her tail, and glared at Brie as if to say, *Whoa, girlfriend. He's mine.*

"Well," Brie said, a bit taken aback. "Somebody loves her Ned, doesn't she?"

"No question about it," he said.

Later that night, after walnut time, I checked in and found the two of them quiet and content, watching TV and exchanging occasional hoots and soft chatter. Kasey turned her attention to grooming Ned, checking for hangnails, picking lint off his pajamas, licking his hands, and just plain snuggling. Finally, she wrapped herself around his neck, making a completely new sound. It was deep and throaty, almost gorilla-like.

"Hooo hooo."

Everything about her face and body language communicated the meaning, but we called Megan Monkey the next day, ostensibly to ask for a translation.

"That, Ned and Ellen, is the sound of complete happiness." She told us what we already knew, realizing that we really just wanted to share this huge event with her.

It had taken three full months to soldier two steps forward. I held my breath, waiting for the one step back.

17

No Pain, No Gain

"IS IT A DULL, ACHING SORT OF PAIN?" ASKED NED'S PHYSI-cal therapist. "Or is it a localized, stabbing sort of pain?"

"Well," he said, "there's the constant, underlying, sucks-to-be-you sort of pain. And then there's the lightning-bolt-ripping-through-my-entire-body sort of pain. It's like my tongue is on fire, and my hands are stuck in an ice bucket. Sometimes I can't stand the drive to rehab. Or I get there and I can't do any meaningful exercises."

It was terrible to witness Ned experiencing these excruciating rushes of nerve pain that had plagued him since the accident, growing steadily in both frequency and ferocity.

"We've tried everything," I said. "Medication, massage, hot packs, cold packs—nothing seems to help. Nothing except . . ."

"Except what?" the PT prompted.

"Monkey," said Ned, smiling at her baffled expression. "She's a trained service animal. She does all kinds of stuff for me, but mostly . . . she's a friend."

"And she's able to distract you from the pain?"

"That was the original idea," I said, "but it goes way beyond that. At first, we didn't notice anything different, but after she'd been close to him through a few of these episodes, I noticed . . . rather than perching on his shoulder with her tail wrapped around his neck, she positions her body on his chest, right over his heart.

She keeps very still and just—I don't know. The anguish is so visible in Ned's face. But with Kasey there, his breathing slows down. That contorted expression is gradually more relaxed. It's . . . quite a thing to see."

"Kasey's like a medicine for me," said Ned with affection and pride. "She comforts and relaxes me like no drug. It's like she actually understands what I'm going through."

Unfortunately, Ned's pain had gone beyond the scope of Dr. Kasey. He'd come so far in the two years since doctors told him he'd never even breathe on his own. Now he was talking and able to pick up a few finger foods with his left hand, and was working on his left foot.

"This pain is really slowing me down," said Ned. "It's . . . it's debilitating."

We kept searching for a solution.

"MRIs are showing a cyst in the spinal cord," the doctor told us. "That's likely impinging on nerves, setting off the increased pain."

"So what's the action plan?" asked Ned.

"One option is to rework the original head and neck fusion and insert a microscopic shunt. But I'll be honest with you, Ned: with your diminished respiratory function, any kind of surgery is extremely serious. Any time we go into the spinal cord, there's the risk of additional damage. That said . . . this procedure could improve your quality of life by reducing the pain."

That night after walnut time, Kasey tucked herself in next to Ned's neck, quietly contemplating his earlobe and grooming his hairline, as if she knew we were in too serious a mood for play.

"The harsh reality," I said, "is that things are going to get worse before they get better. This is major surgery, followed by several weeks in rehab. It means being away from home for weeks and weeks, being poked, prodded, stuck, and stared at by doctors and medical students. I'm not saying you shouldn't do it, Ned. It might be a godsend. Or it could be . . . not."

"It's a gamble," he said soberly.

"Yes. And the stakes are high. It was an easy call last time. I mean, how much worse could it get? But you've come such a long way, Ned. You've got a lot to lose."

"I'd make a deal with the devil if I had to. Seriously, Mom— it's that bad. The only thing is . . . I don't want to jeopardize what Kasey and I have accomplished, you know?" Ned pushed his cheek into her warm rib cage. "How could she understand if I just disappear? She'll be confused and lonely, and then who knows what it'll be like when I come back. Four months of bonding down the drain."

"I can take care of Kasey, Ned. Right now, we're talking about you."

"Honestly, I'm all in," he said.

"I wish I could tell you it'll all work out fine. Or that the alternative is any better."

"Mom, the pain is . . ." Ned shook his head tightly.

"It's your decision. You have to do what you feel is right for yourself."

"I need to do this," he said firmly.

The words "I can't take it" are simply not in Ned's vocabulary, but the agony was unrelenting and had clearly become unbearable. Arrangements were made, all the pre-op questionnaires and blood tests accomplished, the clipboard-wielding case manager satisfied. On the day before the surgery, I packed a few essentials in a duffel bag, and Ned sat close to Kasey's cage, talking softly to her, telling her he'd be home soon.

"Be a good girl, Kasey. And don't you worry, I'll be back soon," he promised. As difficult as it was, he finally said, "Bye, Kasey."

He rolled out the door, leaving her bewildered and alone. It's hard to say how much she understood, but I'm sure she could tell he was anxious and sad.

"Pay attention to her, Mom," Ned told me as we left for our old stomping grounds at Mass General. "Give her apples. And don't put off cutting her nails."

"I've got it covered, Ned. I promise."

Ned moved into his room, and we met with the doctors, anesthesiologists, and assorted staff. I returned home late that night to find poor Kasey wandering her cage, forlorn and unsettled. When she saw me, she peeped a happy hello. Then she saw I was alone and her expression fell.

"So sorry, Kasey," I said. "He's not coming home tonight."

She tiptoed from one side of her cage to the other, deeply concerned.

"Peep? Cluck?" she fretted.

The unwelcome development seemed to sink in then. Kasey scrambled to her bedroom shelf and turned her back to me.

"Don't play with her too much while Ned's gone," Megan Monkey advised. "We don't want you to replace Ned as her number one."

No danger of that. Kasey wanted nothing to do with me.

I gave her a few walnuts from my pocket, adhering to the same rituals we always went through. SCI patients cling to routine, and Kasey depended on Ned's nighttime drill as completely as he did. But tonight, the key element was missing. She watched me reproachfully as I closed the drapes, turned off the TV, set the radio to Ned's favorite station, and hit the "sleep" button so it would automatically shut off in thirty minutes.

"Good night, Kasey," I said softly. "He'll be home soon. I promise."

"THE SURGERY WENT WELL," a post-op nurse told me. "He's a fighter."

"Now what?"

"The first few days in ICU are going to be tough," she said. "But I guess you know that."

I nodded. It was all too familiar: the hovering residents, the octopus of IVs and monitor hookups, including a tube down his throat. We were back to blinking through the alphabet cards.

"Hi, Ned. How are you feeling?"

K A S E Y   O K?

"She's fine. We're taking good care of her."

Ned progressed quickly and was moved to our favorite floor, White 12. Whenever he was there, he was the youngest patient by fifty years, so all the older folks loved him. He flirted with the nurses and fascinated the doctors with his unusual case. I, of course, was comfortable being in the familiar surroundings; Megan and I knew where all the bathrooms and vending machines were. Everyone welcomed him and made a big fuss about all his progress. As soon as he could speak again, he couldn't stop talking about Kasey.

When he was stable enough, Ned moved back to Spaulding for rehab. We posted pictures of Kasey all around the room, and Ned interrogated me daily about her care.

"She's fine. Happy as a clam," I kept assuring him. "If I stay late, Megan stops by to take her out for walnut time."

"Kasey and I get along pretty well," Megan told Ned over a bowl of mashed potatoes. "She lets me know I'm down with Maddie and Anna in the hierarchy. Gives me a little pounce every once in a while, just to show me who's boss. But I wear lots of big jewelry for her to play with, so she's okay slumming with me if no one else is available."

"She's accepted you," he said. "That's good."

But I felt sorry for Kasey. She missed Ned terribly. I arrived home one night and heard soft voices in Ned's room.

"I know it's scary. I get scared, too."

"Purrup pip?"

"I know you're lonely, but he'll be home soon."

"Seeeee kit kit."

"It's okay. Neddy will be all right."

"Hi, Mads."

I leaned in the doorway and smiled, surprised to find her there, speaking so benevolently to her arch-nemesis. I was even more surprised to hear Kasey pip-pipping back without any screeching or saber-rattling. She gripped the side of the cage and Maddie rubbed her little fingers.

"I thought you were giving her the cold shoulder," I said.

"She seemed lonely." Maddie shrugged. "Anna and I have been stopping by to say hello."

"That's good of you. I'm sure Kasey appreciates that. And Ned will, too."

"I gave her a few walnuts. I hope that's okay."

At the sound of the w-word, Kasey slapped the side of the cage, looking for more.

"Looks like it's very okay with her." I laughed. "Does this mean there's hope for a future relationship for you two?"

Maddie rolled her eyes and assured me in teenager parlance, "Um, *no.*"

"Hmph," Kasey agreed.

I was pleased to see Kasey developing bonds with the girls, but I worried—and so did Ned—that there might be an equal and opposite effect on his relationship with her.

"Kasey might be standoffish—even peevish at first," Megan Monkey warned us. "She doesn't understand why Ned would abandon her and betray her trust."

The suggestion took me back to my days as a working mom. I missed my kids while I was away, but when I came home, I found them so testy and sullen it made me want to leave again.

"But does that mean they'll be starting from scratch?" I asked Megan Monkey on the phone that night.

"We'll have to wait and see," she said, and wished me luck.

I've never had much talent for "wait and see." And I couldn't bear the thought of going back to square one with Kasey. It was beyond daunting. Okay, I said to myself, the wheels slowly turning. She's a service animal . . . She's *Ned's* service animal. What does that mean? What *can* that mean? And then it hit me. The ADA! I'd learned all about the Americans with Disabilities Act at the Shepherd Center. Kasey was a service animal, so she could go wherever Ned went! They couldn't keep her out!

It was my *aha!* moment.

The next day I arrived at the hospital. Kasey, nestled in her carrying case, was slung over my shoulder. I glanced at the nurse's station down the hall. My dad always said, "When in doubt, walk in like you own the place."

So I did.

There was a little bit of friction with one Nurse Ratched who rallied a security guard to make some noise, but Ned wasn't the only one who'd come a long way. I was on a mission of mercy with a monkey carrier under my arm and righteousness on my side. I was used to getting screeched at by someone who needed to assert her place in a hierarchy, so bureaucrats didn't scare me a bit.

"Geez, Mom," Ned said in amazement. "You're fierce when you want to be."

"I promised I'd bring her."

The looks on both faces—man and monkey—were worth whatever verbal skinning I'd had to take and dish out.

"Hi, Kasey," Ned crooned. "How's it going, girl?"

Kasey trilled at the sound of his voice.

"Kasey, leash?" I said, and she was more than happy to comply, eager to scramble out and see the strange surroundings.

After the initial burst of happiness and hellos, she switched to spy mode, checking under the bed, peeking inside the drawers on the nightstand, making an open-and-shut case of the closet door. She scaled the IV poles and made sure everything was in good order, pulled the suction machine off the wall and handed it to Ned.

"Eck?"

"Thanks." He laughed. "Don't mind if I do."

She danced back and forth on his bed a bit, then settled in comfortably on his shoulder. There was a sudden knock on the door and it burst open without waiting for an answer. Kasey leapt from Ned's shoulder to the end of the bed with one of her infamous pounces—*Hey there! Who do you think you are? I'm in charge now!*

The look on this poor fellow's face was unbelievable. He'd come in to check Ned's vitals and found a monkey giving him the evil eye. He was out of there faster than a speeding bullet.

The visit energized Ned. True to form, he worked his you-know-what off in PT and OT and was ready to come home after five weeks of rehab. All our worries were for naught. Kasey hailed him with a hero's welcome. *Peep-peep*ing happily, she sailed straight for his shoulder, back in love, standing by her man with even more gusto than before.

The surgery was a resounding success and paved the way for progress that wasn't possible before. Ned was in a lot less pain and gradually became aware of newly awakened feeling in his right arm and hand. It was difficult, but he could now raise his right arm, wiggle his fingers a bit, and actually pick up objects with that hand.

Kasey seemed immediately savvy to this new development. At first the jerky movements sent her skittering off, but soon I noticed she seemed to hang out on Ned's left shoulder more, baiting him to bring his right arm up to pet her, the same way hanging out on his right shoulder always made him raise his left hand. She was always up for new games, and she astonished us all by inventing a few.

She loved to wrestle, making sumo faces at Ned as she squared off with him, then rolling back on his chest for a belly rub. She brought toys to his lap and made him reach for them instead of placing them in his hand. Sometimes when I was on pest patrol, she took the flyswatter from my hand and pressed it into Ned's, then scampered all over the room (once she'd munched down the offending fly), collecting plastic rings on her hands, feet, and tail. The new game required Ned to hold the flyswatter upright while Kasey slid the rings down the handle one by one.

Having discovered a cup Ned had used to snack on some granola one evening, Kasey tipped the last few crumbs into her mouth, then ambled over to her man, regarding him intently.

"Humm . . . pip?" she wondered.

She tilted the paper cup to Ned's lips. He spit a walnut into it. Kasey immediately tipped it back to her own lips and downed the walnut.

"What made you think to spit the walnut in the cup?" I asked.

"Seemed like she wanted me to, so I did."

"Ned . . . look . . . ," I whispered.

I wasn't sure he could feel what she was doing, but Kasey methodically moved each finger on his right hand until he was holding the cup. As I watched in disbelief, she dragged his arm up to his mouth and tilted the cup to his lips.

I couldn't wait to call Megan Monkey the next morning.

"That's incredible," she said. "We never trained her to do that. Cups would be too easy to spill. That's why we train them to use a bottle with a straw."

"How is she coming up with this stuff?" I asked. "It seems like she's purposely challenging Ned's capabilities, but . . . is that even possible?"

"Kasey watches everyone, every day, every moment. She wants to help. I can't explain it other than to say . . . wow." She laughed, nonplussed. "That is one tuned-in little monkey."

Even the simple repetitive motion of petting her was therapeutic.

"I'm really pleased with what I'm seeing," the occupational therapist told Ned. "I'd like to do some additional upper body work."

"Bring it on," Ned said with a grin, and they did.

He stepped up to whatever they threw at him, working to build strength and capability on both sides.

"I'm definitely feeling stronger through here." He indicated his middle. "I've got that sitting balance whipped. Can't quite sit on a regular chair, but . . . someday. I can see it."

"Ned, that's huge," I said. "I'm so proud of you."

The physical therapists wanted to see how he would do in a standing position, using a special harness that essentially hung him from an overhead lift, but Ned shook his head.

"I don't know. I tried that about six months ago," he said. "I was strung up like a rag doll over the treadmill—arms dangling, my head hanging. I couldn't even feel them moving my feet. It was totally lame."

"But you've been working that core," she said, setting her hands on his torso. "There's a lot more strength through here."

He considered it for a moment, then gave the plan a circumspect nod.

I could tell he didn't love the process of getting rigged up, but suspended erect in front of the mirror—upright largely on his own power—he watched himself like he was seeing an old friend, a man he knew from another life. With help from the therapist and a carefully positioned walker, Ned purposefully moved one foot forward, then the other. The pace was glacial. Agonizingly slow to watch. But my son's face was a portrait of pride and determination. One foot. Then the other.

I held my breath.

Another step. Another. And then another.

A deep shiver traveled the length of my spine.

I don't see him walking, the shaman had said. *But I don't see him not walking*.

18

Just Before Dawn

"I HAVE NEWS," SAID CHARITY.

"Oh?" I glanced up from a fresh batch of Monkey Chow.

"I passed my board exams."

"Oh . . . wow . . ."

Charity had graduated nursing school shortly after she started working with us. (Could it have been over a year ago?) For one reason or another, she'd put off taking her boards. Until now.

"I did it," she told us, beaming with pride and excitement. "I'm finally a real RN."

And the real world was ready and waiting. She had a hospital job lined up.

"Charity, that's . . . that's wonderful. We're so proud of you."

I tried to sound supportive, but everything inside me wanted to wail, *No! You can't leave us!* She was one of the precious few PCAs I'd found who was medically adept, dependable as day-break, and a pleasure to have around.

"Congratulations, Charity," said Ned. "I'm glad for you. But selfishly, I wish . . . sheesh. I'm really going to miss you."

"You're not getting rid of me that easy," she said. "I'll be around."

"You better. Seriously. Visit. A lot."

"I will, I promise." Charity gripped his hand, her eyes filled with emotion. "I'll never forget you, Ned. Kasey, too. You've been such an inspiration to me."

I reluctantly began interviewing potential replacements for Charity (a treasure for whom there really was no replacement) and scheduled a semi-likely candidate for a trial day.

But by 10:30 A.M., I knew we weren't going to make it.

"I'm hungry," she announced. "I think I'll have some eggs."

"Actually, it's time for Ned's shower," I said.

"It's time for eggs," she informed me, rifling out pots and pans, chopping onions and peppers, toasting English muffins. She scooped a heaping bowl of ice cream to go with it all and spread out at the kitchen table to chow down and read the morning paper.

"Um . . . I don't think this is going to work," I told her as politely as I could.

She finished her brunch without looking up and left while I was getting Ned into the shower. Oh, well. This wasn't as bad as the girl who'd left him in the scalding water while she played with her ponytail in the bathroom mirror.

The hiring process was further complicated by the Monkey Factor.

New aides seemed to put Kasey off her game; instead of snuggling with Ned to watch the Sox, she wandered around his bed and wouldn't settle down. If the new aide touched Ned to reposition him, Kasey screeched and pounced inside her cage.

"Sounds like it's hard for Kasey to see strangers touching her man," said Megan Monkey. "She wants to make sure he's safe. She wants that person to know Ned's spoken for."

So now, in addition to excellent references, experience, a modicum of personality, and a penchant for the Red Sox, we had to add "must love monkey" to the list of qualifications.

Kasey quickly proved herself to be an uncanny judge of character, partly because she picked up on Ned's reaction. When he was too tactful to express his true opinion, Kasey voiced hers without restraint. When she just plain didn't like someone, she gave them the cold shoulder, even if the oblivious applicant cooed and clucked and gawked like this was the Bronx Zoo. If we were desperate or foolish enough to bring this person in for a trial day, Kasey reiterated her veto by lunging back and forth in her cage, screeching.

By green bean time, we'd have moved on to the next candidate. The talent pool dwindled, and sole responsibility for Ned's care more frequently fell to me.

I loved my son. I considered his care a privilege. I hope that goes without saying. When your child is in need, you rise to the occasion. You just do. You can't *not*.

As Ned always said, "I'm not complaining. Just reporting."

But Ned was a foot taller than me and a whole lot heavier. During the day, I had to operate the lift that got him in and out of his wheelchair, help him shower and shave (which was tougher on him than it was on me, I'm sure), feed him on schedule, move him to his PT mat and help him stretch, see to his various waking needs and the various needs of the girls, along with regular household chores, which in our somewhat irregular household, included caring for two apoplectic dogs and a diva monkey.

At night, Ned had to be turned twice to avoid the bedsores that plague many SCI patients. The protocol had been drummed into my head during my Shepherd Center education: pressure sores are incredibly painful—and incredibly dangerous. Because of the patient's impaired circulation, lesions are slow to heal, opening the door for potentially lethal infection. A person can actually die as the result of a bedsore. In Atlanta, Megan and I witnessed horrific examples, patients in dire straits as a result of less than hypervigilant home care. We were henceforth the Skin Police, determined to see that Ned never had even a teeny, tiny skin breakdown. I bird-dogged every little wrinkle and seam, edging on a pillowcase, nubby socks. The worst culprit—remaining in one position too long—was a risk we eliminated by repositioning him on a regular schedule, including turning him at 1:30 A.M. every night and 5 A.M. every morning. Without fail.

Every aide caring for Ned was indoctrinated with the creed. Our reward: at this writing, Ned has incurred *zero* pressure sores. When he was in Mass General, the chief neurosurgeon smiled at me and said, "His skin looks remarkable. You're obviously doing a great job there, Mom."

Probably a small moment for him, but I positively preened. It meant so much to have someone of that caliber notice the quality of care I was dedicated to providing for my son.

Even when I had to do it alone.

Sole responsibility for Ned's care was a daunting physical task, not to mention the emotional number it does on a person to go without sleep, without help, without the freedom to take a walk for several days and nights in a row. I'm ashamed to say how much it burned me out at times.

This is why I had such huge appreciation and respect for a good PCA or nurse.

I'd logged a lot of miles in her shoes.

"MOM, ARE YOU SURE you don't want me to come over?" Megan asked one summer night. "Maddie said your late shift flaked out again."

"She twisted her ankle. I tried really hard to sound sympathetic."

"Yeah, I bet. This is what—two nights in a row?"

"She swore she'd be in tomorrow night," I said. "We're okay. Thanks anyway, Megan. You've been a gem this week. As usual."

I hung up the phone and dragged a load of towels from the dryer. "Okay" was probably an overstatement, but for God's sake, even a Go-to Girl is entitled to a life of her own once in a while. There was really nothing to do but do it. After walnut time, Kasey hopped lightly to my shoulder, and Ned said the same thing he said to her every night: "Good night, Kasey. I love you. Hang tough."

Kasey waited patiently as he raised his left hand and extended his index finger. She grabbed the finger briefly, pulled it gently to her chest, then let go. A purposeful and poignant good night between special friends. It was a luxury to turn off the light and climb the stairs with the two of them breathing in deep, contented sleep.

I stumbled out of bed at 1:30. Again at 5:00. Headed downstairs at 7:45 to start the day.

Breep. Breep.

My heart sank when I heard the voice-mail alert from my cell. Voice mail prior to 8 A.M. is never a good thing at my house.

"Hi, Ellen." The daytime aide inserted a pallid cough for dramatic effect. "Won't be in today. Got the flu or something. I'll give you a call later and let you know about tomorrow."

I closed my eyes, took a deep breath. *Okay. We're okay.*

Prepping breakfast for Ned and Kasey, I scrolled through my mental Rolodex. Forget emergency backup. Anyone who was any good was already working. I was head nurse for another sixteen-hour day.

Ned had physical therapy scheduled, which meant most of the day would be spent on the trip into Boston. I checked my desk

calendar to see what would have to be canceled: dentist appointment for Maddie, Anna's softball game.

Coffee with one of my consulting clients.

I don't remember now if it was the client developing an exit
strategy or the software start-up seeking a way to break from the
pack. Many of the local companies I worked with had branched
off from companies where I'd worked a long time ago in a galaxy
far, far away. I'd done my best since Ned's accident to maintain
working relationships with my colleagues, but the ones who knew
me best were getting used to last-minute cancellations.

Anything that took me farther away than the mailbox was out
for today. An afternoon nap was a distant dream. Bad news for
anyone in my path after 3 P.M.

"Good morning, Ned. Good morning, Kasey." I pushed the
curtains aside to allow the morning light in and went about taking Ned's vitals.

"Hi, Mom. What . . . the aide's a no-show?"

"Guess it's you and me against the world."

"World's in trouble," he said. "You're scary when you don't get
your nap."

Ned took the news well, considering he now faced hanging
with his mother for another day, starting with the shower.

"Thanks for being a good sport about it," I said.

"That's just my primal instinct for self-preservation."

Breep. Breep. My heart sank again.

"Hi, Ellen," said the overnight aide. And then in my weary
head there was a buzzing through which I kept hearing words I
could not possibly be hearing. ". . . won't be in again tonight . . .
sprained my ankle so . . . doctor said to stay off my ankle
completely for several weeks."

"Several weeks," I echoed. "As in . . . four . . . five . . ."

"At least."

"Oh . . . wow. I'm really sorry to hear that." And I was. Really, *really* sorry.

My mind raced through the most recent round of applicants and interviewees. None of them had passed muster. Even if I found someone today, I'd have to stay up for several nights to train him or her. But if I had help during the day, I thought, maybe I could tough out the night shift until I was able to reel in one of our old regulars. Or maybe I'd have to break down and call an agency.

After physical therapy at Spaulding, Ned and I got coffee at Dunkin' Donuts and dropped by CVS to pick up a few things. Thank God, Megan stopped by that evening.

"How was your day, Mom?"

"Sometimes you have to be like a shark. Just keep moving."

"Go to bed," she said. "I'll hang out with Ned and Kasey."

She didn't have to tell me twice.

Next morning I was looking forward to the cavalry when the phone rang.

No. Not happening. Bad dream.

"Hi, Ellen." Cough, sniffle, cough. "Still down with the flu. Wouldn't want to bring the bug over to Ned, so . . . you know. Maybe I better stay home the rest of the week."

I drew a line through another day on the desk calendar and went to take Ned's vitals. Kasey was in full voice, trilling a happy morning song.

"Kasey, must you?"

"Come on, Mom," Ned said. "We're a team. We'll get through this."

"Sure. Of course." I smiled and tried to sound genuine. "We'll make the best of it. It's such a beautiful day," I said. "Let's go out on the terrace and soak up some sun."

We spent the rest of the morning outside watching Kasey embark on an extensive bug-hunting safari.

"Daddy longlegs are her favorites," Ned observed as she greedily snatched one off a potted plant and systematically pulled the legs off, a macabre twist on the traditional "he loves me . . . he loves me not." She munched the legs one by one, rolled the body between her palms like a meatball, and popped it in her mouth.

I cringed. "Oh, that's just gross."

"You eat crab legs," said Ned. "What's the difference?"

"If you really believed that, Ned, you'd be much cheaper to feed."

"Mom, look at her now."

I glanced up just in time to see her snatch a fly right out of the air. She clutched her prey tightly to her breast, then raised her fist to eye level. She opened her thumb ever so slightly, peeking in to make sure she had her victim, and out it flew.

"Kitz!" The huntress snatched it out of the air again and popped it in her mouth.

"Geez, she's quick," said Ned. "Oh! Look, Mom. She shimmied up the umbrella pole and got a Japanese beetle."

"Aaaarrrrrr." Kasey skipped over to Ned with the fresh hors d'oeuvre.

"Hear that?" said Ned. "That's the victory growl."

"Our Megan says we should have business cards printed up: Capuchin Critter Control. Or Primate Pest Removal."

Kasey took Ned's water bottle from the umbrella table, carefully deposited the beetle inside, screwed the cap back on, and gave it a vigorous shake. When she saw the thing still flittering, she scooped a handful of dirt from a terra-cotta planter and stuffed that in for good measure.

"Preep?" She offered the cocktail to Ned.

We laughed until we had tears in our eyes.

"Well, this is good entertainment," I said after a while, "but I need to make lunch."

As I started toward the door, I felt a thump and squeeze on my leg and looked down to find this little creature clinging to my calf, latched on for a ride, the way she had with Megan Monkey.

Ned laughed because it looked so funny.

I laughed because it felt so good.

I MOVED THROUGH the rest of the day like a machine; put supper on the table, cleaned up after, got Ned onto the lift and into bed—pushing myself through my regular evening chores. When I tried to put Kasey back in her cage after walnut time, she clung to Ned's neck with both arms and her tightly wrapped tail, beseeching me with big eyes.

"She's certainly a lovebird tonight," I said. "Kasey . . . let go. Kasey, cage."

With his face muffled by Kasey's freshly fluffed tail, Ned couldn't say anything, but he smiled a sheepish smile up at me. Exhausted as I was, I couldn't bear to separate them.

"Ten minutes." I sighed and futzed around the room, picking up, counting the seconds till I could call it a day. "Okay, time for bed, you two."

She hopped to my shoulder, and I allowed them their good-night moment before I put her in her cage. After that I was on a tear, barking orders like a drill sergeant.

"Dogs, pipe down or I'll get the spray bottle. Girls, take the trash out to the curb."

My cell phone rang, and Megan's name appeared on the caller ID.

"*What?*" I snapped.

"Never mind." She hung up, and I envisioned her backing slowly away from the phone, hands in the air.

"Mom?" Ned called. "Could you please—"

"Ned, for the love of God!" I pushed my fingertips against my temples, trying to keep my voice from going any shriller. "I've moved your feet to five different positions. Pick one."

"I was going to ask you to turn on the radio."

"Fine! Why don't I come running right now and do that?"

I strode into the room, flipped off the TV, set the radio, and flicked on the night-light. Kasey clucked and slapped the side of her cage. *Well, I never!*

"Knock it off," I warned. "You've had your walnuts. It's time for bed."

"Mom. Chill," Ned said gently. "Would you please calm down?"

"Yes, Ned, I will calm down. I will be perfectly calm. *When I'm sleeping.* Good night."

"Geez. Good night," he mumbled.

I was unconscious before my head hit the pillow. The alarm jolted me awake.

One-thirty A.M.

I could hardly move.

All those sharp words, brusque good nights, and nasty

comebacks haunted me. The evening played and replayed in my head. I hated how uncaring and selfish I'd sounded. Now the girls were asleep; I'd have to wait till morning to apologize. But perhaps Ned would wake when I turned him, and I could tell him.

I dragged myself out of bed and down the stairs.

"Mom, you were really harsh tonight," he said before I could get any words out. "I know you're tired, but you don't have to take it out on us."

"You're right. I'm sorry," I said, but his stony silence let me know how hurt he was. "Look, I've got some fence-mending to do. I get it. But it'll have to wait till morning."

I straightened the pillows and covers and helped him get repositioned and adjusted his sleep apnea machine.

"I'll be right back with some water for you."

In the kitchen, I stood for a little while, staring out the window, watching dead leaves drift across the dark surface of the pool.

"Ned?" I whispered as I crept softly into his room with the water, but he was dozing already.

I dragged myself back up to bed, but I was exhausted beyond sleep. I tossed and turned, threw off the covers and pulled them back on, thrashing back and forth between stinging guilt about how mean I'd been and aching awareness of the unfairness of it all.

It isn't fair. I shouldn't have to do this. This is wrong.

Self-pity is such a slippery slope; I try not to step anywhere near the edge. But as I lay there, I was engulfed in sadness—not just for myself, but for all of us.

Wrong, wrong, wrong.

The word hammered through my head.

It was *wrong* that my son had to live his life at the mercy of these strangers. *Wrong* that my life had to be consumed with finding and training them. *Wrong* that our family life had been hijacked by their comings and goings. It was unthinkable that my girls were always put second in my priorities, their home turned upside down and invaded by outsiders who ate our food, sat on our sofas, used our bathrooms. The girls couldn't stay up late to watch a movie in their own family room because some aide was in there at midnight, bogarting the remote. Megan couldn't spend an undisturbed evening with her husband without feeling like she should race over to help me. Jake was away at school, feeling like he was out of sight and out of mind, relegated to the role of the "other brother," off in the corner of every conversation.

And Ned—oh, God, what Ned had to endure in the course of a day.

I complained about being chained to the house—*he* was the one for whom any outing was a major undertaking. He saw only those friends who came to see him, and he had to sit there listening to me blather on to every new trainee about the Hoyer lift and bedsores and all the broken aspects of his body, what he needed to eat, how his toenails should be cut and his private needs attended. He endured the indignity of some woman he'd never met and might never see again giving him a shower.

And if the stranger didn't show up, he had to be with *me*.

I love my mother dearly, but I couldn't fathom being stuck with her 24/7 for weeks on end without respite, having to depend on her to tie my shoes, put on my pajamas, or simply turn me over in bed. With all that my son endured, how could I spare one bitter thought for myself? But how could I pretend the life

I'd loved, the business I'd built, the freedom I'd fought for meant nothing to me?

The tossing and self-flagellating went on until five. The alarm went off, and I heard a soft sigh from Guy and Bailey. Familiar with the drill, they stretched and yawned, padding along the hall behind me as I pulled on my bathrobe and headed down the stairs. Looking up from the landing, I saw their sweet faces in the half-light, chins on paws, waiting on the top step.

"I'll be back, girls."

I shuffled through the kitchen to Ned's doorway and stood for a long moment with all that reality still crashing down around me. I didn't want to do this. Shouldn't have to. But I did have to. That was the only reality that mattered. I opened the door, and in the sliver of light that spilled in, I caught a glimpse of Kasey's face peeking out from under her covers. She offered a tiny peep of recognition, and I leaned my forehead against the side of her cage.

"Oh, Kasey . . . ," I whispered hoarsely, "how are we going to do this?"

She looked down at me, and as her beautiful, expressive eyes drew me in, she tilted her head and made two small sounds I'd never heard before. First she pursed her lips and repeated in soft, quick succession a sound just this side of a kiss. Then she crooned quietly.

The strange lullaby started as a high-pitched warble and slid down to a deep, mellow purr. Any words I might put to it by way of translation—*I love you* or *I'm here*—would be trite and inaccurate, but I suddenly understood what Ned had said about Kasey being medicine to him. It was the empathy that transcends language. The culmination of millions of years of compassionate instinct. Everything that can't be said with blinks or letters or the lame evolution of words. There was healing in it.

I stood for a long moment, allowing it to wash over me.

No *aha*. No lightning bolt. Only a simple knowing of what was and is and would always be.

I could do this. I would do this.

And I did.

I wish I could report there was a skip in my step as I climbed the stairs after tending to Ned, but I was still beyond . . . whatever is beyond weariness. Prostration. Siberia. But Guy and Bailey were waiting for me on the landing, and when I got up again two hours later to start another day, they were there again.

So was Kasey. Yodeling her little morning song.

I suddenly heard myself humming along.

19

Of Moms and Men

I F THERE'S ONE THING NEW ENGLAND KNOWS HOW TO DO, it's autumn. Frosty mornings turn into Indian summer afternoons. Spectacular colors invite us out into the crisp, cool air. There's a shift in the way people think, the way they drive, the way they talk to one another. Summer lethargy gives way to a fresh, invigorated stride. School starts, and everyone settles into a seat on the big yellow bus back to the real world.

"I love this road in the fall," Anna told me on the way to school. "The trees are so beautiful. This was always a good one for the leaf project."

I smiled at the memory of the dreaded freshman "leaf project," a ninth-grade rite of passage. Forty-eight different leaves had to be collected and catalogued, each with a written description of its unique characteristics. And of course, this usually happened with flashlights and bitter complaining at ten o'clock the night before the project was due. Any mother in Concord can tell you exactly where to find the gingko, sweet gum, or quaking aspen.

Autumn is in the details. Veins of gold on a red leaf. A single blade of persistently green grass in a patch of brown. Each breath of crisp, dry air brings both lungs to life. You can feel the oxygen reaching the brain.

The terrace outside Ned's room turned out to be one of the best investments I ever made. He sat in the sun watching Kasey hunt bugs while Guy and Bailey kept well out of Kasey's way and made themselves crazy chasing squirrel shadows and bunny trails.

"I think we'd better buck up and hose down Kasey's cage once more before it gets cold," I told him. "You might want to move back."

Hosing down the cage was an onerous chore during which overspray and choice words often hit the wrong target. I got into grubby clothes, pulled on rubber gloves, and dragged out the stepladder, scrub brush, and a bucket of Simple Green. Watching his five-foot mother wrangle the six-foot cage was entertainment for Ned. The cage rolled easily to the terrace door, but he laughed and teased me as I struggled to maneuver it over the threshold, and I laughed and teased him back as I took up pruning shears and cut the plastic cable ties that secured the corners. I pinched my finger and muttered a swear word.

"I heard that," Ned called over his shoulder.

"Watch it, buddy. I'm getting the hose, and I know how to use it."

"Just don't spray the open windows like you did last time."

"Everything's closed up," I said. "I'm a fast learner."

With the cable ties and spring locks released, I opened up the cage and climbed the stepladder to hose down the whole works before I set to scrubbing.

"Remind me," I said. "What fool said it would be fun to have a monkey?"

"Same fast learner who sprayed the open window."

"Oh, yeah." I toted my brush and bucket over and attacked the floor of the cage on hands and knees. "It's probably a good thing I didn't know what I was getting myself into."

"Think of it this way," said my son, the optimist. "How many people can claim 'excellent monkey cage cleaner' on their résumé?"

My résumé. The thought made me laugh out loud. "Excellent communication skills" had expanded to negotiating with dogs and translating monkey-speak. My "people person" sensibilities now included predicting the future of PCA applicants and reading the minds of teenage girls.

"That's not my only hidden talent," I told Ned. "I can also wrestle with case managers, provide salon services for monkeys, repair wheelchairs and other devices, run my own home health agency, and manage pharmacies. Any start-up would be thrilled to have me."

"I'm happy to have you, Mom."

He said it so seriously, I sat up and pushed my sweaty bangs from my face so I could look him in the eye when I said, "Thank you, Ned. I'm happy to be here."

Kasey peeped her two cents' worth from under the umbrella table, where she was busy torturing a centipede.

"It must've been tough to give all that up," said Ned. "The whole corporate and then your own company thing."

"It was," I said honestly. "I miss the challenges, ideas, interesting people. The thrill of the chase. But I'm not really interested in high tech anymore. Or any conventional job."

"What about an unconventional job?"

"I already have one." I laughed. "I guess I'd like to find some way to apply everything I've learned about—oh, a lot of things. Advocacy, spinal cord injuries, animal-human bonding. Even if I could go back to the corporate world . . . I'd miss being here. I actually like being around my kids." I finished scrubbing and set the brush in the bucket. "Ned, I never even pretended I had it all when you were little. I knew what I was missing. And I know what

I'm missing now. Bottom line: nobody has it all. There's always a trade-off. You make choices. You take one path or you take the other—and sometimes you don't even get to decide where you go. But you do get to decide who you are."

"The trick is being *who you are* when circumstances yank you off track."

"Exactly. And that's true for everybody."

I stripped off the rubber gloves on my way to the spigot, feeling terribly wise and philosophical until I turned on the water without getting a firm grip on the nozzle. The hose took on a life of its own, flipping and leaping all over, soaking me to the skin. Ned roared with laughter, and Kasey took refuge on the back of his neck, scolding me when I let fly another blue streak of choice words.

ALWAYS A TRADE-OFF.

My kids understood that having Kasey significantly added to my workload, but knowing what she brought to Ned's life, they were always good sports about it. Everyone has moments, of course, but I'm consistently amazed and moved by how mature and selfless my children can be. Over the years, I've been MIA for countless games, horse shows, prom pictures, sports banquets, and Back to School Nights.

Unable to get coverage for Ned, I missed what turned out to be Jake's last college football game. So I didn't see him go down. Hard.

"They're getting somebody to look at the scans," he told me on the phone from the ER.

"I'm sorry I wasn't there."

"It's okay. I understand," Jake said. Because that's what he and the girls always said, and it always stabbed me in the heart.

"Tell me what happened."

"I don't know, I just—I didn't even see the other guy was about to hit me. His helmet caught me right on the side of my knee, and it hurt like . . . like . . ."

"Like getting hit in the side of the knee."

"By a cement truck. Geez. It was excruciating. I thought maybe I could walk it off. Tried to go back out."

"Oh, no . . ."

"Don't worry," Jake said. "I turned around and came right back. I knew something was really wrong."

The following Monday, I took him to his orthopedist in Concord. Jake was no stranger in that office. Football is a pretty tough sport when you're as good at it as Jake was. In addition to various torn ligaments, abrasions, and contusions over the years, he'd torn his left shoulder the fall of his senior year in high school. Surgery. His freshman year in college, he tore his right shoulder. Matching scar on the other side. Now, three games into the season—he was hurt again.

"This can't be it," he said, as we waited for the doctor. "Not this year. I was starting."

His team and coaches were counting on him. He'd gotten into Bentley partly because they'd wanted him to play football. And beyond all that, football was his passion, a huge part of his life, his reason for breathing. He always gave it everything he had.

The doctor breezed in with a big smile. Our hearts soared. "The ACL is torn," he said. "That means surgery. I'm sorry, Jake. Your season is over." Crash and burn.

His season, maybe his football career, was done. Jake shut his eyes and clamped his jaw, fighting back his emotions, but his neck and cheeks flushed deep rose.

"Let's talk about the logistics," I said, knowing that if he had to speak at that moment, his misery would be complete.

We talked about dates, preliminary physical therapy, follow-up appointments. They issued him a pair of crutches to hobble around on in the meantime, and we stumped out to the car. He was quiet on the way home, but as we pulled into the driveway, I squeezed his arm.

"I'm so sorry, Jake," I said. "I know this is really hard."

He took a deep breath and said, "Well . . . it could have been way worse. I could have torn the meniscus or cartilage—done serious damage, like some of my teammates have. Torn ACL's not the end of the world. The surgery is arthroscopic. I hear it's not that bad."

He got out of the car in a tangle of crutches and long arms and legs, and we stood in front of the house, talking for a bit. Jake said all the brave rah-rah things a person is supposed to say, but the undertone in his voice and the slump of his shoulders seemed heartbreakingly defeated.

"It's okay, Mom," he said. "It's just my knee. It's not like . . . like Ned."

"It's just your knee," I repeated and nodded. "But I love your knee as much as I love his. And what happened to Ned doesn't make what happened to you any less painful."

I reached up and gave him a hug. I was suddenly too choked up to speak, full of unspoken sadness for every moment of his life I couldn't be there for him. He hugged me back, full of *Yeah, I know. I get it.*

He always did.

"You know what's weird," he said as we walked toward the house in the Indian summer sun. "The mom part of your life is all . . . upside down."

"What do you mean?"

"Most moms are all about the kids when the kids are little and not so much when they get older. You were totally doing your own thing when we were little, and now you're microscopically involved in every aspect of our lives."

"Is that a complaint?"

"An observation," he quickly filled in. "There was never any doubt about how much you love us."

It was a pretty good observation, actually. The more I thought about it, the more profound it seemed. And I was about to be reminded that the path I'd chosen—along with the path I hadn't— was full of unexpected turns.

20

The First Day of
the Rest of Your Life

JAKE'S COLLEGE FOOTBALL CAREER WASN'T WHAT HE'D hoped it would be, but he didn't mope. He plowed on through toward graduation with growing enthusiasm about the commencement of real life. He and I had a lot of long conversations about where he'd go in life and which path he'd choose to get there. I was thrilled to see him with his head on straight and his possibilities unlimited, but it brought to the foreground big questions about how Ned could move forward to forge a meaningful, productive life.

Back when we were at Shepherd, just a few days after he'd spoken for the first time, Ned was scheduled for a "career counseling" session. I wasn't sure it was such a great idea. It seemed to shine a light on everything that was now *not* possible for him. Did he really need that when every breath, every word, every day was such a struggle? I couldn't even think about the flaming wreckage of my own career at that point. We had more immediate fish to fry.

Ned was open, but he approached the discussion with characteristic caution.

"I see you were a senior at the University of Arizona prior to your accident," said the counselor. "What were you planning to do with your degree?"

"Sports marketing," said Ned, slowly getting each word out.

"What led you in that direction?"

"I played a lot of sports all my life . . . and I like people."

The counselor shared some stories of other Shepherd patients and what they'd gone on to achieve. Ned contemplated all that for a long moment before responding.

"Well . . . I like the idea of motivating people . . . being a mentor. Like Lute Olson . . . UA's basketball coach. The guy's a legend . . . inspires people . . . gets them thinking . . . gets them going."

The counselor nodded, waiting for him to get the words out. Back then, speaking was still an exhausting effort.

"Before the accident," he said, "I took the Dale Carnegie course . . . learned about public speaking . . . got involved in Big Brothers."

"That's great, Ned. So maybe you channel all that into education or journalism or public speaking. You'll have to retool the logistics. You might have to think in baby steps, but the big picture is still possible. You're learning a lot right now. There may be a way to use this experience to your advantage in the long run."

There was a glint of something in Ned's eyes. Recognition. A spark of electricity.

"I'll think about it," said Ned, and I could see the gears turning.

Over the next two years, fighting to hang on in the here and now, we didn't talk much about that remote "long run." This extraordinary path was not Ned's choice, and the arduous journey was filled with pain and effort. But every once in a while, I saw that spark.

My pragmatic side kept telling me, *This is how it is. Denial won't do anyone any good.* But my heart couldn't accept the idea that my athletic, talented son would be confined to this house, his room, that chair for the rest of his life. I kept searching for the most innovative doctors, the latest therapies, believing things could get better. (I still am. I still do. I'll never quit.) This was *Ned*—the passionate go-getter, the boy with way too much energy. There had to be more to his life than hanging out with Mom and the monkey. There were dark moments when he mourned his lost dreams, but quitting simply wasn't in his DNA.

Ned was still Ned.

Genuine and caring. A young man with purpose and conviction. His charisma and sense of humor were still very much intact.

"Ned, I've got everything all set for the morning," I said as I bustled about getting him ready for bed. "Allison will be here, which is always a good thing." Allison, a bright, incredibly competent—not to mention fun—nursing school graduate, had joined Team Ned a few months ago, and we were thrilled that she had. "But I've got to get moving right away."

"Why?" he asked.

"I've got a horrific dentist appointment in the morning. You know how I hate the dentist. Megan suggested Ativan."

"Mom, what the heck are you scared of?"

"I have to have a crown—the whole novocaine needle thing coming at my mouth . . . really terrifies me."

He looked at me in total disbelief. "Mom, you—after everything you've been through—are scared of a needle? Come on!"

"Well," I cleared my throat, "it's much worse than that. That needle is really long. It's coming right at me. I'm totally trapped in the chair. I can't get out . . ."

"Okay, Mom, whatever drowns your boat."

With Kasey's help, he'd gotten a lot of his gung ho back. He just needed the right on-ramp back into the real world, and in my mind the most important thing was his ability to communicate.

Getting Ned on the computer was a goal from our early days at Shepherd, and he took a good, hard swing at everything assistive technology teams pitched his way. The sip-and-puff Morse code thing, eye-gaze, and then voice-recognition technology. After a while, the effort became more depressing than it was worth, and we had to focus on other things. But with the increased motor control he'd gained—partly from petting Kasey—he was eventually able to hold a fork in his left hand and feed himself, which made me wonder . . .

"Ned," I said, casually broaching the topic, "instead of trying to find ways around the keyboard, maybe we should work on a basic hunt and peck."

He considered it, then nodded. "It's a concept."

Ned's vision is better when he's looking up, so we set the monitor high. He rolled his chair up to his desk and went to work. Every "LOL" and "OMG" was laborious and slow, but he trudged through it. His brain gradually rewired to compensate for his vision issues, allowing him to see his laptop screen fairly clearly. Ned looked forward to getting on the computer every afternoon at five, keeping up with friends on Facebook, staying up on the scores with ESPN.com. Eventually, he was answering email and even texting on his phone. In weightless, boundless cyberspace, he didn't need a ramp or a lift. He was free to explore the world, go wherever he wanted, make his voice heard.

Now the question came around again: *What do you want to do with your life?*

The first inkling of an answer came when Teddy's sister Heather clinked her glass with a spoon and announced to all of us at a family get-together that she was expecting a baby.

"I'd like you to be the baby's godfather, Ned. It would mean a lot to me. You'd be so great. Plus, it's really a family tradition," she said. "Since my mom is Jake's godmother."

"I . . . *Wow*. I'm really—I'm very touched, Heather. I'd be happy to. Thrilled, in fact." Ned beamed broadly, and there was a general round of joy and congratulations at the table.

That night, he told me soberly, "Mom, this is the most important responsibility I could possibly have. I'll be here for Heather like she and Teddy were for me after the accident. And I'll be here for the baby, to love him and guide him through life."

The affirmation was empowering. It was about giving. It was more than a baby step.

At the christening, the priest gestured out over the congregation, asking, "Who stands for this child?"

"We do," Ned answered with a solid nod to Kate, Quinn's godmother, and rolled up to the front of the sanctuary.

I'd never seen anyone stand taller.

WHEN THE FENWAY PARK INVITATION was presented, we hardcore Red Sox fans thought we'd died of bliss and gone to Home Plate Heaven.

"Ayla, one of Kasey's college roommates, is throwing out the first pitch," said Megan Monkey. "We'd love for you to come out onto the field with us."

Ned's eyes widened. "*Sweet!*"

"I figured you'd feel that way." She laughed. "I told Jill you're the biggest Red Sox fans I know."

"Fans?" I said. "Megan, Ned's father was such a Sox lover, I had 'GO SOX' chiseled on the back of his gravestone."

"It's been a long time since we went to a game," Ned said quietly.

Over the past two years, many friends had generously invited us to Celtics, Red Sox, and Patriots games, promising special seating and accommodations. We always had to say "thanks, but no thanks." The logistics and pain, the whole fraught procedure of getting there was just too daunting for Ned. But in the seven months since Kasey arrived, he'd made significant progress, physically and emotionally. He could move both arms and hands, control his neck and torso, even kick both legs. His spirits were high, and he was ready to take his first real step back out into the real world, with real people. What better way to do it?

Something he'd always loved and always would: a Red Sox game.

The Green Monster, the cheering crowd, the 2004 World Champion banner flying in the breeze, Pesky's Pole, players warming up—sheer paradise. Megan Monkey and Judi Zazula, the cofounder of Helping Hands, met us on the way in. Ned, Megan, and I were thrilled to walk in with them. We were proud to be a Helping Hands success story, grateful this organization had truly become a part of our family.

Ayla was adorable in her Red Sox diaper cover and threw an impressive curveball for someone the size of a relief pitcher's bicep. Naturally, the place went crazy when the crowd caught sight of Ayla sitting on Judi's shoulder. Boston area TV stations played and replayed the clip for days.

"It's not exactly Fenway," Megan Monkey said a few weeks later, "but how would you and Kasey like to throw out the opening pitch at a Spinners game?"

"Are you kidding? We'd love to!" said Ned. "Plenty of great players start out in the farm league. Red Sox of tomorrow."

"Excellent," said Megan.

"Maddie's been playing catch with her," I said, "and she's got that down. Do you think we can get her to throw?"

Kasey's answer was a dainty *"Um . . . no."*

"Okay. Plan B," said Megan Monkey. "Ned, you throw it."

He considered it for a moment. "That's . . . an idea."

Okay . . .

I excavated a dusty baseball from the bowels of our basement, and we spent hours practicing on the terrace. Ned's first few throws thumped to the ground in front of his chair.

"Gaugh, that was lame," he groaned. "Let me try it again."

And again. And again . . . until the first few throws became the first few hundred.

"Go, Neddy! Woo-hooo!" the girls cheered on the sideline, dodging fouls as necessary.

Before long he could throw a pretty believable pitch about five feet into the yard.

"All right," said Ned. "Now we need to work on aim."

"Wait, wait. Ned, you're doing great," said Maddie, "but you have to work on how you *look* when you throw it. Don't grimace. Try to look intent but happy."

"Intent but happy." Ned nodded with a grimace. "Got it."

The big day dawned, brilliant and hot. Megan Monkey, Jill, and our handlers (there are always handlers) led us down onto the field. We took Kasey out of her carrying case, and she hopped up on Ned's shoulder, instantly curious to see and smell the huge crowd.

She peeped and nuzzled Ned's ear. *So many pockets, so little time . . .*

On cue, the whole entourage followed Ned out to the pitcher's mound. The ride was a little bumpy, so Kasey scrambled up to my shoulder—then burrowed inside the back of my shirt.

"Oh . . . oh, dear . . ."

I was suddenly hearing the story inside my head: *So I'm standing there in front of thousands of people with this monkey down my shirt . . .*

"Kasey, this is no time to be shy," I whispered over my shoulder. "Come on, Kasey . . . what happened to that whole diva thing?"

As we reached the pitcher's mound, Kasey thrust her head out of my collar and scrambled over to Ned's shoulder with a backward glance at me and Megan Monkey. *Let me show you how this is done, girls.*

The crowd went wild.

"Ready, Ned?" The catcher positioned himself, and Ned gave a confident nod.

With a look of fierce (but happy!) concentration, he chucked the ball neatly into the catcher's mitt. Another roar went up, warm, congratulatory, and full of all-American baseball hot-dog joy.

The game commenced, and we headed into the stands to watch the first inning, but we were mobbed with kids of all ages who wanted to see Kasey up close. Ned smiled and shook hands and fielded a million questions.

"How old is she?"

"In her twenties. Almost as old as me."

"Does she sleep with you?"

"We're roommates, but she has her own bed."

"Can she do tricks?"

"She does her job. That's pretty tricky sometimes, I guess."

Amazingly patient and open, Ned made one connection after another. The experience seemed to feed him. By the time we left, he was simultaneously energized and exhausted.

"You were so great with the kids," said Megan's mother-in-law, Terry, who teaches fifth grade. "My class would be thrilled to have you and Kasey visit."

"Absolutely." Ned was immediately *game on*. "We'd love to."

The children sent a packet of twenty-three handwritten invitations, and I posted them on a bulletin board so Ned could see them as he diligently prepared for the program, practicing a few key tasks with Kasey, identifying some main points he wanted to make about spinal cord injuries and the difference between a service animal and a pet.

"I'm stoked," he told me as we loaded Kasey's carrier into the car. "This is exactly what I always wanted to do, Mom. Get out and talk to people. Inspire, educate, motivate. And Kasey gives me this platform that'll really get kids listening."

Listen, they did. Naturally—instinctively, even.

The children were mesmerized by Kasey, who delighted them with her bravura personality from the moment she and Ned rolled into the classroom. Megan Monkey started the program with a bit of background on how the monkeys were trained. Then it was Ned's turn.

"Thank you so much for having Kasey and me here today." He looked out over the wide-eyed audience. "As you can see, Kasey's my helper monkey. She's trained to do lots of things for me, but she's also my friend."

A ripple of breathless giggles went through the room when Kasey purred and curled her tail around Ned's neck. She brought his finger up to her heart and licked it.

Yeah, it's cool. We're tight that way.

A timid hand went up, and Ned nodded.

"How come you can't walk?"

"I had a really bad car accident a few years ago," said Ned. "It hurt my spinal cord, and your spinal cord is like the telephone wire to all the muscles and nerves in your whole body. So now I can't walk. But I haven't given up hope. I'm working really hard to get strong again."

More hands went up, and he patiently answered one question after another.

"What does Kasey like to eat?"

"How fast can you go in your wheelchair?"

"Does Kasey have brothers and sisters?"

As the children waved and vied for Ned's attention—"*Ooo! Ooo! Ooo!*"—it was comical how much they resembled a certain curious monkey I knew.

"What's her favorite toy?"

Oh, boy.

I produced the pink purse. Kasey whipped out her lipstick, hopped on Ned's shoulder, and gave his crown a vigorous itching. The children cooed with delight. She took out the mirror to admire herself, and they roared.

"Is Kasey ever bad?"

"She's like you," I said. "Never bad, but occasionally naughty."

We shared a few of her misadventures, and of course the kids got a kick out of that.

"Before we wrap it up," said Ned, "I want to talk to you about something really important. Having Kasey is fun, but I want you to be serious about your safety so you'll never need a wheelchair or a helper monkey. When I was in the different hospitals I was in, I saw a lot of kids who'd fallen and hurt their heads. You've got to wear your helmet when you bike or skateboard or Rollerblade. Always wear your seat belt. Never dive into the water unless you know for a fact how deep it is. If you don't know how deep it is, jump in feetfirst. Even if you can see the bottom, there might be ledges on the side of the pool or sandbars in the ocean. After car accidents, diving accidents are the second most frequent cause of spinal cord and brain injury."

The children listened solemnly, but Ned and Kasey left them laughing. As he said good-bye, she dove into his vest and popped her head up under his chin, basking in the delighted applause.

When the fat packet of thank-you notes arrived, Ned called me, Maddie, and Anna to his room to help open and read them all.

Thanks, Ned and Kasey! You're awesome!

Keep working hard, Ned and Kasey! You rock!

Dear Ned, I hope someday you'll walk and play baseball again.

Dear Ned and Kasey, I promise I will wear my seat belt and helmet!

"Wow . . ." Ned looked up, moved and emotional. "Mom, if just one kid remembers to buckle up or grab that helmet because of me and Kasey—if it prevents one bad thing from happening to one family—how incredibly great is that?"

"Very," I said. "It's very . . . incredibly great."

"You know what else is cool," said Anna. "It's like 'what goes around comes around' because that program at our school two years ago—that's how Kasey came to live here."

"You're right," I said. "We've come full circle."

It was like another lifetime, but I remembered with razor clarity what it felt like to see that single point of light. I leaned back in Ned's big armchair, and Bailey jumped into my lap.

"Hey, you. Such a snuggler." I smiled and scratched her behind the ear. "Ned, did Bailey just sneak in under Kasey's radar or have they reached some kind of truce?"

Hearing her name, Kasey stood on Ned's lap, casually scoped out the situation, and lightly leapt over to my knee. Bailey tensed and lay shivering as if an arctic blast had blown in, but Kasey cuddled up as nice as you please. I held my breath, petting both of them at once.

"Girls," I whispered, "can you believe this? Look how nice Bailey and Kasey are sitting here together. I think they've bonded!"

Anna rolled her eyes. "Mom, look at Bailey's face. She is terrified."

"Kasey's such a faker," said Maddie. "You can tell she's sitting there planning to do something evil to the dog."

"It's true, Mom." Ned burst out laughing. "The monkey's an evil genius."

So much for my "We Are the World" moment.

THE BOSTON CELTICS were honoring Helping Hands as part of their "Heroes Among Us" program—a huge honor for Megan Monkey and the entire team. Celtics management was presenting the award during a special time-out at the next game, and we were invited. With the Celtics in the midst of a dramatic comeback season, energy was high and tickets almost impossible to get.

"And we'll be down on center court," said Ned, making it sound like the top of the world.

"I haven't been to a Celtics game in forever," I said. "Your dad and I always had season tickets. And those were amazing days for the Celts—Dave Cowens, Larry Bird, Kevin McHale—all the greats."

Their numbers were retired up there in the rafters now, but the building was still full of fond memories. I was excited about going, but I'd begun to realize that each new and wonderful place we were invited to presented unique challenges. My Megan and I had to do a bit of advance recon to make sure there was adequate space for Ned to drive his wheelchair, and to plot an easy escape route in case Ned was overcome with pain. It was important to have a detailed game plan spelled out so Ned knew where, when, what, and why.

The Celtics handlers met us at the players' entrance the night of the game and took us up in the secret elevators where no mere mortals were allowed—only players and their families. Ned cruised by the Celtics Dancers, who smiled and waved and went back to warming up. With Kasey snug in her carrier, we went to our VIP seats and watched the rip-roaring start of the exciting game. Just before the time-out was called, we were taken down in the Elevator of the Gods, through a secret passageway, and out into the glaring light and deafening sound at the end of the court. The high muckety-mucks in their courtside seats pulled their feet under their folding chairs and greeted us as we rolled into position.

"About one minute," said the handler, and Megan Monkey indicated the carrier.

There was a collective reaction from the fancy courtsiders when Kasey scrambled up my arm and hopped to Ned's shoulder. The handler touched my elbow, and we watched Ned and Megan Monkey roll out across the parquet floor. A roar went up and carried them to center court. We could barely hear the announcer on the loudspeaker, introducing Megan Monkey, telling about the important work of Helping Hands, introducing Ned and Kasey. Up on the JumboTron, Kasey dove inside Ned's vest, then popped her head up, mugging for the cameras.

Another roar, twenty thousand people on their feet, stamping, whistling, cheering.

Oh, Ted . . . All I could do was stand there and breathe it all in. *Look at our son.*

Ned practically floated back off the court, instantly mobbed by well-wishers. By the time we left, he was physically wiped out but euphoric.

"This is important, what we're doing," he said on the way home. "Bringing attention to spinal cord injuries, which is huge. And I like giving something back to Helping Hands after everything they've done for us."

Ned's head was filled with ideas about venues where he could take his message, and his fire for it was contagious.

"There's a whole world out there," he said. "A whole world of people who'll listen, once Kasey gets their attention. And we can tell them what we did together, what a person can accomplish even when a doctor or anybody else says you can't. I want to tell them that if you assemble the right team . . . you can accomplish just about anything."

"AND THAT'S WHY we're here tonight," I told the roomful of sharp suits and cocktail dresses. "I hope that when you hear the story of my family's journey, you'll better understand the vital work being done by Helping Hands, thanks to your generous support."

I'm no stranger to the podium. In my professional heyday, I'd addressed corporate functions, sales conferences, and partner meetings with audiences from five to five thousand. It was different sharing such a personal journey. I was a little nervous at first.

"Kit kit purrrrrr," Kascy said at my elbow. *You still got it, Mom.*

It didn't take me long to get my groove back.

I'd found a whole new something to give.

I prefer the intimate settings where I can see people's faces. My energy seems to expand as I watch them light up, get wide-eyed, laugh, and cry in all the right places. It's best when Ned and Kasey are there with me, being the stars they are. I just set the stage, let them do their thing, then step in again to help field the Q&A once everyone has been completely charmed by both of them. The human-animal bond is so basic—so primal—people are instantly smitten the moment they see those two together.

It was appropriate, I guess, that Kasey belongs to the primate group called New World monkeys, because she would one day bring an entirely new world to Ned. In many ways, she had been out there in the world needing him just as much as he was trapped inside himself needing her. The well-disguised romantic in me likes to think that Kasey couldn't have been placed with anyone else. Be it fate or God or dragon luck, Ned and Kasey were meant to be together.

21

Amazing Grace

RON AND MEGAN ARRIVED RIGHT ON SCHEDULE FOR Thanksgiving dinner. Maddie and Anna appeared in holiday finery. Jake greeted friends at the front door.

Kasey welcomed Judy and her family with what we call the Monkey Salute: she sits up on her haunches and takes her right arm, crosses it over her belly, clutching a few chest hairs, and raises her left arm up over her tilted-back head in an arc (sort of a cross between a hula dancer and Tonto).

"You know, I just learned from Megan Monkey recently that monkeys do this greeting in the wild. The hair on their underbellies is considered their fairest or lightest, so they're flirting and showing off the most beautiful part of their body to those they like. Right above their eyes is another special spot—they pull their forehead back and waggle their eyebrows to show superiority to others. Look, she's doing this to the dogs right now!"

Then, of course, it was time to check out her pals. Kasey first tried to extract Teddy's gum, then went for Judy's ring, sniffing and turning it, examining each stone like a certified gemologist—all of which turned out to be a distraction so she could swipe Judy's watch.

I returned her to her abode, where she could play while we ate. (She tends to be that dinner guest who adds a little too much to the conversation.)

Ned rolled up to the table, laughing, talking, welcoming everyone in a very man-of-the-house sort of way. Quite a contrast from a year earlier when he'd remained in his room after tersely explaining to me that "Thanksgiving isn't a whole lot of fun when you can't feed yourself."

A therapist had bullied him into using a sling device that raised his arm the way a puppeteer would raise the arm of a marionette, but that was so not Ned. Now that beast was out in the garage "archives" with everything else he'd conquered, rendered obsolete, and kicked to the curb. The sip-and-puff mechanism he struggled to implement, a handicapped-accessible bowl with a suction cup that anchored it to a tray, a contraption we called the "cough-o-lator" (you do *not* want to know)—every time we retired one of these relics to the archives, it was a great victory. The only thing missing was the wretched halo. I can only hope it was re-cycled for playground equipment or beaten into a plowshare.

Once Ned got comfortable with something that worked for him, he was slow to give up on it, but he despised anything that made him look more disabled than he had to. This kept him motivated, kept him trying new things, and though it sometimes took a while, he was able to master pretty much every new thing he took on.

When it was time to say grace, Ned led us in a prayer of thanks, then picked up his glass to propose a toast. Before he even said anything, the small act was a celebration.

"Thank you all for coming today," he said. "And thank you all for being here for me the last few years. Your support kept me going."

Ned moved his gaze around the table, connecting with each of us for a brief, meaningful moment—Megan and Ron; Maddie and Anna; Jake; Judy and Wes, her husband; Teddy and his brother Kyle; Heather with baby Quinn—all the major players. Team Ned.

He raised his glass. "I'm the luckiest man in the world."

We all raised our glasses, "Hear! Hear!" and "Cheers!" sounding through audible sniffles.

As the feast commenced, Judy asked me about our holiday plans.

"We're going to have a wonderful Christmas this year if it kills us." I laser-beamed a no-nonsense look at my offspring. "You'll all have fun and like it."

I was fully prepared to resurrect the spreadsheet. Ned would assist with online pre-shopping; Megan to cross-reference for cost control; Anna would compile menu requests; Maddie was to cross-ref with a comprehensive grocery list; and Ron and Jake were back on decoration detail.

"Mom," said Ned, "don't forget to add Kasey to the gift and stocking-stuffer matrix."

"Yes. Will do." I made a mental note. "Have you prepared your requests for Santa?"

Maddie and Anna were prepping formidable lists. (They'd been very good girls this year.) Jake, Ned, and Ron were all about entertainment, electronics, and manly accoutrements.

Megan had made her request months earlier.

A stroller.

"How about you, Mom?" Megan scooped mashed potatoes onto Ned's plate. "Or should I say Gr—"

"Don't say it." I raised my hand. "I'm so not ready for the g-word."

"Mom, all your friends are totally over the moon about being Grandma. Or Mimi or Grammie or whatever."

"I'm too busy mothering to get all over the moon about anything. I'm happy because Megan's happy. It's not about me."

"Won't the baby call you 'Nonnie' anyway?" said Anna.

"Nonnie is my mother."

"Do like that fashionista I read about," said Maddie. "She goes by 'Glamma.'"

"How about 'Nana' as a placeholder?" Megan said. "Then we'll let the baby decide."

It was such an eminently practical yet sensitive suggestion.

"You," I told my daughter, "are going to be a terrific mom."

HOLIDAY PREPARATIONS proceeded in a blur, and Christmas Eve fell peaceful and snowy.

Outside, that is.

On this side of the door, I of course was bustling around the house getting last-minute wrapping done and making a few treats for our evening tradition of opening our "family" gifts. But, before we got started, I remembered that I had promised Ned that I would give Kasey a bath. It was the last thing that I wanted to do, but it was really necessary.

As I was bringing her into the kitchen, she spotted Jake, who had already settled in on the couch in the family room to watch the football games. She immediately stood up on my shoulder, wildly saluting. She launched herself practically across the room, where she jumped onto Jake's shoulder and securely implanted herself. If Ned wasn't going to protect her from bath time, Jake was the next best thing. Meanwhile, Maddie, who was sitting next to Jake, nearly screamed in terror and jumped off the couch. Playing catch was one thing. Getting up close and personal was another. Maddie was not yet anywhere near snuggling terms with Kasey—and she might never be. Meanwhile, I had to pry Kasey off Jake's neck to get her in the tub.

Just then Anna came bouncing into the kitchen. With Kasey in the tub, I mentally prepared for a small screech and certainly a pounce at Anna as she walked by. But no—she got a huge *peep-peep* from Kasey and a vigorous monkey salute. Anna greeted her back. "Hey, Kasey!" Then she popped her head into Ned's room. "Hey, Ned!" she said. "Merry Christmas!" She grabbed the camera and started snapping a few pictures of Kasey, who was clapping her hands in the soapsuds and splashing water everywhere. Now that was real progress. Except, oops—I spoke too soon. Kasey suddenly jumped up on top of the faucet and gave Anna a mini pounce and an evil grin. *Look who's got Mommy's attention now!* she seemed to brag, and then went right back into the water. Anna sarcastically—but with a smile—retorted, "Okay, Kasey, you win!" Someday, Maddie, Anna, and Kasey are all going to look back on their old sibling rivalry days and laugh. Or not.

"Okay, Kasey. Spa time's over."

I delivered a freshly fluffed monkey to Ned. He and Jake had strategically positioned themselves in the family room for optimal viewing of two different games on separate TV sets.

Moments later, Megan and Ron arrived with their newest addition to our Animal Kingdom: a miniature schnauzer puppy. His real name was Sergeant, in a nod to Ron's police career, but we all called him Barky or "The Schnauz." All we needed was yet another dog, but they had been determined to have a puppy (sort of "in training" for the new baby), and of course they were certain Mom would dog-sit whenever the need arose. (Did I ever actually *say* I'd dog-sit?)

Poor Barky—who was a really nice little schnauzer—probably wondered how he got so lucky. Guy and Bailey had totally rejected him from the first moment he walked in the door five months before. They were much too sophisticated to play with a mere puppy.

And Kasey found a new target to fill the role of lowest life form on the planet. But there Barky was for his first Christmas at the "petting zoo," as Heather and little Quinn refer to our home. It wasn't long before the new dog, who clearly suffers from an identity crisis—*Here, Barky! Here, Sarge! Here, Schnauz!*—was dashing throughout the house, running under the coffee table, knocking over presents, and trying desperately to get someone's attention.

"Okay, guys. Turn the tree lights on and bring the first round of gifts in. Here's the color-coded list. I've got about thirty seconds to clean Kasey's cage before—"

"Mom. Relax," Ned said evenly. "Everything will be easier if you're calm."

"Seriously," Jake said. "This is supposed to be fun, remember?"

"You're right." I made a conscious RPM adjustment.

Kasey reclined in her fresh golden coat, black tufts perfectly coifed, regal cheekbones sleek and chiseled. Seeing her on the shoulder of her pet man, I was moved by the beauty of this extraordinary creature and the bond of friendship that had evolved between the two of them.

Jake and the girls carted in the gaily wrapped mother lode.

This, of course, got Kasey's attention.

With the help of Allison, Ned had done all his own shopping this year, cruising the mall in his power chair, and he took immense delight in handing a gift to each sibling and opening his own gifts without help from anyone. Kasey needed no assistance stripping the paper off her shiny new play doctor kit.

"Ooo! Ooo! Ooo!" She unzipped the case and whipped out a large plastic syringe. *Nurse! Five cc's of peanut butter—STAT!*

Sweet and childlike at moments like this, Kasey reminded me of my children when they were about three. The world was her oyster; everything was out there for the taking. The way she delighted in exploring the simplest things—new toys, a dollop of hummus, a package to unwrap—kept us mindful of how wonderful the world is when you maintain a monkey's-eye view. Looking at her in the glow of the Christmas lights, I said to myself . . .

That little stinker is—

Too late.

While I was taking the slow boat from sentimental to savvy, Kasey had trained her eye on Ron's wineglass, plotted her trajectory, and pulled off the aerodynamic maneuver with James Bond panache. Before you could say "survival of the fittest," she'd catapulted to the coffee table, downed the dregs of Ron's wine, snatched a shrimp with one foot and a handful of cashews with the other, and executed a gymnastic double-wahoo flyer back onto Ned's shoulder.

Everyone howled, and Kasey made some cheeky remark around a mouthful of shrimp.

Megan checked the folded gift tag on a colorful, oblong package and handed it across the coffee table.

"Ned, this one's from Charity. She dropped it off yesterday."

Ned tore the paper away and laughed out loud. "Barrel of Monkeys."

The old-school children's game. I peeked inside the red barrel at the huddle of bright yellow monkeys.

"How do you play again?" I asked.

"Like this."

Taking one by its little hooked arm, Anna hooked the hooked arm of its brother, who hooked up a sister, who hooked up an aunt, an uncle, a godfather, a friend, forming a chain of linked arms and round faces.

"See?" She dangled the long chain from her finger. "They have to hang on to each other."

I straightened my shoulders and cleared my throat.

"We have one more important item on the agenda," I said. "'Twas the night before Christmas, and all through the house . . ."

AS WINTER TURNED TO SPRING, Megan grew rounder—and more vocal—but she wore it well.

"I'm so ready for school to be out," Maddie said as Easter approached.

"I'm so ready for this baby to be out," Megan said without sympathy.

Grace Marion Holsinger was born on an April afternoon: seven pounds, six ounces, perfect from nose to toes, and instantly the center of the universe.

Maddie and Anna doted on her, vying for Favorite Aunt position from day one. Jake, my gentle giant, turned to marshmallow whenever he laid eyes on her. Ned was getting to be an old hand at the baby thing and nestled Grace comfortably on his lap while she stared up at him with huge blue eyes. Kasey was enthralled with this strange new being and studied Grace with impressive self-discipline. Quivering with the desire to groom and pick at the newest member of the tribe, she nevertheless clutched her little fists against her breast.

I was amazed at the purely animal sense of gentleness, protectiveness, and play that came over us all around the new baby.

"Ron and I actually went out for date night this week," Megan told me, "but all we did was talk about the baby."

"Have you decided about going back to work?" I asked.

"July," she sighed. "I wonder if Gracey would like it under my desk."

Early in the morning on Memorial Day, I came down to wake Ned and found a text message from Megan on my cell: *4:45 AM: Grace has 103.7 fever. Taking her to ER.*

As I ran toward Ned's room, another message came: *Doctor doing blood workup. Waiting for results.*

Since we brought him home, I'd never left Ned alone in the house for more than a few minutes. Until now.

"Ned? Ned, wake up. I need your help."

Kasey stirred in her bedroom, and he mumbled awake.

"What's up?"

"Grace is very sick. Megan needs me. I have to go."

"Okay. Of course. Go ahead. I'm good."

"Are you sure?"

"I'll be fine, Mom. Do what you need to do."

"Okay. Here's this." I thrust his special medical alert alarm into his hand and rolled Kasey's cage close to the bed so they could keep each other company. "If the day nurse doesn't show up—"

"Yes, yes. Go!"

With a nervous glance over my shoulder, I left them, but in the kitchen, I stopped and stared at another incoming message from Megan.

White count high. Need to do spinal tap. Come soon.

"Oh, my God . . . ," I whispered, my heart hammering. "A spinal tap on a five-week-old baby?"

Poor Grace. And poor Megan, seeing that needle in her baby's tiny, perfect back. I threw myself together and dashed out the door. As I ducked into my car, another message came:

Spinal meningitis.

I squeezed my eyes shut, not wanting to see the words.

Not for Grace.

Not for Megan and Ron.

The scene in the ER was chaotic. Every hospital worker in the area was pulling on yellow contagion-prevention garb. Human hands disappeared into latex gloves. Faces were reduced to surgical masks and sharp, concerned eyes. There was a great deal of motion around Grace's small form, but it seemed as if there was very little sound, like a movie with no soundtrack, only muted effects and hushed voices.

"Mom . . ." Above her own mask, Megan's eyes were dry and terrified.

"What do we know?"

"They don't know. Maybe it's the viral kind, but maybe it's the bacterial kind, which is . . . It's bad, Mom. It's really serious."

"Yes. That's . . . bad."

I wanted to comfort her, but any reassurance would have insulted the situation. We were two women who knew too much for platitudes.

"What's the action plan?" I asked.

"They're taking her to Mass General, where the infectious disease team will take charge. The doctor said they're the best in New England."

"Okay. All right. Mass General. Good."

Megan nodded. "We know where all the bathrooms are."

I had a thousand questions for the doctors, but there was no time. A swarm of EMTs and paramedics in blue suits swooped in and instructed Megan and me to step back while they surrounded Grace with tubes and equipment, inserted a second IV, and positioned the respiratory monitor on the stretcher, nudging Grace's pacifier against her lips to soothe her screams. I felt Megan's entire body go tense.

"Megan?" the ER doc asked from inside her mask. "Are you all right?"

Megan was quiet for a moment, leaning into me just a little.

"I'm fine," she said. "My mom's here."

A tidal wave of emotion swept through me, and it took all my will to keep my eyes from showing it. There was heartache for my daughter and my daughter's daughter, but woven through it was the acute awareness of what a privilege it was to care for one another. And woven through that was profound pride and appreciation for my little girl, now a mother.

My mom's here.

As if that made hope a safe place. As if all the times I wasn't there didn't matter, and no one had kept score of all the times I'd counted on her to be there for me.

"Megan?"

We turned to see Ron hurrying down the hall. They had a quick hug, but they were already moving. A medical team swept Grace through the swinging door.

AS WE PACED the familiar halls at Mass General, test results were very slow to trickle in. It was going to take forty-eight hours for cultures to grow to make a final diagnosis. Meanwhile, no one was taking any chances, and through an IV in her little tiny hand Grace was inundated with harsh anitibiotics and other medicines. The hours dragged by. Megan and Ron never moved from Grace's side, while Terry and I rotated through giving them a few hours of sleep here and there. It was really so sad to see such a little baby, so defenseless, so very sick.

Finally after two-and-a-half agonizing days, the doctors ruled that it was viral meningitis, thank God—although that in and of itself was no trivial thing. So they forged ahead with treatment. The next morning, Grace's temperature was almost back to normal, and she was pronounced "out of the woods." Remarkably, she seemed no worse for wear.

Megan stood between her baby and the wall of monitors and machines, watching over her daughter. She had just hung up from talking to Jake. Maddie linked arms with her on one side, Anna on the other.

"I feel like a zombie," said Megan.

"You kinda look like one," said Anna.

Maddie wordlessly produced concealer and lip gloss from her purse.

When Ned called for an update, I gave him the latest.

"Tell Megan I'm here for her," he said.

His voice was heavy with concern, but there was strength in it, the solid sense of self-worth that comes from being someone who's there for someone else. Beyond all the astonishing progress he'd made physically, perhaps the most important thing Ned had recovered since those moments he lay utterly in the dark was his ability to be a real brother again.

"Megan's exhausted, but she did great," I said. "I'm so proud of her, Ned. From the moment we got to Mass General, she kept her cool, asked all the right questions. Total Mom in Charge."

"Some men are born to greatness," he said philosophically. "Mothers have greatness thrust upon them."

"I think that's *others*, not *mothers*."

"Not in this family."

I smiled a weary smile. "See you later, Ned. Say hello to Kasey for me."

Megan turned from the window when I clicked off the phone. "How's Ned?" she asked.

"He's good. He wishes he could be here."

Such an understatement.

This was one of those moments when his captivity chafed painfully, but it was also moments like this that kept driving him to work harder and reach past his physical limitations to the limit-lessness within. He pushed himself every day to be smarter, stronger, and more helpful to others. He became the mentor and role model he'd always dreamed he could be. The truth is, the best of Ned came out in his captivity.

I hope to say the same for myself someday. I'm working on it, but candidly, I'm cranky a lot. At times the cabin fever rages. But every day, I see flashes of light, like doorways opening in the dark. In those instances I see all that I've gained: a wealth of life experience, advocacy skills honed to machete sharpness, a more resourceful style of living, a fully present style of mothering. I'm discovering new ways to share what I've learned passing through one refining fire after another.

I've learned to manage now, worry later.

With five kids, two dogs, and a monkey, there's never a dull moment at my house. The next so-called emergency (as opposed to the genuine five-alarm swivets) is always just around the cor-ner. I manage what I can and ignore what I can't. It's all about triage, a mental filing system that shuffles everything into de-scending order: Kasey's cage position, Ned's non-urgent issues, the girls' daily dramas, Megan's micro-traumas, and Jake's dilemmas.

If I allowed myself to get caught up in each and every little thing, I would seriously have to be institutionalized. Then I'd be of absolutely no good to anybody.

I've learned to live and breathe by lists and spreadsheets.

Life is complicated; it requires organizational tools. I have a where-and-when spreadsheet for chauffeuring the girls to their various sports and social activities, a who-takes-what spreadsheet for administering pharmaceuticals to various people and dogs (myself included), and a Hail Mary spreadsheet for PCA schedules and hours. I have spreadsheets for non-reimbursable medical expenses, Christmas gifts, menu planning, grocery shopping. You name it, I can plug it into a spreadsheet. I find that measured grid very comforting. Taken as a whole, life gets overwhelming at times, but you can do what you need to do—one little box at a time.

I've learned the beauty of a daily routine.

Go ahead. Dare to be boring. There has to be an eye of calm within the chaos. The strict structure of Kasey's feeding schedule is a comforting framework for Ned's day. And mine. The key is including pleasant things in the schedule. Those pleasantries are small—walnut time, a nap—but every bit as important as the routine maintenance tasks.

I've learned to see the humor in almost any situation.

Because crying gives me a headache and doesn't do a bit of good, I avoid it at all costs. Even in the problematic moments, for the sake of your own sanity, there are times you have to accept life for the grainy misadventure it is and just laugh at its absurdity.

I've learned to accept help.

This is a tough one for the typical Power Mom—and for a control freak—but everyone loses when we let pride get in the way. My friends are the life raft I cling to every day, and my kids continually amaze me with the generosity and love they share. Why rob someone of the opportunity to be an angel? When people rise to the occasion and reach out to help, I've learned that the right response is: "Thank you."

As I watch my family grow, I cherish all these steadily evolving miracles I'm lucky enough to live with—not the least of which is Kasey.

Somehow this funny little creature restored our courage and rescued our joy.

She couldn't make Ned walk again, nor could she restore his independence. She couldn't change the realities or the forever-ness for us all. But Kasey, so wise and sensitive, turns the simple tasks of life into a life worth living.

She reminds us that pure love, trust, and respect are what really matter to keep going, just by being there for Ned.

And for me.

For all of us.

We link arms and love each other, and when it all falls apart—as it inevitably does—we find a way to live through it. We find a way to laugh.

And then we begin again.

The Rogers/Sullivan/Kokos/Holsinger Family

Ron, Sarge, Megan, Grace, Ellen, Kasey, Ned,
Anna, Maddie, Bailey, Jake, and Guy

Afterword by Ned Sullivan

"The world makes way for a man who knows where he is going."
—RALPH WALDO EMERSON

NOT TOO LONG AGO, I LISTENED TO THE OUTGOING MESsage on my cell phone. "Hey, it's Ned," the voice said, loud and clear and fast. "Leave a message!"

I played it a few times. I couldn't believe it. I'd recorded it before my car accident in June 2005 and never had a reason to change it, or listen to it, since. I was floored. This was the voice of someone else—someone I now refer to as Ned 1. He's the guy I was before the accident.

Ned 1 was a pretty optimistic, upbeat guy. People described me as a go-getter, and I was. I have my mother partly to thank for that. She was always advising me and encouraging me, and that helped me form a positive outlook. I liked to share that optimism with others, to help motivate them. I knew what I wanted to do in my life, and I had a plan, with specific goals and strategies, on how to get there.

Then the accident happened and I became Ned 2. I felt like I had fallen off a giant cliff and plummeted into a deep, dark canyon. I couldn't breathe, I couldn't talk, I couldn't move. I wanted to give up. I was so frustrated and angry at my injury.

There were so many things wrong with me, so many things that made me so fundamentally different than I had been before. When I finally was able to speak, I could only talk v-e-r-y s-l-o-w-l-y and softly and with a different sound altogether. Once I could eat solid food, I had to be fed. It was always so unappealing and humiliating to be fed. I had to become a lefty, when Ned 1 had been a righty. I was also frequently in tremendous pain that would completely overcome me. It could be really lonely, and I often felt very isolated. Plus I spent about sixteen hours a day in bed. And that was on a good day. I could no longer walk or play sports or go out to bars and parties with my friends. Just getting out of bed each day was a serious challenge.

Some people might hear all this, assume I am unfortunate, and feel sorry for me. But while it may seem like I am not lucky, my accident has actually made me very lucky.

Since those early horrible days, I have made huge physical and mental progress. I am able to be up and about eight hours of the day. I can now pick up a slice of pizza, or a hot dog, and eat it myself—a small step, but being able to feed myself is huge. Everything tastes much better that way! I can actually put on my own gloves. I can text message my family and friends. I can play games on my cell phone. Above all, I am alive and doing better than anyone ever expected after such a terrible injury.

While I had to work hard to achieve these steps, I have to give a lot of credit to the tremendous support I fortunately received from my inspiring friends and family—my mother, who has devoted so much of herself to helping me and cheering me on, and my sister Megan, who has upended her life for me. Ron, Jake, Maddie, Anna, Nonnie, Nana, Aunt Lynn, and Bob have been there through the good days and the bad. My friend Teddy, who told me to "be there" when he came back from Europe—I hung on to those words through even the most difficult hours, and I *was* there when he got back, and I am here now. Kyle, Heather, and Quinn, my amazing godson; Annie and Kate; Bri, Wes, and Judy; Jane and Chris; Terry and Ron; Paula, Kim, Karen, and so many others were always there for me. Their visits, phone calls, text messages, cards, letters, and packages have been beyond motivating. I thrive on their love and encouragement.

I am also lucky to have had such excellent medical care from the get-go. From what I'm told, the doctors and nurses at University Medical Center in Tucson did a great job while they were working to keep me alive. Then everyone at Mass General, Shepherd, and Spaulding—all the doctors and nurses and therapists—were incredible.

Perhaps the luckiest thing of all was connecting with Helping Hands. One afternoon when I was going through major rehab at the Shepherd Center in Atlanta, my mother came rushing into my room excitedly. She couldn't wait to tell me about something my younger sisters had just told her about on the phone—their school had been visited by Helping Hands: Monkey Helpers for the Disabled. They'd learned that capuchin monkeys made wonderful service animals for people with spinal cord injuries and other mobility issues. In the few hours since she'd spoken to my sisters, my mother—who can sometimes get ahead of herself, God bless her—had already decided that we should have one. I remember thinking, *A monkey? Really?* It seemed far-fetched, but I wasn't going to rule it out.

While it may sound strange, if I hadn't had the accident I wouldn't have gotten Kasey, and without Kasey, my life would be boring, pain-ridden, purposeless. Unlucky, lucky. And I would never have met Megan Monkey and everyone at Helping Hands who have been so outstanding. First they donated Kasey to me, and then they helped us integrate her into our family. But more importantly, they have become real friends.

Since Kasey came along, I have been able to regain some of my old perspective. I often say that Kasey is like medicine, or a booster shot against depression. Some of that comes just from her sheer cuteness. I watch her play with her toys and chow down her food, and it lifts my spirits. My mom recently put a little hammock in her cage, and when Kasey takes her blankets up there and snuggles in with just her face peeping out, she is so cute it hurts. She's also adoringly affectionate toward me. There's nothing like the warm, soft cheek of a monkey pressed against mine to take my mind off my problems. It took months for this to happen, but now that Kasey trusts me, and knows that I trust her, she snuggles with me in a way that comforts me and makes me forget any pain or pessimism that I have been fighting. I am also no longer lonely— she is always there to hang with me. We can talk to each other and keep each other company even when everyone else in the house is busy or out. It's huge.

Most importantly, she has helped me rekindle my plans of being a role model to others. By going out into the community with Kasey by my side, I can bring an increased awareness of spinal cord and brain injury prevention to a really large audience. Maybe we can even get a few more kids to buckle up or wear their helmets. Hopefully we can inspire others to keep working, to keep trying, to never give up. I know where I am going and I have a plan and the strategies to succeed.

It's probably hard to imagine all this—it's even hard for me to imagine it—but Kasey has made all the difference in the world to my recovery. She brought back the important part of me that I thought I had lost in the accident. She feeds my soul. She keeps me going when I feel like life is too hard and I want to give up. She has helped me make a conscious choice to "fall up"—to take

my accident and all its consequences and use them as an opportunity to help and inspire others. She has helped me pick myself
up and propel myself forward. Even when I am in terrible pain or
I am so frustrated by what I seemingly can't do, her presence is
always in the back of my head, the image of her beautiful face or
the sensation of her arms and tail wrapped around my neck. With
Kasey I can hang tough. With Kasey, we can make a difference.
Together.

"Better to light a candle than curse the darkness."

—Chinese proverb

A Note from Megan Talbert

Executive Director
Helping Hands: Monkey Helpers for the Disabled, Inc.

I REMEMBER IT WELL. MY MONKEY MOBILE PHONE RANG AT about 8 p.m., and a quick check of the caller ID told me it was Jill Siebeking calling. Jill is an occupational therapist and placement specialist at Helping Hands: Monkey Helpers for the Disabled, the nonprofit organization that I direct. She coordinates the Monkey Helper Placement Program, including the recipient application process, from start to finish.

"Meg, I met the greatest guy today—I love him," she said. "I really hope he qualifies to get a monkey." Jill's voice had a level of excitement like a kid's on Christmas morning.

I remembered that Jill was to visit the home of Ned Sullivan and his family in Concord, Massachusetts, that afternoon. We are always thrilled at Helping Hands when we can meet an applicant during the process, and we aim to make pre-placement home visits whenever possible. Although our application includes video and phone interviews, they do not compare with meeting an applicant and his or her family in person.

"Ned is so sweet and his family is so warm and caring," Jill went on. "His mom is a hot ticket—she is really motivated but is definitely going to need 'the Talk.' I want to make sure she realizes what she is taking on with a monkey, because she has so much going on in her life."

"The Talk" Jill referred to is a straightforward reality check we at Helping Hands often have to deliver that might go under the heading "What to Expect When You Are Bringing a Monkey into Your Home." We feel very strongly that we need to prepare all of our recipients, their families, and their care attendants for not only the heartwarming, laughter-inducing moments that come with a monkey helper, but also the hard work and sometimes frustrating moments that come with a monkey, as well.

Let me flash back several months earlier to the beginning of my conversation with Ned's family about our service monkey program. My first communication was with Ned's older sister, Megan Holsinger. She told me that Ned had been injured for less than six months and was still in rehab in Atlanta, but the family hoped to arrange a visit to their home as soon as Ned arrived back in Massachusetts in a few weeks.

I explained to her that one of our most important policies at Helping Hands is to wait to begin the application process for spinal cord injury patients until one year post-injury. After such a devastating injury, a rehabilitation hospital is just the first step in recovery and learning.

Coming home from rehab, people who have suffered paralysis must then learn to live with their injury outside the hospital setting. Everything from environmental modifications to the home for accessibility, finding reliable attendant care, and medication adjustments can be very stressful. Add to that the extreme emotional toll that a spinal cord injury can take on the patient and his or her family, and you can imagine how terribly difficult the first year post-injury can be.

Ned's family had the best intentions trying to speed up the application process for him. Although we explained our reasons for wanting them to slow down and adjust to this new change, the family was eager to share some news of a monkey helper to cheer Ned up (and needed some positive news for themselves, as well). Unfortunately, just weeks after Ned returned home to Massachusetts from Atlanta, he required an additional five-month hospital stay at Spaulding Rehab in Boston for pain management and other issues.

In short, it would be late the following summer when Jill would make her first visit to Ned's home, and several months later when I had the pleasure of meeting this extraordinary young man and his family.

My first impression of the residence on Elm Street was that it was a home filled with warmth and lots of energy. We were welcomed like old friends and could feel the family's excitement in the air. Little did they know, I had a surprise in store for them, as a small friend of mine named Kasey had made the trip to Concord with me that day. I couldn't wait to introduce her to Ned. I felt then that this would be a great match, but I had no idea about the possibilities this placement would hold and the ultimate relationship that Ned and Kasey would build together.

On the wall in my office at the Monkey College hangs one of my favorite pictures of the duo, taken just moments after their initial meeting. Ned and Kasey, with their hair the same shades of blond, look like a match made in heaven. Ned is so handsome, looking down at his new friend, who is happily perched on his shoulder, studying the room and chewing on a nut. It was a moment I will never forget.

The story told in this book is one of hope, perseverance, laughter, and most importantly, family. I am honored to have the opportunity to add a few words and to have this extraordinary group of people as part of the Helping Hands family forever.

. . .

IN CLOSING, I WOULD LIKE TO WRITE . . .

To Kasey: My littlest girl and my buddy for many years . . . you make me so proud. I look forward to years to come when I walk through the door of that pretty house on Elm Street and hear you call hello when you recognize my voice.

To Ellen: I laugh when I remember your initial confidence during the application process, as I thought to myself: *Oh boy . . . what a task she has ahead of her!* Our relationship has grown over the years and I am proud to call you a friend. You are an example to mothers across the country of unconditional love, selflessness, and strength. "Megan Monkey" will always be there for you and your family, to support you in any way I can.

And finally, to Ned:

Ned, you are my inspiration. It is a privilege to get up every day and come to work at Helping Hands because of people like you. From the first days of the placement, when you were most concerned about what *you* could do to make Kasey happy—and not at all concerned with what Kasey could do for you—I knew what an incredible man you were. Your life, recovery, and determination are proof that *miracles do happen*. I feel lucky to have you in my life and look forward to the many years of joy, laughter, and healing that we have ahead of us.

Megan L. Talbert
Executive Director
Helping Hands: Monkey Helpers for the Disabled, Inc.
www.monkeyhelpers.org

Helping Hands Mission Statement

E STABLISHED IN 1979, HELPING HANDS: MONKEY HELPERS for the Disabled, Inc. is a national nonprofit 501(c)3 organization that breeds, raises, and trains capuchin monkeys to provide daily assistance to people living with spinal cord injury or other mobility impairments.

Helping Hands supports each service monkey and his or her human partner during their many years together through interactive mentoring of the placement, and close supervision of the monkey's behavioral, nutritional, and veterinary needs.

Relying on private contributions, Helping Hands provides these specially trained service animals and their lifetime support free of charge to recipients.

www.monkeyhelpers.org